COURTLY AND QUEER

INTERVENTIONS: NEW STUDIES
IN MEDIEVAL CULTURE
Ethan Knapp, Series Editor

COURTLY AND QUEER

*Deconstruction, Desire, and
Medieval French Literature*

∾

Charlie Samuelson

THE OHIO STATE UNIVERSITY PRESS
COLUMBUS

Copyright © 2022 by The Ohio State University.
All rights reserved.

Library of Congress Cataloging-in-Publication Data
Names: Samuelson, Charlie, author.
Title: Courtly and queer : deconstruction, desire, and medieval French literature / Charlie Samuelson.
Other titles: Interventions: new studies in medieval culture.
Description: Columbus : The Ohio State University Press, [2022] | Series: Interventions: new studies in medieval culture | Includes bibliographical references and index. | Summary: "Focuses on high medieval verse romance, associated with Chrétien de Troyes, and late medieval dits, associated with the work of Guillaume de Machaut. Courtly and Queer considers these genres both alongside each other and in relation to deconstruction and queer theory"—Provided by publisher.
Identifiers: LCCN 2021048000 | ISBN 9780814214985 (cloth) | ISBN 0814214983 (cloth) | ISBN 9780814281987 (ebook) | ISBN 0814281982 (ebook)
Subjects: LCSH: French poetry—To 1500—History and criticism. | French literature—To 1500—History and criticism. | Courtly love in literature. | Queer theory. | Narrative poetry, French—History and criticism. | Romances—History and criticism. | BISAC: LITERARY CRITICISM / Medieval | LITERARY CRITICISM / LGBTQ
Classification: LCC PQ178 .S26 2022 | DDC 841/.03309—dc23/eng/20211221
LC record available at https://lccn.loc.gov/2021048000
Other identifiers: 9780814258248 (paper) | ISBN 0814258247 (paper)

Cover design by Laurence J. Nozik
Text design by Juliet Williams
Type set in Adobe Minion Pro

CONTENTS

Acknowledgments		vii
INTRODUCTION	Verse Romances and *Dits,* Poetic and Sexual Indeterminacy	1
CHAPTER 1	Reflexive, Ambivalent, Queer Subjects	27
CHAPTER 2	Medieval Metalepsis: Queering Narrative Poetics	70
CHAPTER 3	On Sameness, Difference, and Textualizing Desire: Queering Lyric Insertion	111
CHAPTER 4	Queer Irony in Chrétien de Troyes and Guillaume de Machaut	158
CODA	Slashes	207
Bibliography		211
Index		225

ACKNOWLEDGMENTS

I have been extremely fortunate to benefit from the wisdom and generosity of many friends in the profession. Early versions of parts of this book were read by Matilda Bruckner, Sophie Marnette, and Julie Singer. I am indebted to these friends for their guidance and support, as well as to, in particular, Christine Bourgeois, Sarah Bowden, Paul Rockwell, and Simone Ventura. This project has been reworked at two very happy homes: the Department of French at King's College London and the Department of French and Italian at the University of Colorado Boulder. For their friendship and support, I profoundly thank my colleagues at both institutions. Working with The Ohio State University Press has also been an absolute pleasure, and I am most grateful to Ana Maria Jimenez-Moreno and Ethan Knapp.

Four brilliant minds, and kind hearts, stand out for their contributions to this project, and my gratitude to them is eternal. Thanks to Deborah McGrady for her attentive readings, her open mind, and her exceptional generosity to young colleagues. Thanks, too, to Noah Guynn for his unparalleled rigor and unflagging support, as well as his persistent good humor. I also profoundly thank Sarah Kay, who was probably more patient with me than she should have been, who read countless pages, who encouraged an overly ambitious project from the start—and who effectively taught me what I know about critical thinking. Finally, my loving thanks to Simon Gaunt, a very dear friend and mentor, who died as this book was in the final stages of production. Medieval

French studies lost an infinitely brilliant and generous scholar, and many of us lost a great friend. This book, this medievalist, and this person are a hell of a lot better for Simon's having been here, and he will be deeply missed.

This book is dedicated, with love, to Raphaël.

NOTE ON TRANSLATIONS, CITATIONS, AND PERMISSIONS

All translations from medieval French are my own. Verse narratives are cited by line number. In texts with inserted prose letters, I provide the letter number, followed by the page number. For some paratextual elements (i.e., Christine's *Ballades de plusieurs façons*), I provide page and line numbers. Where there could be any confusion, I always provide a page number. Translations from critical works in modern French are also my own; I have provided the original only when it seemed particularly useful.

I am grateful to Boydell and Brewer for permission to reproduce small elements from my "Affirming Absence and Embracing Nothing: On the Paradoxical Space of Heterosexual Sex in Medieval French Verse Romance" (*Arthurian Literature* 36, 2021, pp. 79–104). Parts of my "De la filiation à la subversion: Les modalités et enjeux des répétitions dans *Aucassin et Nicolette* et *le Roman de Silence*" (*Florilegium* 30, 2013, pp. 1–25) are also translated, adapted, and reprinted with permission from the University of Toronto Press (https://utpjournals.press).

INTRODUCTION

Verse Romances and *Dits*, Poetic and Sexual Indeterminacy

This book focuses on two medieval French literary genres: verse romance, whose heyday ran from the mid-twelfth century through the thirteenth, and where the towering figure of Chrétien de Troyes looms large; and *dits*, best known for the fourteenth-century work of the "Master," Guillaume de Machaut. I argue that considering these genres together opens up important new perspectives on how each self-consciously interrogates the indeterminacy both of language and poetics and of gender and sexuality. This book studies, then, how the sophisticated poetics that are the hallmarks of each genre not only relate to each other but also overlap with their *queerness*, which, for now, I will define as all that resists the notion that courtly literature seeks to present gender and sexuality as coherent and/or normative. In this introduction, I first justify bringing verse romances and *dits* together, by emphasizing how critics have approached them in similar ways. Second, I describe how this book understands, respectively, poetic and sexual indeterminacy. Finally, I explain the logic behind the twisty itinerary it takes in indulging the deviant poetics and sexual politics of verse romances and *dits*.

VERSE ROMANCES AND *DITS*

While verse romances and *dits* have emerged as two of the most studied and taught genres of medieval French verse narratives, no full-length study has examined the relationship between them.[1] Rather, as regards courtly verse narratives, criticism often assumes a break of sorts occurring sometime in the mid- to late thirteenth century.[2] These almost contiguous genres are, accordingly, considered separately. They nonetheless have some basic similarities. The name of each genre, for instance, initially stands out for its capaciousness. In the twelfth century, and sometimes later, *roman* referred to any writing in any vernacular, while *dit*, in the thirteenth century and after, refers to words either not sung or not necessarily sung.[3] Both terms would then gradually acquire firmer meanings, as they become associated with longer texts where didactic pretensions give way to self-conscious literary sophistication.[4] Francis Gingras (188) and Douglas Kelly (*Art* 316) thus estimate that between 1150 and 1170, romance was acquiring an increasing distinctness as a literary genre. There seems, with the *dits*, to be a "sort of fracture-line . . . around the middle of the fourteenth century," as "*dits* gradually approach . . . the proportions of romance" (Lechat 11). Around the 1340s, *dits amoureux* emerge as a more recognizable—and recognizably—literary genre.

When speaking in this way, we must, however, be cautious, since medieval authors and scribes seem less preoccupied by the ascription of texts to genres than today's critics. Many texts today considered to be *romans* or *dits* are only labeled as such by modern scholars.[5] Furthermore, many texts that, in the Middle Ages, either refer to themselves or are referred to as *romans* or *dits* do not conform to our modern conceptions of these genres—and this even after each genre had begun to acquire elements of distinctness.[6]

According to Kelly, "The problem for modern readers derives from the fact that the Middle Ages did not have a theoretical conception of genre" (*Art* 318). Yet, with these two forms of verse narratives, the problem seems to run deeper, since they have proven particularly difficult to define. Indeed, for Gingras, romance is "a genre whose resistance to any classification is frequently observed" (21), while R. Barton Palmer considers the *dit*, "much like the novel," to be "defined by its resistance to over-limiting definition" ("Guillaume de Machaut" 247). Both genres are hard to delimit, in large part because

---

1. Some critics draw distinctions between them: e.g., Cerquiglini-Toulet, "Clerc" and *Engin* 23–32, 107–38.
2. See e.g., de Looze, *Pseudo-Autobiography*, 6, for critical accounts of Jean de Meun's *Rose* as turning point.
3. For *roman*, see Gingras 49–94; for *dits*, Léonard 33–52.
4. For romance length, Gingras 461. For brevity of pre-1340 *dits*, Léonard 196–203. For didacticism of early romance, see e.g., Nichols 52. For didacticism in pre-1340 *dits*, Léonard 20–27; for didacticism in late medieval *dits*, Kay, *Place*.
5. Léonard, for example, shows how some 40% of pre-1340 *dits* are only labeled as such by modern critics (343).
6. For *dits*, see Léonard 401–16. For *roman*, see e.g., Gingras 178–89.

each incorporates elements associated with other genres. "The *dit* . . . absorbs, reorients, and even personalizes themes and narrative motifs borrowed from other secular and learned traditions," writes Palmer (247), while for Matilda Tomaryn Bruckner, romance has a "taste for a wide array of materials combined through intergeneric mixing of all sorts" (*Shaping Romance* 1). "The essence of romance is its protean adaptability," she argues (208), while *dits*, for Michel Zink, are a "protean genre" (*Subjectivité* 64; also Léonard 29).

If both genres are literary *mixtions*—to employ a term Jean Froissart (*Prison amoureuse* 1694) and Christine de Pizan (*l'Advision* pp. 13, 73, 82) each use—they nonetheless particularly rely on one ingredient: lyric poetry. Romance mines the "latent narrativity" (Vance, *Mervelous* 88) of troubadour and trouvère lyrics. *Dits* also grow out of lyrics; in fact, suggests Jacqueline Cerquiglini-Toulet, they tend do so more organically than romances (*Engin* 23–31). Bracketing for now differences in how they relate to troubadour and trouvère songs, I would note how the proximity of both genres to lyric poetry becomes particularly stark when, as of the thirteenth century, lyric pieces began to be inserted into larger texts. For while they could find homes in all sorts of places, critics have overwhelmingly focused on examples taken from verse romances and *dits* (cf. Boulton, *Song* xiii–xiv).

Faced with this state of affairs, whereby verse romances and *dits* are particularly indebted to lyric poetry but prone to absorbing material from almost anywhere, criticism of both genres has effected a similar move, by defining each genre in terms not of what goes into it but rather how it acts on different *matières*. Both genres function more as verbs than nouns; they denote processes done unto heterogeneous parts. Thus, for Claude Luttrell (68) and Kelly (*Art* 307), *conjointure*, defined as "the poet's own coherent arrangement of disparate material," emblematizes the romancer's task. Romance, according to such a conception, is a "secondary mode of literary expression," as it incorporates and reflects on different materials *au second degré* (Zink, *Subjectivité* 30).

Yet, for Cerquiglini-Toulet, "the *dit* is a genre defined by *second degré* play; in other words, it is a genre that operates via discontinuity" ("Clerc" 143). For this pioneering critic, *dits* self-consciously dramatize sutures in order to call attention to how they act on heterogeneous materials. This may seem diametrically opposed to Kelly's understanding of *conjointure*, as one is about constructing the smoothest whole, the other the intellectual pleasure to be derived from a text's bumpiness. Yet Cerquiglini-Toulet does attend to how Machaut's *Voir Dit* "vigorously brings together disjoined elements" at the same time as it "disjoins . . . elements that could have appeared . . . in a continuous manner" ("Clerc" 141). Likewise, Kelly stresses how the influential twelfth-century theologian Hugh of Saint Victor exhorts the artist both to bring together things disjoined and to disjoin things put together: *disgregata coniungere* and *coniuncta segregare* (*Art* 21, 40). Bruckner emphasizes, too, the "play in [romance] between the whole and the fragment, the continuous and the discontinuous" (*Shaping Romance* 215). Rather than associating romance with continuity and *dits* with discontinuity, both seem, therefore, to preempt Georg Lukács's notion that "the novel is the paradoxical fusion of heterogeneous and discrete components into an organic whole which is then abolished over and over again" (84; also Segre 31).

The *second degré* nature of both genres nonetheless points to something basic but crucial about them: their oft-remarked self-consciousness or metaliterariness. Each has a tendency to represent signs as "problematic: ambiguous, contradictory, misleading, and deceptive," as Bruckner writes of romance (*Shaping Romance* 220). And because both genres thematize the complexity of signs, they appear particularly "literary"; both are associated with the "triumph of writing within a medieval culture ... profoundly marked by orality" (Baumgartner, *Récit médiéval* 3, on romance). In both, moreover, someone must undertake this literary work. The emergence of the self-conscious author, the development of her/his craft, and the importance of her/his point of view are of course tied to the gradual emergence of the individual subject, also a commonplace for scholars of both high medieval romance and late medieval *dits*.[7] What's more, "by integrating reflection on the work of the writer, romance at the same time defined the task for the reader" (Zink, *Subjectivité* 31). This statement holds just as true for *dits*, where critics, foremost Deborah McGrady, have studied the relations between the author and her/his readers.

The literary "inventions" we might ascribe to these genres do not stop here. Both genres have, for instance, played a key role in developing the distinction between the (often unreliable) narrator and the implicit author.[8] Yet, for all each genre did for literature, this is probably not what they thought they were up to. Centuries before any conception of *l'art pour l'art*, these medieval texts are intimately connected with such intellectual domains as logic, theology, philosophy, ethics, and the law. Indeed, if in verse romances and *dits*, the text "is true only because *I* say it is," as Cerquiglini-Toulet writes of the latter genre ("Clerc" 155), there is always an overriding concern with intellectual questions larger than the individual, to which s/he reacts. Even this notion that truth is in the words of the speaker is itself replete with philosophical, theological, legal, and ethico-political significance; it is by no means exclusively, or even primarily, literary.[9] Ditto for what we might today call semio-

---

7. See e.g., Zink, *Subjectivité*; Hanning for romance; and Hanf and Wolfzettel for *dits*.
8. E.g., Krueger "Author's Voice"; Brownlee, *Poetic Identity*; Swift, "Poetic 'I.'"
9. See e.g., Hunt, "Abelardian Ethics"; Miller; de Looze, *Pseudo-Autobiography*; Moreau.

logic concerns. Scholars have shown how the status of the sign is implicated in such disparate (though often overlapping) domains as theology, philosophy, logic, the law, politics, and economics—to name just some of the big ones.[10]

To outline the contours of the intellectual engagement of verse romances and *dits* is a task far beyond the bounds of this introduction (or this book). Here, I am merely calling attention to how the foremost experts of each genre describe their relationship to learned culture, language, and other literary genres in broadly similar ways. This overlap in critical conceptions of these genres may, in turn, be leveraged to open up new avenues of inquiry. One might, for example, study how the two genres interact at given historical moments, looking to manuscripts such as Fr. F°. v. XIV.3 of the National Library of Russia, which contains *le Roman de la Violette* and the *Dit de la Panthère* and may have formerly contained *Athis et Procelïas* and belonged to Philippe le Bon.[11] One might reflect, too, on why Jean Renart's *Escoufle* and Jean Maillart's *Comte d'Anjou* call themselves *dits* when they seem to be romances (Léonard 42, 33). Or why Huon de Mery, in the *Tournoiement Antechrist*, refers to "Les diz Raol et Crestïen," or the anonymous author of the *Hunbaut* to "Les bons dis Crestïen de Troies" (Schmolke-Hasselmann 35, 37). Such a study would no doubt focus on the fate of verse romance in the age of *dits*, looking at fourteenth-century verse romances, the place of verse romances in late medieval libraries, prosifications of earlier romances, allusions to verse romances in *dits*, and so forth.

This is not, however, the path this book takes. Nor is my primary goal to argue that when verse romance fizzles out, it funnels not only into prose but also into the *dits*. This literary historical suggestion has been advanced (e.g., Kelly, *Art* 309–11; Zink, *Subjectivité*) and will be considered here. Yet, I am more concerned with how the juxtaposition of verse romances and *dits* opens up new ways of thinking about what each does. It does so, in part, by inviting us to use the best criticism of one genre to expose gaps in our knowledge of the other. In particular, this means mustering the energy critics have brought to the representation of gender and sexual politics in romance, and bringing it to the *dits*—where, with the exception of work on gender in Christine de Pizan, these issues have gone understudied. In the opposite direction, it means imagining a future for verse romance not overshadowed, however implicitly, by a less intricate and more moralizing prose romance. It means considering

---

10. For logic, see Kay, *Courtly Contradictions*; Brown, *Contrary Things*; Vance, *From Topic*; Greene, *Logical Fictions*. For philosophy, Kay, *Place*; Armstrong and Kay. For the law, Bloch, *Medieval French Literature*; Burgwinkle, *Sodomy*; Gravdal. For ethics and politics, see e.g., Haidu, *Subject Medieval/Modern*; Rosenfeld, *Ethics*.

11. Todd vi–xii in his edition of Nicole de Margival's *Panthère*.

how a *dit*-like involution might steal the day—and evaluating what this would mean for the political implications of verse romance.

Above all, though, this book seeks more generally to offer new readings of verse romances and *dits* that bring to the fore the indeterminacy of language and of desire—and of their interplay. But what do these abstract formulations mean? I'll tackle them in order.

POETIC INDETERMINACY

To frame, much less define, the indeterminacy of poetic language is necessarily contradictory, a task as impossible as it is obligatory. We might nonetheless begin where Paul de Man does his 1979 *Allegories of Reading*. In the opening essay, de Man attempts "to distinguish the epistemology of grammar from the epistemology of rhetoric" (7). Following Kenneth Burke, he sees rhetoric as a "subversion of the consistent link between sign and meaning that operates within grammatical patterns," and with Charles Sanders Peirce, he describes "the process by which 'one sign gives birth to another'" as "pure rhetoric, as distinguished from pure grammar, which postulates the possibility of unproblematic, dyadic meaning" (8, 9). For de Man, "grammar and logic stand to each other in a dyadic relationship of unsubverted support," while "rhetoric radically suspends logic and opens up vertiginous possibilities of referential aberration" (7, 10).

This opposition between a positivist grammar and a deviant rhetoric, which serves as de Man's *point de départ*, is also more medieval than he acknowledges. It echoes, for instance, Thomas of Chobham's early thirteenth-century notion—here summarized by Rita Copeland and Ineke Sluiter—according to which "grammar and dialectic deal with a stability of meaning," while "rhetoric governs the ambiguation of meaning" (38). Of course, ancient and medieval rhetoric and grammar are vast, heterogeneous domains. For Copeland and Sluiter, a fundamental distinction can nonetheless be made between the two, particularly in their treatment of figurative language, a domain to which both lay claim. "Grammar," they write, "in its drive towards correctness, treats the figures and tropes last as a form of deviation from correctness," whereas rhetoric "treats figurative style as the last of its compositional components or canons, as if to suggest that the edifice under construction is now ready for its surface, its outer walls, its uppermost layers" (32). The emphasis is thus opposite. Figurative language represents, for grammar, "a deviation from a proper 'norm,'" while "in rhetoric it is the amplification of form and meaning," a twist to be celebrated (35).

In this book, I focus on the deviance of language, which—in a medieval and a deconstructive framework—may be embraced by rhetoric but derided and repressed by grammar. Yet, when approaching medieval texts, this distinction quickly proves overly schematic.

Consider, for example, Alain de Lille's *De planctu Naturae*. In this twelfth-century Latin treatise, the highly moralistic Nature embraces a grammatical outlook. She is obsessed with "correctness," both grammatical and ethical. This personification loudly "condemns," as William Burgwinkle summarizes it, "some figures as metaphors of unnatural sexual practices, especially *metaplasmus* (highly irregular grammatical change), *barbarismus* (mistakes in forms of words, such as gender) and *syneresis* (contracting two syllables into one), since they suggest the mutability of all language and coupling" (*Sodomy* 181; original italics). Yet, Nature "freely acknowledges using *antiphrasis* and oxymora . . . rhetorical figures which, one could argue, also subvert the natural order she claims extends even to grammar" (181). Nature's argument appears, then, to be tripping over itself, and Alain's text might even be described as torn between the grammatical outlook embraced by Nature and a rhetorical one, which resides in what Burgwinkle calls "those gaps" that "mak[e] abjection look glamorous" (*Sodomy* 194). Such a reading would, moreover, be consistent with how, "for Alain, rhetoric, even more so than the other *artes*, plays a contradictory, morally dubious role," as Noah Guynn has shown (101).

To overlay Alain's text with the governing opposition of grammar to rhetoric will, however, not get us far. It even smacks of Nature's uncompromising binarism within the text. Indeed, the brilliance of various readings of Alain's treatise—like those of Scanlon, Burgwinkle, and Guynn—lies in how they resist containing the text's deviance by resorting to any such neat solution. Rather, these assessments seem to me to function more deconstructively. Famously hesitant to define deconstruction, Derrida nonetheless proposes in *Psyché: inventions de l'autre* (which is dedicated de Man) that deconstruction may function like Francis Ponge's *Fables*, "en tournant ces règles dans le respect de ces règles mêmes afin de laisser l'autre venir ou s'annoncer dans l'ouverture de cette déhiscence" [by turning the(se) rules in the same direction as they were already turning in order to let the other come or emerge in the opening formed by this dehiscence] (vol. 1, 59). Derrida's notion of moving with the rules of a text but taking them too far to see what emerges lines up with Burgwinkle's strategy for reading the *De planctu*. "I propose," he writes, "to follow Alain's own prescribed reading and writing practice: push the word to its allegorical and etymological limit, chart the text's assault on its own logic, and read it against the grain" (172). For Derrida and Burgwinkle, the binary of reading "with" or "against" a text does not, therefore, hold up. To follow modalities inscribed in texts to their "limits" amounts to dramatizing gaps, to reading "against the grain."

Similarly, in this book, I attempt to read with the rhetoric of texts, which also means reading against them. At the most basic level, this amounts to troubling any simple equation between courtliness *qua* mode of literary texts and the political ambitions of medieval courts. In the *Origins of Courtliness,* Stephen Jaeger describes "the flowering of literature" that emerges in the second half of the twelfth century as

> the expression of a movement aimed at taming the reckless assertiveness of the European feudal nobility, at limiting its freedom in manners and morals, at restraining individual willfulness, and at raising this class from an archaic and primitive state of social and civil life to a higher stage, imbuing it with ideals of modesty, humanity, elegance, restraint, moderation, affability, and respectfulness. (3)

Yet, I study how courtly texts not only construct but also deconstruct these lofty ideals. I am interested, that is, in how one facet of texts commonly referred to as their "courtliness"—namely, their literary sophistication, as valued by courts—does not necessarily function to promote the political ambitions generally ascribed to these courts. Rather, literary sophistication can self-consciously unravel the desire for control and order underpinning conceptions of "courtliness" like Jaeger's.

This probably still seems abstract. I am also hardly the first to highlight courtly literature's subversive potential. It makes sense, then, to specify this book's contribution by contextualizing my reading practice in relation to criticism of each genre.

Verse Romance

"If I were to characterize in a nutshell the main critical issue that animates this book throughout," writes Bruckner in *Shaping Romance,* "I would point to the role played by repetitions and its variations, the values and meanings we assign to them in medieval textuality" (1–2). My readings focus, too, on repetitions, defined in the most general way as the recurrence of similar language, themes, or motifs. Nothing surprising here, as repetition has long been considered crucial to verse romance. According to Norris Lacy, for example, the analogies and "numerous and brief echoes" that dot romances, even if they do not "bear an essential relation to the work's meaning," make texts "fuller and richer" (*Craft* 110). Kelly agrees (*Art* 64). Such repetition, he argues, plays an important role in fostering the "thematic" and "topical" unity of texts.

Bruckner stresses, though, how "repetitions and variations supply not only the links that connect the various parts" of romances "but also an implicit commentary that emerges out of [their] interplay" (*Shaping Romance* 216). Unlike Lacy and Kelly, Bruckner does not understand repetition as primarily or necessarily speaking to the cohesiveness of texts. Rather, for her and others—in particular, the tremendous feminist critics of the nineties—it often foments a more ambiguous commentary, even generating what Sarah Kay has called "counternarratives" (*Chansons de Geste* 52).

This is notably the case when we chew on the manifold *aventures* that are the stuff of romance. When—to look to an example Bruckner emphasizes ("Interpreter's Dilemma")—we wonder to what extent the Demoiselle Entreprenante in the *Charrette*, who stages her own rape but fails to seduce Lancelot, might recall aspects of Guinevere's plight (but surely Guinevere isn't engineering her own abduction?) or point to something about Lancelot's (is he attracted to Guinevere because he pries her from other men? Does he prevent a rape or is he nearly raped himself?), we are engaging with repetitions that are more provocative than self-evident. In her studies of the notion of the *droite voie* (straight path), Zrinka Stahuljak has nonetheless argued that, too often, nagging issues in romances are flattened out by critics ("Chrétien de Troyes" and *Thinking* 75–109). Stahuljak considers how, within texts, the *droite voie* only emerges "après-coup" for the adventuring knight: only when "the error or the folly of erring . . . is incorporated into how the adventure is comprehended" ("Chrétien" 130). The "regularity" of "moralizing" readings of Chrétien's romances, she suggests, functions similarly ("Chrétien," esp. 115). Like the knight, the critic straightens out—and thus distorts—the *errance* of romance by casting it *a posteriori* as a *droite voie,* whether in ethical, aesthetic, or other terms.

I am interested in troubling artificial *droites voies* that have persisted in romance criticism. My readings focus on incendiary issues that are raised by repetitions but have been underdeveloped by critics, the precariousness of "resolutions," and ambiguities resulting from the interpenetration of narrative levels. None of these notions, I should (or shouldn't) say, is original in its own right. Yet, each tends to have been restricted to certain texts and presented as the exception rather than the rule. My goal, therefore, is both to open up new readings of individual romances and to counter a persistent tendency to associate romance with order, with emphasis on its unredeemable deviance.

Let me unpack this. It seems, for instance, to be a commonplace that "romance emphasizes the open-ended nature of its organization and meaning" (Bruckner, *Shaping Romance* 104, on the *Charrette*). Not only, for example, do different episodes in the *Charrette*—like that of the Demoiselle Entreprenante—raise issues that they don't resolve, but the larger romance also leaves dangling the central problem of adultery, which is only explicitly discussed when the antagonist Méléagant falsely accuses Kay, not Lancelot, of having slept with the queen. Yet, while we know this about the *Charrette*, other romances deflect equally pressing issues in ways less familiar to criticism. For example, midway through *Erec et Enide*, the spouses stumble upon the predatory Count Galoain, who is overcome by Enide's beauty.

> Haÿ! fait li cuens, mout me poise
> Quant vos alez a tel vitance,
> Grant duel en ai et grant pesance . . .
> Bien sai et voi que vostre sire
> Ne vos aimme ne ne vos prise. (3312–14, 3326–27)

"Oh!" says the Count, "it quite bothers me when you go about in such a shameful way; I feel great pain and great sorrow. . . . I can clearly see and understand that your husband doesn't love or value you."

Although Enide has no interest in Galoain, she pretends to accept his advances in order to buy time to warn Erec. She even says to him, "Trop ai menee ceste vie, / Je n'ain mie la compaignie / Mon seignor" [I've lived this life for too long; I do not appreciate my husband's company] (3391–93). Galoain's function here is analogous to Méléagant's in the *Charrette*; the antagonist brings up a central issue—in this case, the acceptability of Erec's treatment of Enide—around which the romances dances. Rather than reading *Erec et Enide* as serving to reconcile a broken couple (as it is generally read), I attempt, therefore, to tease out antagonistic "counternarratives," like Galoain's, which trouble the basic terms of the protagonists' union.

I also query notions of resolution. It is often held that "closure in romance . . . involves the bracketing of subversive elements within the romance narrative and the production of a seemingly unbreakable moral and political consensus" (Guynn 8). *Erec et Enide* would, again, be a case-in-point, as anything subversive about the text—namely, Enide—seems drowned out when Erec is finally crowned with great pomp. Indeed, whether stressing the significance of his coronation or critically analyzing her relegation to the background, scholars largely concur that this concluding sequence serves as a genuine attempt to resolve things: whether we like it or not.¹² Therefore, if we think we know that the conclusions of Chrétien's works are "notorious for opening up as many questions as they claim to resolve," I would caution against overstating the extent to which critics have troubled the resolution provided by different romances.¹³ As regards the four completed romances attributed to Chrétien, the first two have proven relatively immune to such readings, since *Cligés*'s epilogue is often read as so abrupt and outlandish as to disqualify itself—and, in any case, it does not trouble Cligés and Fénice's union so much as it does her posterity. Because discussion of the *Charrette*'s epilogue is generally concerned with the enigmatic figure of Godefroi de Leigni, and because Lancelot and Guinevere's love cannot be lived in the public eye, scholarly debate about the satisfactoriness of Chrétien's resolutions has, in fact, focused on one romance, *Yvain*, where things seem to wrap up too quickly and neatly.¹⁴ Yet, the precariousness of *Yvain*'s *fin* may be more the rule than the exception in the world of romance. Indeed, I shall argue that such romances as *Erec et Enide, Cligés, Silence, Guillaume de Dole*, and *le Roman du Châtelain de Coucy et de la Dame de Fayel* stage conclusions that are just as wobbly. And this is to say nothing of texts like *Partonopeu*, which both wear their open-endedness on their sleeves and self-consciously reflect on their inability to provide a legitimate *fin*.

If the *voie* is not *droite*, and the *fin* not the *fin mot*, this troubles the ostensible narrativity of romances, as the romance text "both progresses and resists progression" (Bloch, *Etymologies* 184, on Béroul). With Howard Bloch, I am inclined to conceive of verse romance's antilinear thrust in relation to lyric tradition. Indeed, like the formidable *Thinking Through Chrétien de Troyes*, this book approaches verse narratives as "long poems," where the interest lies in what is suspended and unresolved (Stahuljak et al., 13–14). Reading romances more as narrativized verse than as verse narratives does not, however, entail overlooking issues of narrative poetics, but rather challenging the association of medieval narratives with key features today associated with narrativity, such as mimesis. I shall, therefore, emphasize what Bruckner has called the "mirroring" characteristic of interactions between "the diegetic and the extradiegetic"; many of the repetitions analyzed will be between narrative levels (*Shaping Romance* 207). The canonical example of such repetition comes from the *Charrette*, where the line "Come cils qui est suens antiers" [as he who is entirely hers] (4, 5656) describes both Chrétien's relationship to his patron

---

12. For Erec's coronation as resolution see e.g., Maddox; Haas; and Maddox and Sturm-Maddox 115–19. For Enide's sidelining, Ramey; Burns 151–202; McCracken, "Silence" 121–24.

13. Bruckner, *Shaping Romance* 214, referring to the epilogues in particular.

14. See Cheyette and Chickering 75–77 for summary of this debate.

Marie de Champagne and Lancelot's submission to Guinevere. Yet, similar to how *Yvain* has held an outsized place in critical discussion of unreliable endings, the *Charrette* seems to have been overly privileged when it comes to repetitions across narrative levels. In readings of *Erec et Enide, le Bel Inconnu, Partonopeu de Blois, Silence,* and Christine's *Duc des Vrais Amans*, I show how metalepsis—understood in the narratological sense as the interpenetration of narrative levels—is more prevalent than it appears. And as in the *Charrette*, it tends to reflect important yet intractable ambiguities.

So, repetitions that nag, texts that meander from and impede the *droite voie*, unstable *fins*, and convoluted narrative poetics: what amounts from this conception of verse romance? Two entrenched notions are taken to task. One is the author. My intention is not to rehearse the lack of evidence proving that, say, Chrétien de Troyes was one man who penned the five romances attributed to him (Kay, "Who"; Stahuljak et al.). Rather, I propose to explore how texts themselves inscribe resistance to what Foucault calls the "fonction auteur" [author function] (83), where the "author function" refers to the discursive operation by which cohesive authority is posited behind texts. Yet, unlike A. C. Spearing, my quibble is less with the ascription of cohesive subjectivity to narratorial "I's" than with the gesture of associating authorship with order. For despite much introspection by medievalists about the status of the author—best exemplified by Virginie Greene's edited volume—medievalists still seem largely to assume that authorship is, true to the origins of the term, about authority: whether that of an author, a text, or even political forces. Indeed, as Greene observes, even those seemingly most circumspect about the author have not so much fundamentally queried the "author function" as they have rebranded its ways of generating authority. For example, "in submitting medieval authors . . . to his merciless skepticism," the great Roger Dragonetti has "implicitly constructed other medieval authors: the brilliant forgers who imagined the schemes and invented the names" ("What Happened" 217).

In querying whether romances are about generating authority, I focus—particularly in the final chapter—on the trope of irony, long held to be essential to the toolkit of the greatest romancers. Contrary to a tendency to understand the trope as signaling the author's ability to masterfully manipulate language, I turn to a de Manian understanding of it, according to which irony figures the impossibility of controlling meaning. For de Man, that is, irony calls attention to how language does not, and cannot, mean in a direct, stable, or positive way; "true irony," by extension, is resolutely negative and cannot be harnessed by anyone. Similarly, I suggest that the romance author is not asserting his/her mastery of language but achieving precisely insofar as s/he submits to the impossibility of mastering larger forces, including but not limited to language. I explore how romancers and romances showcase—and resist, accept, even embrace—the futility of efforts to exercise control over language, texts, the self, or others. Indeed, it may be only teleologically that the romancer has emerged as an individual firmly asserting him/herself.

Yet, if this book does not read romance as about the power of the individual, it is equally wary of that of patriarchal discourse. *Courtly and Queer* inherits from the paradigm-altering work of feminist critics the notion that romances foment counterreadings, or "doubt, rejection, [and] resistance" (Krueger, *Women Readers* 30). Yet, I focus on those counternarratives that— almost paradoxically—inhabit the center of romances. For if such critics as Roberta Krueger have situated the subversiveness of female speech and reading in opposition to "the values of male aristocratic culture," this may be understood as conceding—even reifying—the notion that "romance played an essentially conservative role in transmitting patriarchal ideology and class privilege" (*Women Readers* 3, xiv). Krueger views her task as "read[ing] against the grain of romance's dominant ideological structures" (*Women Readers* 32), while my concern is with how reading *with* romances is to read *against* them.

Certainly, it has been recognized—in many ways—that "the role of writing" in the "gradual centralization of political power" that took place in the twelfth and thirteenth centuries is "highly ambiguous" (Bloch, *Etymologies* 14). Often, however, those critics who have emphasized the ambiguity of romance poetics have placed less emphasis on the political implications of deviancy, instead tracing a path whereby literary play speaks to self-reflexivity and thus to the achievement of authors or texts (e.g., Bloch, *Anonymous Marie*; Dragonetti, *Mirage*). Yet, because I am convinced that, as (even) de Man observes, "poetry does not give up its mimetic" or referential "function . . . at such little cost" (*Blindness* 182), my goal is to follow the rhetoricity of romance not back to the author or the text but rather to issues of gender and sexual politics. This is, of course, not the first book to operate at the junction of rhetoricity and gender and sexual politics. Guynn's argument that high medieval allegory "plays on the instability and unpredictability of its own meaning in order to authorize more aggressive and more violent forms of social and political control" (4) is a particularly deft example of how we might consider in tandem poetic indeterminacy and political struggles. Unlike Guynn, I will, however, emphasize how poetic indeterminacy not only brings to the fore the tenuousness of "social and political control" but also relishes in its incoherence and its impossibility. I contend that, almost paradoxically, the "courtlier" a romance appears—the more it uses language in the sophisticated ways seemingly so valued by medieval courts—the more incendiary its gender and sexual politics often are. What I mean by incendiary politics I momentarily bracket, though, as we look more briefly at poetic indeterminacy in *dits amoureux*.

DITS

Many of the arguments just outlined about verse romances will not need to be developed to the same extent about *dits,* as they seem more clearly to apply. Of course *dits* are "long poems," narrativized verse rather than verse narratives. In texts like the *Voir Dit,* as Cerquiglini-Toulet has contended, "the narrative text in its entirety unfolds, like a Japanese flower, from the lyric pieces" (*Engin* 24). *Dits* more explicitly resist the imposition of features today associated with narrativity than romances, too. It is harder, for instance, to pin down spatio-temporal referents, and to do so often seems beside the point. For example, Nicole de Margival's *Dit de la Panthère* is, by all accounts, less about his love for an actual lady than a meditation on Adam de la Halle's lyrics. There is also less impetus to read *dits* as *droites voies.* So often they seem to go basically nowhere—as in the *Panthère. Dits* have, moreover, been described as circular rather than linear in movement. Cerquiglini-Toulet argues, for instance, that the *Voir Dit* is modeled on the rotations of Fortune's wheel (*Engin* 56–63). *Dits* are less-than-straight in other ways, too. Froissart's *Prison amoureuse* is presented as almost haphazardly assembled by its narrator, Flos, who fumbles around to locate the scattered parts of his text; this *dit* appears as anything but cohesively compiled. There is also little temptation to read *dits* through their endings. The *fin* of Machaut's *Fonteinne amoureuse* is notoriously ambiguous; it asks, "Dites moy, fu ce bien songié?" [Tell me, was this well dreamt/conceived?] (2848). Inconclusive *fins* are, though, by no means restricted to this *dit.* Fishier than *Yvain*'s *fin,* the *Voir Dit,* for instance, culminates in "an ironically jangling sequence whose ludicrously overdetermined affirmation of concord conveys . . . the discord that characterises the end of [Guillaume] and Toute Belle's relationship" (Swift, "Poetic 'I'" 29). Probably no need, moreover, to bother demonstrating how narrative levels interpenetrate in *dits.* For in these texts known for their use of "features" associated with "postmodernist fiction" (Palmer, "Metafictional" 26), "la narration de l'aventure" often becomes entangled in "l'aventure de la narration," to borrow from Jean Ricardou's description of the *nouveau roman* (Cohn 108).

If much of my argument about verse romances already aligns with critical conceptions of *dits,* we might conceive of them as rendering more explicit elements of verse romances that the conventional narrative moving from verse to prose romances has obfuscated. Yet, juxtaposing these genres also invites us to think about other, generally less moralizing ways in which artificial *droites voies* have persisted in criticism of *dits.* Helen Swift has, for example, cautioned against presuming "the implied 'unifying presence' of the poet," which has underpinned many a critical account of Machaut's *dits* ("Poetic I" 20; also

"Picturing Narrative Voice"). McGrady has also recently taken aim at the "oneness" of both the Machaldian "I" and his *oeuvre*. Focusing on the *Jugements*, she shows how digitizing Machaut's manuscripts exposes a "fragmented, damaged, and dis-articulated textual body" that "only loosely resembles the 'Machaut' we have constructed over time" ("Textual Bodies" 17).

These studies are, in my view, particularly exciting, because they resist any straightforward association of authorship with order or cohesion. There can nonetheless be a tendency to locate order in the disorder of *dits*. McGrady has, for example, earlier argued that when the *Voir Dit* confronts us with apparent disorder, which critics once attempted to resolve, Machaut is both "subduing his readers and challenging them to disseminate, disperse, recoup, and rewrite a hybrid and resilient text" (*Controlling Readers* 13). Laura Hughes summarizes this argument as follows: "The deliberate disordering that is the fundamental architecture of the *Voir Dit* would discourage any readerly meddlings from disturbing the author's textual authority" (194). For McGrady, Machaut thus strategically embraces the text's disorder, even if this disorder comes to reflect his authority. Hughes's own clever argument takes a similar form. For her, "each interruption of time and narrative, each surprise of formal interplay, as well as the instances of creative chaos" everywhere in the *Voir Dit* "puncture the warp and weave of a stable textual experience," pointing to a "virtual sphere in which the entirety of the *Voir Dit* could exist, preserved and unbounded" (207, 205). The absence of the *droite voie* thus gestures toward another plane, where things are "virtually" worked out. McGrady, Hughes, Swift, and others have, with brio, therefore paved the way for reading with the disorder of *dits*. Yet, similar to Guynn's argument that allegorical texts stage un-control to sanction greater control, there can be a tendency to return to a complex and indirect association of authorship with control and authority, which I shall resist.

As with romance, this may sound abstract. Yet, it arguably betokens more literal readings of *dits* than those to which we are accustomed. Over the last decades, critics have devoted much effort to prying apart the various levels of the *je* in *dits amoureux*. We have learned to distinguish the "I-protagonist" from the "I-narrator" and the "author" (see e.g., Brownlee, *Poetic Identity*). The fact that these distinctions would, over the centuries, be so important to literature does not mean that they were the *fin* of late medieval authors, and the impulse to distinguish permutations of the *je* merits being questioned. This does mean that, say, Machaut is as silly as the narrator hiding in the bush in the *Behaingne*. Rather, it means that the choice, characteristic of fourteenth-century *dits,* to stage an insipid protagonist-narrator does not—as if by a dialectic reversal—necessarily speak to the brilliant author's control over his text.

Rather, I argue that *dits,* like romances, are often ironic in the de Manian sense, whereby

> ironic language splits the subject into an empirical self that exists in a state of inauthenticity and a self that exists only in the form of a language that asserts the knowledge of this inauthenticity. This does not, however, make it into an authentic language, for to know inauthenticity is not the same as to be authentic. (*Blindness* 214)

While there are important differences between the narrator-protagonist and the implicit author (here, Baudelaire), de Man is arguing that they are each powerless when faced with the instability of their language, their selves, and their world. Similarly, I shall argue that *dits* reflect (on) the pain of being unable to be "authentic" in language.

While the ensuing chapters will develop this notion, taking more seriously the silly *je* so often on the surface of *dits* already brings us full circle, in a manner: back to the notion that *dits* are more engaged in consequential reflection on gender and sexual politics than is generally thought. For if we are not really striving to look through to the implicit author, we are confronted with the amorous protagonist that *dits amoureux* never quite do without. The place of love in *dits* is routinely discussed in some form or another. Yet, critics have often appeared more intent on reconstructing, rather than troubling, what Machaut or Christine means by Love.[15] Too rarely have the feminist and queer perspectives that scholars have shown to be so fruitful when approaching romance and other genres been brought to bear on *dits* (with the exception of feminist work on Christine). Granted, such *dits* as the *Dit de la Panthère,* the *Fonteinne amoureuse,* the *Voir Dit,* and *la Prison amoureuse* may appear more interested in the literary than the erotic. This does not, however, necessarily betoken a seconding of eros. Rather than prioritizing letters over love, *dits amoureux,* I argue, radically interrogate the discursivity of desire, which brings me to this book's second main contention.

SEXUAL INDETERMINACY

In her foundational *Chaucer's Sexual Poetics,* Carolyn Dinshaw reflects on how "love, sex, gender, and literary activity are intimately, metaphorically related in the Middle Ages" (14–15). The commonplace that love was invented—or, more

---

15. See Kelly's notion of "good love," which is "asexual," in *Machaut* 21–93; or Leach 132–96.

accurately, "came into its own in Europe" (Karras 26)—in the twelfth century suggests that they were, in fact, never before so "intimately" bound up with one another. This raises the question not only of why love would become the subject *par excellence* of courtly letters, which largely belongs to Occitanists, but also that of what its "intimate, metaphoric" ties to "literary activity" betoken. Critics such as E. Jane Burns have warned how "studies that read woman as a metaphor for male poetic invention effect a surprising and subtle erasure of female subjectivity" (13). Understanding issues of gender and sexuality as metaphors can, that is, become a pretext for not attending much to the "intimacy" of relations between poetics and gender and sexual politics, as the latter become a way of speaking about the former without this being a two-way street. As much about sexual indeterminacy as it is poetic indeterminacy, this book vies not to collapse one into the other.

Recourse to a modern theorist has helped me in this balancing act. The "underlying assumption" of Lee Edelman's 1994 *Homographesis* is

> that sexuality is constituted through operations as much rhetorical as psychological—or, to put it otherwise, that psychological and sociological interpretations of sexuality are necessarily determined by the rhetorical structures and the figural logics through which "sexuality" and the discourse around it are culturally produced. (xiv)

Yet, if sexuality is contingent on rhetoric, rhetoric depends just as much on sexuality. Indeed, for Edelman, sexuality is never "simply ancillary to the ... unfolding of some trans-historical deconstructive insight into the structural contradictions at work in any representational system as such" (225). Rather, in stunning readings of—in particular—de Man's work on rhetoric, Edelman shows how obsessively he "returns" in his "own figural constructions to the very site of ... erotic speculations" (233). Whether we think we are discussing poetics or sexual politics, Edelman thus suggests, "the body of writing and the writing of the body remain locked in what we might ... choose to call an embrace" (235).

Edelman is perhaps more sweepingly theorizing something akin to Dinshaw's notion that, in Chaucer, "literary representation is understood in terms of the body" (15). Yet, he also takes a tack that Dinshaw does not in her 1989 volume, by arguing that homosexuality is the privileged site for analyzing the rhetoricity of sexuality and the sexual politics of rhetoric.

> By attending to the construction of "homosexuality" as the reified figure of the unknowable within the field of "sexuality," this book will explore how

"gay sexuality" functions in the modern West as the very agency of sexual meaningfulness, the construct without which sexual meaning, and therefore, in a larger sense, meaning itself, becomes virtually unthinkable. (*Homographesis* xv)

Yet, "medievalists know," as James Schultz writes, "that if they claim to have found homosexuals in the Middle Ages they will provoke cries of outrage and nothing else they say will be heard" (51). Edelman's "modern West" cannot therefore include the medieval period, where "sexual meaningfulness" and "meaning itself" must be conceived in relation to something other than homosexuality. Perhaps this "something other" is sodomy, which medievalists such as Burgwinkle and Robert Mills are careful not to equate with homosexuality, but which seems invariably to overlap with it? There can be a tendency to stage a binary opposition between the normative and the sodomitical, and to read into the latter much of the "agency of sexual meaningfulness" that Edelman locates in homosexuality. Witness, for example, such claims as,

> Over the course of 1000 years, (*c.* 500–1500), when almost any sexual act or impulse which did not focus on sex exclusively in terms of procreative potential was branded as sodomitical, all readers conveniently find themselves in the same crowded boat, cast out one and all as sodomites. (Burgwinkle, "État présent" 79)

Two scholars have particularly objected to conceiving of medieval sexuality in terms of the binary opposition of the sodomotical to the normative—or even in binary terms *tout court*: Schultz and Karma Lochrie. Schultz is interested in how "the study of courtly love adds an important chapter to the histories of sexualities that were *not* peripheral" (xvii; original emphasis). He sees recurrent emphasis on marginal sexualities as having entailed undue neglect of the "center," which has led scholars to project an anachronistic notion of normative sexuality onto the medieval period (xvii). Rather than falling in love with an opposite gendered body *qua* heterosexuals, "courtly lovers are," for Schultz, "aristophiliacs: they fall in love with nobility and courtliness" (xx). For her part, Lochrie is equally suspicious of the "heteronormativity," implicit and explicit, "of modern scholarship," which "ends up creating its own modern categories where they did not exist before" (xvi). Heeding the call, increasingly loud in queer theory (e.g., N. Sullivan 119–35; Marcus), to critically interrogate the history of sexual normativity, Lochie argues that there was no unmarked norm in medieval culture. She vies to "drive a methodological wedge between the modern identity formation we call heterosexuality, which is heteronormative, and past sexualities, which were not governed by heteronormativity," but were, instead, "unexpectedly plural" (xvi, xix).

From the groundbreaking work of these scholars, I inherit the desire to probe the tenuousness and messiness of the center, in a move that resists a tendency to concentrate on sexualities at the margins or beyond the bounds of courtliness. Yet, inspired by much feminist work on medieval French literature, I am wary of any impulse radically to dissociate medieval and modern gender and sexual politics: even quite suspicious of what Aranye Fradenburg refers to as "discontinuist historicism," or "the idea that different periods of time are simply and radically other to one another" (87). In concluding her study of "medieval marriage, masochism," and their relation to "the history of heterosexuality," Sarah Salih writes of "proper marital sex" in late medieval England:

> This is heterosexuality, but not as we know it; or rather, since modern heterosexuality is not a singular or coherent formulation, this is not the face that it prefers to show to the modern world. (147)

I study how "courtly love," which is not a "singular or coherent formulation" either, intersects in important ways with both "modern heterosexuality" and influential critiques of it. As Salih implies, denying this risks reifying "modern heterosexuality" (and/or "courtly love") into something artificially stable. It is also, I believe, imperative to insist that critical analysis of interfaces between medieval and modern sexualities can be as sensitive, subtle, and important as insistence on historical differences—perhaps especially when the points of contact are quite counterintuitive. My focus is, therefore, on "a medieval past that is strange to modernity even though it is at the heart of modernity," to quote George Edmondson's subtle take on the relationship of the one to the other (152).

Consider, by way of example, the group which, going by the collective noun *losengiers,* represents the rivals of the *je* at court (Baumgartner, "Trouvères" 171; also Koehler 43–44). Kay has studied the wrongdoings of which troubadours accuse them. These "slanderers" or "gossipmongers" can badmouth the lady, menace the *je*'s amorous or poetic ambitions, or spew enmity in a manner "not specified at all" ("Contradictions" 218). The menace of *losengiers* is therefore not strictly restricted to the realm of the amorous; yet these figures, as Emmanuèle Baumgartner has observed, "are often likened to false lovers [*faux-amants*], that is to men who get what they want from women . . . by using lying, insincere language, which is nonetheless impossible to identify as such" ("Trouvères" 174; see also Dragonetti, *Technique poétique* 272–

78). *Losengiers* thus tend to use their words to stir up trouble in the world of *fin'amor*. *Losengiers* or "*mesdisans*—and the very frequent use of this substitute for *losengier*, where the prefix *mes-* denotes deviance, is revealing—expose the nagging possibility of a gap between the signifier and the signified: here, true love, *la fin'* or *la bon'amor*" (Baumgartner, "Trouvères" 175).

Terms such as *faux amants*—as opposed to the *vrai, fin*, or *bon amant*—point, like the *mes-* in *mesdisans*, to a binary opposition in courtly letters. You can be a true or false lover; you can speak well or badly as a lover yourself or about other lovers. Not unlike modern heterosexuality, *fin'amor* does, then, have—or creates—a foe to which it is diametrically opposed, and the persistence with which medieval French courtly texts denounce *losengiers* suggest that they embody this role more so than any other group.

In a wonderful piece on Christine de Pizan's *Epistre Othea*, Claire Nouvet sheds more light on these sketchy *losengiers*. She notes how, for Christine's Cupid, "the deceiver is less interested in the actual seduction of women than in the narrative of this seduction. His driving impulse, in other words, is not erotic but narrative" ("Writing" 288–89). Nouvet also observes how *losengiers* displace their own problem onto women. The slanderer lacking in "integrity" accuses the woman of lacking integrity: of not being "whole," thus "ascribing guilt to the part that it itself constituted as the 'guilty party'" (291, 292). Nouvet does not, therefore, ignore the complexity of the interactions between *losengiers* and women. She also pulls no punches in highlighting the (generally male) courtier's complicity with them. For the courtly lover or author, by violently denouncing *losengiers*, is *like* them, insofar as s/he is constantly slandering those guilty of slandering (296–300). S/he generally does so, moreover, by "turn[ing] an open hypothesis, the hypothesis of deception, into a certainty: the knowledge of deception" (299). Both *losengiers* and "true lovers" are, that is, similar, because whether denouncing lovers or *losengiers*, one party frequently posits as certainly true what it merely wishes to believe (or to claim).

These *losengiers* seem quite foreign to us. Yet, they can match up well with key concerns of queer theory. Edelman makes much of the invisibility of "homosexual difference":

> Unlike gender difference ... which many feminist and psychoanalytic critics construe as grounding the notion of difference itself, "homosexual difference" produces the imperative to recognize and expose it precisely to the extent that it threatens to remain unremarked and undetected, and thereby to disturb the stability of the paradigms through which sexual difference can be interpreted and gender difference can be enforced. (*Homographesis* 11–12)

Like homosexuals, *losengiers* cannot be visibly identified—if only they had horns, exclaims Bernart de Ventadorn ("Non es meravehla s'eu chan," 33–36, p. 62)—and this causes great anxiety. For medieval "true lovers" as for heteronormativity, the solution is to attempt to morph this indeterminate category into a sort of determinate category; hence, in courtly texts, the use of the term *losengiers* as if it were at all self-evident. In the modern arena, Edelman argues that gay men even, and paradoxically, become determinate in their indeterminacy:

> The gay male body . . . must be *marked and indeterminate at once*; consequently, it is imagined to be marked *as* indeterminate with the result that indeterminacy effectively ceases to *be* indeterminate and becomes, instead, the gay male body's determinate mark. (*Homographesis* 237; original emphases)

Losengiers are like homosexuals insofar as they are only a determinate group to the extent that they figure indeterminacy. This is Nouvet's point: this hazy group (who are they, and how can we identify them?) troubles both the meaningfulness of amorous rhetoric (do I say what I feel?) and the determinacy of meaning more generally, both by spouting "fake news" and by resembling in uncanny ways righteous lovers. *Losengiers,* like modern queers, equally confront courtliness with the potential meaninglessness of sexual behaviors, as they "screw" but don't love women.

Medieval *losengiers* and modern queers are nonetheless uncomfortable bedfellows. In no small part because *losengiers* seem generally misogynistic (see, however, Krueger, *Women Readers* 196–216 for "the feminist reader as *médisant*"). Since *losengiers* are at the heart of the court, stressing their queerness also conflicts with a tendency to situate queerness at the margins. It must reckon, too, with their elite status. Perhaps most importantly, *losengiers* clash with ways in which queerness has historically been approached by rejecting any implicit equation of queerness with same-sex desire, with sexual behaviors more generally, or with recognizable—and imperative—political claims. At one level, that is, there is no reason to think (generally male) *losengiers* are interested in sleeping with other men. Rather, they are more likely to be menacing because they have too much sex with women; they potentially overindulge in, or overprivilege, the *factum*. To return to Derrida's description of deconstruction, *losengiers* can take too far the attraction to the female body, thereby deconstructing the relation of the sexual and the discursive. Or alternately, if (like Nouvet) one views *losengiers* as more interested in discourse than women, they deconstruct the relation of love to rhetoric not only by exposing the potential gap between one's words and one's feelings but also by relegating sex to a secondary position, whereby it is shown to be above all a discursive construct, a narrative phenomenon. Understood in this way, *losengiers* would be guilty of something like "tak[ing] the sex out of being queer," as Leo Bersani has complained of much queer work (42). These opposite ways of interpreting *losengiers* turn on whether one views sexual desire as reflecting a primary engagement with discourse or discourse as manipulated by desire for sex, which is the choice between the sexual and the poetic that this book tries not to make. Yet either way, *losengiers* seem to me to be potentially quite uncomfortable fits with modern queers; for even if queerness's umbrella has considerably expanded in recent years, in particular in medieval English studies, it still seems counterintuitive to locate queerness in a group that is either too straight or not actually interested in sex but instead obsessed with discourse. Just as importantly—and in a notion that resonates with the provocative question recently posed by social theorist Joseph Fischel, is the sex offender "the new queer"? (9)—*losengiers* are a group for which nobody wishes to advocate (or should). There is no movement for the rights of *losengiers*: seemingly no redeeming these deviants.

Losengiers as bad queers, then . . . Only in a manner, though; for, no more than this book is concerned with delimiting what counts as a verse romance or a *dit* am I concerned with "outing" *losengiers*. Sure, we will meet some characters who seem to fit the bill, like the Seneschal in Renart's *Rose*. Yet, it would seem to be missing the point to strive to render determinate a group that is menacing precisely insofar as it mobilizes a profound engagement with indeterminacy. Like Nouvet, I am thus more concerned with the indeterminacy figured by *losengiers*, but which is also most interesting—and dangerous, perverse—insofar as it is not contained by any figure in particular: insofar as it bleeds from antagonists to protagonists, men to women, characters to narrators and authors, as we shall see. In her epochal 1999 *Getting Medieval*, Dinshaw writes that she is interested in "indeterminacies, contradictions, slippages in some major [medieval] cultural phenomena" and the "ways we in the postmodern era in the West—indeterminate, contradictory, and slippery as we are—can make relations with those discourses . . . *in their very indeterminateness*" (11; original emphasis). Similarly, I focus on the indeterminacy of what is perhaps the most major cultural phenomenon—*fin'amor*—and its (appropriately indeterminate) intersections with the indeterminacy today embraced by queer theory.

This book's particular approach to queerness can, therefore, be summarized as follows: I am more focused on the deconstruction of the center—the negativity continuously threatening the courtly lover's most basic and cherished claims—than on sexualities at the margins; more concerned with the corrosive effects of linguistic or poetic indeterminacy on gender and sexuality than the struggles and claims of determinate groups at precise historical moments as reflected in (or repressed by) literary texts; and, by extension, willing to risk emphasizing the immaterial over the material, even the realms of language and the literary over what lies beyond or behind texts.[16] These are, of course, not absolute choices; it is not like I strive actively to ignore, for instance, how aspects of texts relate to contemporary political issues, and such questions will come up time and again. I am also aware that these are risky moves. I risk, in particular, deflecting attention away from the historical evolutions that took place over the Middle Ages and the real existences of those who lived—and loved and suffered—under the sway of medieval courts. And in all honesty, this book is probably not the right place to look for something like the kind of "positivist history and traditional historicism" seemingly dominant in medieval English studies, which Elizabeth Scala ("Gender" 192) and others have critiqued. De Man advocates, however, for a "literary history that would not truncate literature by putting us misleadingly *into or outside it*" (*Blindness* 164; original emphasis). He is fascinated, instead, by how literary language invariably both "fl[ies] away from its own specificity" as literary language and "return[s]" to it (*Blindness* 159). In a similar vein, this book explores how returning to a particular emphasis on language and poetics can mark not a turn away from careful analysis of medieval sexual politics but another radical way of engaging with—or returning to—them. My goal, therefore, is not so much to imply deficiencies in studies that approach medieval queerness in better-trodden historicist modes but to complement our knowledge of it, by emphasizing an insufficiently articulated but unflagging queerness that is inseparable from poetic indeterminacy and inhabits—and infests—the core of a literary tradition that has generally, yet perhaps overly hastily, been understood as predominantly at the service of patriarchy.

A TWISTED PATH . . .

This approach and argument make room for a wide-ranging corpus. I focus on the following texts:

1170	*Erec et Enide*
1176	*Cligés*

---

16. Cf. Freccero's argument about the immaterial (15–30).

1176–81	*Le Chevalier de la Charrette*
1182–85	*Partonopeu de Blois*
1208–10	*Le Roman de la Rose ou de Guillaume de Dole*
1250–1300	*Le Roman de Silence*
1285–1300	*Le Roman du Châtelain de Coucy et de la Dame de Fayel*
1290–1328	*Le Dit de la Panthère*
Before 1342	*Le Jugement du Roy de Behaingne*
1349–50	*Le Jugement du Roy de Navarre*
1360	*La Fonteinne amoureuse*
1363–65	*Le Voir Dit*
1372–73	*La Prison amoureuse*
1404–5	*Le Livre du Duc des Vrais Amans*

I have attempted to strike a balance between canonical and less familiar works; to capture each genre's most intense period of activity; and to give an account that spans, without major gaps, from the second half of the twelfth century to the early fifteenth.

Yet, in this book about troubling *droites voies*, it would be illogical and unhelpful to proceed chronologically. Accordingly, this book is organized thematically. Each chapter begins with a formal issue, probing its indeterminacy and looking to queer theory in order to think about how this indeterminacy bleeds into issues of gender and sexual politics. Each chapter also leverages its specific thematic concern to imagine different ways of conceiving of the relationship between, on the one hand, verse romances and *dits*, and on the other, courtly literature and modern queerness. Indeed, as my argument considers the queerness of form, so too do the specific formal issues examined bear on how it conceives of both medieval literary history and its relation to modern queerness; they bear, that is, on this book's organization and argument. The first chapter is about subjectivity; the second, metalepsis; the third, lyric insertion; and the fourth, irony.

More precisely, the first chapter, "Reflexive, Ambivalent, Queer Subjects," explores how the desiring subject is always-already looking back at itself and implicated in deeply ambivalent relations with both itself and instances of power. This chapter draws on a theoretical framework inspired by resonances between Alain de Libera's *Archéologie du sujet* and Judith Butler's *Psychic Life of Power*. It focuses on three medieval texts: Christine de Pizan's *Duc des Vrais Amans,* Machaut's *Fonteinne amoureuse,* and Chrétien's *Chevalier de la Charrette.* I begin with Christine's *livre*, which has been read as a romance and/or a *dit*, because it so suggestively mobilizes reflexivity both to trouble the contours of the desiring subject and to underscore the ambivalence of her relationship to herself and to power. Queering subjectivity in the *Duc* also opens up new avenues for exploring how earlier male-authored romances and *dits* probe the indeterminacy of the reflexive subject. Indeed, I proceed to argue that the *Fonteinne amoureuse* and the *Charrette* are not so much making breakthroughs in terms of literary subjectivity as they are interrogating the instability and ambivalence characteristic of the reflexive subject. Finally, I reflect on how the ambivalence of the always-already reflexive subject may bear on the relationship of verse romances to *dits* and on that of courtly literature to poststructuralist theory. If, as regards the latter relationship, courtly texts can appear always-already receptive to much queer theory, this may generate an ambivalence that queer studies could strategically embrace.

The second chapter, "Medieval Metalepsis: Queering Narrative Poetics," is about the interpenetration of narrative levels. For the narratologist Debra Malina, metalepsis "forces us to read deconstructively: we must refrain from shutting down meaning, re-containing narrative and its subjects within our usual frames, and instead remain open to unresolvable ambiguities" (19). This chapter studies how metalepsis pushes "us to read deconstructively" in three quite different medieval texts: *Partonopeu de Blois, le Roman de Silence,* and Froissart's *Prison amoureuse*. In dialogue with Butler's *Gender Trouble,* I also contend that metalepsis particularly challenges us to be "open to unresolvable ambiguities" in the realms of gender and sexual politics; unruly narrative poetics correspond to unruly gender and sexual politics. This chapter concludes by thinking about how the figure of metalepsis may help us conceive in new ways of the relations between verse romances and *dits* and between courtly literature and modern queerness. In the spirit of metalepsis, the interplay between these genres (at one level) and between the medieval and the postmodern (at another) fosters an undecidability that powerfully troubles normative notions of before and after, inside and outside, cause and effect.

The third chapter, "On Sameness, Difference, and Textualizing Desire: Queering Lyric Insertion," bucks a tendency to understand the insertion of lyric pieces into narratives in quite binary terms. Such texts as Jean Renart's *Rose,* Jakemés's *Roman du Châtelain de Coucy et de la Dame de Fayel,* and Nicole de Margival's *Dit de la Panthère* can also be understood as both positing and deconstructing the binary opposition between the lyrics and the surrounding narratives. "Sameness and difference, from such a perspective, lose their difference without being the same," as Edelman writes of certain figurations of gay sex (*Homographesis* 70). Indeed, in conversation with Edelman's essays in *Homographesis,* I suggest that the insertion of lyrics into verse narratives not only challenges the criteria of difference used to distinguish the two but also effects a "disorientation of positionality" (183) in relation to the love championed by lyrics; as the desire expressed in songs is further textualized, it is destabilized and exposed to radical critique. Finally, this chapter, which approaches verse narratives that insert lyrics as "long poems" rather than narrativized verse, explores less narrative ways of conceiving of both medieval literary history and the relationship of courtly literature to modern queerness. I suggest that the juxtaposition of verse romances and *dits* and of courtly literature and modern queer theory gets particularly interesting, and messy, when "sameness and difference . . . lose their difference without being the same."

The final chapter, "Queer Irony in Chrétien de Troyes and Guillaume de Machaut," brings together the two most formidable authors of each genre. It focuses on the trope of irony. With de Man, I argue that irony does not simply speak to the author's mastery of language; and with Edelman's *No Future*, I emphasize the suggestive relationship between the negativity of de Manian irony and that of queer desire. This chapter looks to a romance of Chrétien's rarely associated with irony—*Erec et Enide*—and to one always associated with it: *Cligés*. In both texts, I argue that irony is prevalent, but less as an aesthetic technique than as force constantly seeking to unravel the coherence of both these texts and the erotic relationships they describe. Machaut's *Jugement* poems and his *Voir Dit*, which have often been seen as exploring and asserting the status of the author, also mobilize a more chaotic irony that, I contend, communes with the bliss of a radically negative, meaningless, perverse desire. What's more, pairing these readings of Chrétien's and Machaut's texts casts a sort of perverse irony on conventional narratives in medieval French literary studies—namely that of the gradual emergence of the self-conscious author—while also raising the intriguing possibility of whether the relationship between these courtly texts and modern queerness may be conceived of in terms of an ever-negative irony.

Finally, I conclude with a brief "coda," "Slashes," which brings the book's major players back together: verse romances and *dits*, deconstruction and queer theory. I emphasize how these elements relate to each other in particular and powerful ways that nonetheless cannot and must not be worked or straightened out. Similarly, I gesture toward the sort of complex and knotty relations I hope this book will enjoy with other work in the field.

CHAPTER 1

Reflexive, Ambivalent, Queer Subjects

As we saw in the introduction, critics have described the genres of verse romance and the *dits* in similar ways. One element nonetheless recurs in definitions of *dits*, which seems not to apply to romance: *dits* foreground the first person (Léonard 27–32, 158–67). Granted, if romances are generally recounted in the third person, the first is hardly absent, as Sophie Marnette's calculations, for example, reveal (33–38). Countless studies have, in turn, examined the significance of this *je*.[1] Inversely, the third person is perhaps more important to *dits* than it seems. Lechat has, for instance, shown how the *je* is "disseminated and fragmented into various figures, mythological or otherwise" in *dits* by Machaut, Froissart, and Christine (57). The *je* is significantly elaborated through "fictions," largely relayed in the third person.

Beyond the question of how exclusively either genre relies on either pronoun lurks, moreover, a meatier one: that of what the distinction of first- to third-person pronouns portends. Arguing that third-person pronouns "are entirely different from 'I' and 'you,' by their nature and function," the linguist Emile Benveniste has famously contended that they connote radically opposing conceptions of "subjectivity" (256). It is not clear, though, how pertinent Benveniste's assertion is to the Middle Ages. Medieval grammar appears to

---

1. E.g., Krueger, "Author's Voice"; Spearing, *Textual Subjectivity*.

read quite little into the distinction of first- to third-person pronouns.² Conceiving of subjectivity in terms of pronouns may also distort the complexity of the history of the subject, as the philosopher Alain de Libera has recently argued. He writes of Benveniste, "to employ, as he does, the term 'subjectivity' . . . reflects a philosophical decision with a long history . . . a decision that is anything but 'normal,' 'natural,' or 'self-evident'" (*Naissance* 85). In his multivolume *Archéologie du sujet,* de Libera strives to uncover the complex processes through which the *je* has come to install itself "en position de sujet-agent de la pensée" [in the position of subject-agent of thought] (*Quête* 14). For him, the association of subjectivity, thought, and the *je* began to take form in the Middle Ages. Long before Descartes, medieval philosophers were developing what de Libera calls *l'attributivisme*,* or "the explicit assimilation of psychic, noetic or mental states or acts," on the one hand, and "attributes or predicates of the subject defined as *ego,*" on the other (*Naissance* 126).

De Libera's thesis serves, in part, to remind literary scholars of something we seem already to know: that the modern subject was brewing in the Middle Ages. There has also been a strong tendency to study subjectivity in relation to genre, and verse romances and *dits* appear particularly to gesture toward this modern subject, as they are closely associated with the emergence of the individual: as character, narrator, and author.³

Yet, de Libera's "archeology" serves, too, to caution us against this familiar narrative. For him, little is linear in the history of the subject. Rather, it takes the form of rhetorical slides, which he calls "chiasms." He traces how such charged but elusive terms as "subject, substance, hypostasis, suppsoit, I, me, one (*soi*), oneself, conscience, self-consciousness, person, individual, agent, actor, actant, mind (*esprit*), soul, intellect, [and] understanding" have shifted and collided throughout history (*Naissance* 87). The term *subject* is a prime example of such "chiasms." For Aristotle, "the term subject referred to something like a base [*support*] or a substrate whose capacities were purely receptive," as de Libera notes (*Quête* 403). Yet, during the Middle Ages, the subject went from representing that which may be inferred from actions to becoming the principle for these actions. More precisely, two distinct propositions—"all actions require an agent" and "all actions require a subject"—gradually fuse to become "all actions require an agent that is a subject" and "all actions require a subject that is their agent" (*Naissance* 58). And "the inversion or the reversal of the *subiectum* into its ostensible opposite" is, for de Libera, "probably the

---

2. It is, for example, only mentioned in passing in Copeland and Sluiter's anthology.

3. Book-length studies on subjectivity include: Kay, *Subjectivity*; Greene, *Sujet*; Haidu, *Subject of Violence* and *Subject Medieval/Modern*; Zink, *Subjectivité*. Nearly all consider subjectivity in relation to genre.

most extraordinary reworking, in all of the history of philosophy, of a term or concept" (*Quête* 414–15).

A tale of "ambiguities," "cross-contaminations," and "redistributions" (*Naissance* 18), the philosophical history of the subject is, therefore, anything but a *droite voie*. The messiness of the macro-history of subjectivity also corresponds to the equally messy ways by which, for de Libera, the individual subject both emerges and operates. For him, the medieval subject is, to a significant extent, the descendent of Augustine's conception of the *mens humana*. According to the Augustine of *De Trinitate* in particular, the *mens*—translatable as "intellect" or "soul"—is formed on the model of the Trinity. As the three players in the Trinity are united by "mutual immanence," so too for Augustine, "the mental acts known as 'knowledge' and 'love' 'exist in the soul and develop there in a sort of mutual involution'" (*Naissance* 264). The human soul therefore always-already knows and loves itself, and the acts of knowing and loving are not in the soul in the manner of accidents but rather as the soul is. Indeed, the soul is simultaneously *that which* knows and loves itself, *what* it knows and loves, and the *acts* of knowing and loving itself (*Naissance* 216). And if the *mens*—and later, the subject—is subject, verb, and object of itself, it runs afoul of grammatical paradigms, which require that each element be heterogeneous, and of narrative logic, which necessitates the possibility of positing a "before" and "after."

As de Libera argues that neither the macro-history of subjectivity nor the modalities of the individual subject are a *droite voie*, this chapter contends that subjectivity in verse romances and *dits* is no straighter an affair. I turn to texts written by Chrétien de Troyes, Guillaume de Machaut, and Christine de Pizan; yet, rather than understanding works associated with these towering figures as increasingly asserting the power of the mind (and heart) of the individual, I argue that they probe the indeterminacy of—and incoherencies in—the notion of the subject.

These literary texts do so, however, by taking the critical analysis of the subject in directions that medieval philosophy largely does not: by interrogating the subject in its political and psychic dimensions. In order to think about the knottiness of the political and psychic subject, I look to a modern philosopher, whose work on subjectivity complements, in interesting ways, de Libera's. In *The Psychic Life of Power*, Judith Butler posits that an "analysis of subject formation" requires "an evacuation of the first person, a suspension of the 'I'" (29). Like de Libera, Butler is skeptical of the usefulness of grammar when theorizing subjectivity, because grammar requires a subject, whereas her interest lies in studying—and thus not presupposing—the formation of the subject. And for Butler as for de Libera, grammatical logic cannot account for the formation of the subject, because the subject is always-already self-reflexive, both subject and object in relation to itself. Yet, unlike de Libera—or Augustine, or medieval philosophers—Butler insists that this reflexivity is political; the subject is both subject and object of itself, because it is also subject and object of power dynamics beyond it. "The subject exceeds the logic of noncontradiction, is an excrescence of logic" because it "is *neither* fully determined by power *nor* fully determining of power (but significantly and partially both)" (17; original emphases).

The relationship of the subject to itself and to power is thus contradictory; yet Butler prefers to call it "ambivalent." No doubt this is because ambivalence draws us into the realm of the "psychic," which, for Butler, cannot be disentangled from the politics of subjection. Indeed, for her, the subject is not only subject and object of itself and power, but more accurately described as subject and object of "a love or desire or libidinal attachment" for itself and for instances of power (171). This "attachment" does not emanate from an autonomous being; nor is it injected, as a weapon wielded by Power, into presubjected bodies, as Foucault seems to suggest. Rather, for Butler, forms of desire appear to precede the subject or object of affection. In this sense, the subject is almost necessarily queer; for the subject *is* to the extent that it desires, but neither the subject nor the object of desire is, or can be, determinate. Desire does not reflect a straight line connecting two established points, but the "turn" or "recoiling" through which the subject emerges (*Psychic Life* 168).

For Butler, this "sorry bind" (79) fosters intractable ambivalence in the modern subject. In this chapter, I argue that medieval texts treat the notion of the subject with a similarly charged ambivalence. This chapter focuses on three works, selected according to two criteria. One, each is associated with a great author and thus routinely read in terms of the development of self-conscious authorship. Two, each explicitly troubles, in literary terms, what it means to be numerically one, where this basic issue of "oneness" lies at the heart of both de Libera's and Butler's reflections on subjectivity (e.g., de Libera, *Quête* 122–59). The *Charrette* purports, that is, to be requested of Chrétien de Troyes by Marie de Champagne, and Godefroi de Leigni ostensibly pens the final third of the romance. The *Fonteinne amoureuse* presents as the fruit of the collaboration—professional, intellectual, sentimental—between Guillaume and the Prince. In the *Duc des Vrais Amans*, Christine nominally recounts her patron's love affair at his request and in his voice. In each case, challenging what it means for a literary text to be numerically one bleeds, I contend, into deeper critical interrogation of what the subject is.

In developing this argument, I will proceed backward in time. This may better lend itself to resisting the notion of forward-moving progress. It also better reflects the crux of the issue. Indeed, both Butler and de Libera are concerned with looking backward; looking back at the formation of the subject, both focus on how the subject always-already looks back at itself. Moving backward is a practical decision, too, since Christine's *Duc des Vrais Amans* particularly clearly tackles the issues framed here. The *Duc*, which has been considered as a verse romance and/or a *dit*, explicitly troubles the first- to third-person distinction. By all accounts a particularly self-conscious text, it also grapples with issues of gender and sexual politics. While critics tend to consider separately various of these elements, I focus on how they interpenetrate. I read the *Duc* as a verse romance and a *dit* that mobilizes reflexivity to express the philosophically, politically, and psychically dense ambivalence of the gendered and desiring subject.

Queering subjectivity in the *Duc* also opens up new ways of reading the stakes of reflexivity in earlier works. Contrary to a critical tradition that persistently understands Guillaume de Machaut as exploring and asserting the status of the vernacular author, I suggest that in the *Fonteinne amoureuse*, reflexivity reflects a deep ambivalence: both toward his subjection at the hands of the Prince and toward himself. The *dit* explores, too, the complex role of "passionate attachments" (*Psychic Life* 6) in the story of the subject. Finally, I journey back to Chrétien's *Charrette*. Rather than understanding this romance as Chrétien's self-conscious literary masterpiece about Lancelot and Guinevere's love, I read it as about the paradoxical and deeply ambivalent reflexivity of the desiring subject: whether Chrétien, Lancelot, Guinevere, or Godefroi. Far from simply asserting the importance of the individual subject, each of these texts therefore troubles the coherence of this construct; and considered together they allow us to glimpse a less straight medieval subject whose relationship to modern queerness merits careful reconsideration.

LE DUC DES VRAIS AMANS

Few medieval prologues are as jarring as that which introduces the *Duc des vrais amans* (c. 1403). The author did not want to write this text, she tells us, but her patron forced her hand:

>Combien que occupacion
>Je n'eusse ne entencion
>A present de dittiez faire
>D'amours, car en aultre affaire
>Ou trop plus me delictoye

> Toute m'entente mettoye,
> Vueil je d'aultrui sentement
> Comencier presentement
> Nouvel dit, car tel m'en prie
> Qui bien puet, sanz qu'il deprie,
> Comander a trop greigneur
> Que ne suis. C'est un seigneur
> A qui doy bien obeïr . . . (1–13)

> While I had neither the leisure nor the intention of writing a *dit* about love at present, because I have been putting all my efforts into something else that I was enjoying far more, I wish now to begin a new *dit* about another's feelings; for he who requests this of me can, without begging, dispense orders to people more important than me. It is a lord whom I must obey.

Christine is therefore not drawn to her lord's struggles with "Amours" (19). Yet, tell his story she apparently must, and as the prologue concludes, she effects a seemingly bold gesture, choosing to appropriate his *je*: "Et par son assentement / Je diray en sa personne / Le fait si qu'il le raisonne" [and with his accord, I will recount what happened from his perspective, as he describes it] (38–40).

Because no historical model has been identified for the Duke, critics have wondered whether this sequence is "real or imagined" (Altmann 233). Since it recalls other texts where Christine similarly purports to be writing "d'aultrui sentement" (about another's feelings), the latter seems likely (Altmann; Paupert). This tactic appears to get Christine out of a bind. She can remain free of any suggestion that she dabbles in illicit love, thus fostering the carefully crafted image of her as virtuous widow, while nonetheless writing about "Amours," the terrain *par excellence* on which courtly writers strut their poetic stuff.[4]

This familiar narrative occludes, however, the larger questions relating to subjection that this passage raises. Because an "authoritative voice . . . hails the individual" (*Psychic Life* 5), it resembles a scene of Althusserian interpellation. It also exemplifies the ambivalence that, for Butler, lies at the heart of subjection. "Subjection consists," she writes, "precisely in [our] fundamental dependency on a discourse we never chose but that, paradoxically, initiates and sustains our energy" (*Psychic Life* 2). Similarly, while Christine does not wish to be interpellated, this act "initiates" an endeavor, into which she channels

---

4. See e.g., Kelly, *Christine de Pizan's* 107–41; Brownlee, "Widowhood"; Demartini.

much "energy." That Christine both submits to her Lord's will and appropriates his *je* speaks to this entanglement of powerlessness and power. As Butler puts it, "Submission and mastery take place simultaneously, and this paradoxical simultaneity constitutes the ambivalence of subjection" (*Psychic Life* 116).

Butler begins *The Psychic Life of Power* by looking to Hegel, and her reflections on the transition from "Lordship and Bondage" to "the Unhappy Consciousness" seem even more pertinent to the *Duc*'s prologue. She describes the initial relationship between the lord and bondsman as follows:

> The lord postures as a disembodied desire for self-reflection, one who not only requires the subordination of the bondsman in the status of an instrumental body, but who requires in effect that the bondsman *be* the lord's body, but be it in such a way that the lord forgets or disavows his own activity in producing the bondsman, a production which we will call a projection. (35; original emphasis)

Similarly, by adopting her Lord's pronoun, Christine "becomes" him, so as to satisfy his "desire for self-reflection." This is why grammatical paradigms do not hold up; in this hierarchical model, her *je* paradoxically only emerges through the "projection" of his. This prologue, like Butler's text, also gestures toward how desire is bound up with these issues. For in this tale of "Amours, ouquel servage / Est encor son cuer en gaige" [Love, in whose service his heart remains pledged] (19–20), Christine's servitude toward her Seigneur appears elusively to reflect his amorous "servage."

But is it justified to read so much into these forty lines? Yes, I think, because the *Duc* is repeatedly "turning back upon itself," to borrow Butler's formula for describing reflexivity (*Psychic Life* 22, 63, 168, and passim). Just as the *je* repeats such expressions as, "Or m'esteut tourner arriere / A ma matiere premiere" [now I must turn back to my initial material] (635–36), so too is this text persistently returning to this almost primal scene. It alludes, for example, to the issue of not telling one's own tale when the Duke declines to gloat about tournament successes, because "c'est honte de compter / Son mesmes fait" [it is shameful to recount one's own deeds] (1085–86). In a similar vein, when the Duke and his lady finally come together, she exclaims, "Dont pour nous deux me convient / Parler quant ne vous souvient / De riens dire!" [so I must speak for both of us, since you can't come up with any words] (2706–8).[5] Butler's reading of Hegel may help explain the *Duc*'s penchant for self-reflexivity. According to her,

---

5. See Laird and Richards 105–7; Demartini 91.

> As the bondsman slaves away and becomes aware of his own signature on the things that he makes, he recognizes in the form of the artifact that he crafts the markings of his own labor, markings that are formative of the object itself. His labor produces a visible and legible set of marks in which the bondsman reads back from the object a confirmation of his own formative activity. (*Psychic Life* 36)

Christine's awareness of her own "signature," her "markings," seems tangible in this text "littered with clues calling the reader's attention to the author's presence."[6] She even appears to "rea[d] back from the object a confirmation of [her] own formative activity," since, as the narrative concludes, Christine gloats over the achievement she has pulled off. She brags about having told the entire tale in *rimes léonines*, "Pour moustrer son essïence" [in order to show off her learning] (3571). Try to tell a long story using such rich rhymes, she adds, and you'll see it isn't easy (3577–80). As Dominique Demartini observes of these lines, "Christine says nothing about the tale of love she has just narrated and passes no judgment on it"; rather, "she invites . . . the reader to appreciate her poetic *tour de force*" (90). This bondsman has become aware of her signature on the thing she has made.

Yet, the text is "after all, the duke's story" too, as Krueger stresses (*Women Readers* 227). In particular, it remains a tale of "courtly love," of which critics have long argued that Christine is no fan. When advancing this argument about this text, scholars always hold up the same piece of evidence: a prose epistolary, far longer than the seven others included in the *Duc*, where Sébille de Monthault de la Tour vociferously denounces the consequences of adulterous liaisons for women. Sébille is routinely understood as "a porteparole for Christine the author."[7] The *Duc* is therefore generally conceived of as "a narrative poem with two competing segments" (Fenster 469). On the one hand, it is a carefully crafted piece of courtly poetry; on the other, an indictment of adultery, relayed in damning prose. This suspiciously neat dichotomy occludes, however, the psychic and political stakes of the poetic achievement and the literary and psychological complexity of the text's political intervention. Rather than opposing Christine's craftly courtly poetry to her political prose, I propose to read the text in its entirety as a critical analysis of subjection, which stresses the ambivalence of reflexivity in both its literary and psycho-political dimensions. Krueger argues that, "by voicing the *livre* as the

---

6. Demartini and Lechat, referring also to the text's manuscript tradition ("Introduction" 18, in Christine, *Duc des Vrais amans*).

7. Krueger, *Women Readers* 237. See also, e.g., Laird and Richards 111; Brownlee, "Rewriting Romance" 173; Demartini 96. Adams offers a considerably more nuanced reading.

extended monologue of a man in love, Christine can explore the problem of woman's displacement within romance's discourse" (*Women Readers* 229). I shall study the *Duc*'s representation of subjectivity by focusing on the "displacement" of one woman: the prologue's author-narrator.

Christine's initial predicament is persistently—indeed, almost constantly—piercing through the Duke's story, albeit generally more subtly than in the two examples cited above. As the text kicks off, for example, the Duke wishes to fall in love, "Pour ce que ou*o*ye tenir / Les amans plus qu'autres gens" [because I had heard that lovers are considered nobler than all others] (44–45). The *oïr-dire* is a staple of "courtly love." Yet here, it may also recall how Christine is narrating what she overhears. Immediately thereafter, the Duke falls for a lady he has long frequented but for whom he only now feels the pangs of passion. He reflects,

> Si sembloye cil qui nage
> Par mer, cerchant mainte terre
> Pour trouver ce qu'il peut querre
> Pres de soy, et point n'y vise
> Tant que un autre l'en advise. (222–26)

Thus I resembled he who sails the seas, looking in many lands for what he could find nearby; yet he doesn't realize it, until another points it out to him.

The Duke's lofty sentiment takes on a more concrete hue here, as this narrative is literally what "another" describes for him. Sweet love then utterly overwhelms our Duke. He exclaims, "A vivre d'aultre maniere / Vraye Amour m'aprist en l'eure" [True Love taught me, right then, to live in a different way] (292–93). If love radically alters the Duke's course, so too has the Duke forced Christine onto a new path; both must "live another way." As any good lover would, the Duke will entirely submit to this newfound influence in his life, letting Love run the show: "Amours faisoit tout l'affaire, / Non pas moy" [Love was responsible for everything, not me] (1103–4). Yet, in this text, Christine, rather than Love, seems to be "responsible for everything, not him." Perhaps we might, then, compare Christine to Love, the subject about which she ostensibly does not wish to write? In any case, the Duke's amorous behaviors continue softly but persistently to rub up against Christine's predicament. The Duke will, for instance, later fret "Que mon semblant le courage / Demoustroit, maulgré qu'en eusse" [that my appearance betrayed my feelings, despite my best intentions] (1342–43). Similarly, critics have wondered how—and where—the *Duc* betrays Christine's "real" attitudes toward "courtly love." The Duke nonetheless persistently attempts to hide his struggles from view: "et le dueil qu'avoye / Dissimulay et couvry" [and I dissimulated and hid the pain I had] (1555–56). In this text, however, it is above all Christine who is "disguising and covering" her state.

As these examples suggest, nothing is too remarkable about the Duke's trajectory—yet another young aristocrat, overwhelmed by Love. Something more singular is nonetheless occurring, as by persistently alluding to the prologue, the *Duc* subtly allows ambivalence to foment. For the Duke's feelings are, on the one hand, truer and more powerful because they overlap with Christine's predicament; yet, on the other, this reflexivity pulls us away from the Duke by hinting at her distance from his plight.

These reflexive returns to the prologue are particularly crafty in the numerous lyrics inserted into the text. In the seventh *ballade*, for example, the *je* declares,

> Ha! Amours, bien m'as traÿ
> Qui au premier pour moy prendre
> Me fus doulz, puis envaÿ
> M'as si qu'il me fault mort prendre
> Par toy! L'en te doit reprendre
> De porter double visage:
> Mais l'un a couleur de cendre
> Et l'autre a d'un ange ymage. (1859–66)

> Oh, Love, you have sorely betrayed me. Initially, to capture me, you were sweet, and you have since attacked me such that I shall die at your hands. You should be accused of being two-faced. One face is the color of ashes, the other bears the image of an angel.

Yet, Love is not only "two-faced" because it makes the Duke suffer. Rather, in the *Duc,* it is literally so, because this tale of love is the product of the Duke's and Christine's heads coming together, with their differing perspectives. The *je*'s clichéd exclamation is therefore truer than he realizes, but love is also more duplicitous than he figures; for the allusion, by glancing back to the prologue, simultaneously pulls us out of the Duke's suffering, effectively betraying it.

Other lyrics lend themselves to similar readings. The *je* persistently protests that he is entirely at his lady's service; one refrain reads "A vous servir tant com vivray m'oblige" [I pledge to serve you as long as I live] (614), another "A qui serf suis par doulce retenue" [to whom I am a lovingly bound serf] (828). Reflexivity colors these protestations with a similar ambivalence. They are twice true, as Christine serves the Duke who serves his lady, but also duplicitous, since beneath the Duke's amorous *servage* lies the specter of the poet's less glamorous, and less amorous, servitude. Reflexivity infests other courtly clichés, too. In his third *rondeau,* the *je* says of his lady, "vous faites ma vigour soustenir" [you allow me to sustain my vigor] (1240), whereas Christine literally "sustains" the Duke by writing the text. In the fourth *ballade,* the *je* wonders, "Et que feray quant . . . Ne recevray d'Amours fors que l'escume?" [And what shall I do, when from Love I receive but the foam?] (1484–85). Christine might be said to glean only the "foam"—the most superficial part—of this Love, because she is narrating a love story in which she does not partake. In this *ballade,* the *je* also struggles to take leave of his Lady: the refrain reads, "Helas! Comment vous pourray je adieu dire?" [Alas! How shall I say farewell to you?] (1481). The next *ballade* is also about the pain of leave-taking. It begins,

> Adieu, ma redoubtee dame,
> Adieu, sur toutes souveraine,
> Adieu, perfaitte et sanz nul blasme,
> Adieu, tres noble et d'onneur pleine,
> Adieu, vraye loyal certaine,
> Adieu, la flour de tout le monde,
> Adieu sans adieu, blanche et blonde. (1564–70)

> Farewell, my much-feared lady; farewell, sovereign among ladies; farewell, perfect and blameless one; farewell, very noble lady, so full of honor; farewell, true, loyal, steadfast; farewell, flower of the whole world. Farewell without farewell, my fair, blond lady.

While there is nothing surprising about a courtly lover bemoaning the necessity of departing from his lady, another leave-taking of a woman is also lurking in the background here: Christine's renunciation of her pursuits, even her person, in the prologue. In fact, the formula "Adieu sans adieu" wonderfully captures the ambivalence of the *Duc*'s reflexivity. By persistently recalling the prologue, Christine is returning to the moment when she renounced her own *je,* her own desires; she is bidding them (or herself) "adieu." Yet, by repeatedly saying "adieu," she also isn't saying "adieu," because the compulsion repeatedly to renounce her self prevents it from ever being complete. As Butler writes of the Hegelian subject,

The renunciation of the self as the origin of its own actions must be performed repeatedly and can never be finally achieved. . . . The self becomes an incessant performer of renunciation, whereby the performance, as an action, contradicts the postulation of *in*action that it is meant to signify. (*Psychic Life* 49; original emphasis)

Each reflexive return to the prologue both reiterates the poet's renunciation of her agency and undoes this posture, by recalling that there is still a *je* to renounce.

It is not, moreover, only in terms of the *je* that the *livre* treats the ambivalence of subjection. Christine's posturing in the prologue also resonates with the ensuing behaviors of the object of the Duke's affections, the anonymous lady. Like Christine, this lady will, for example, hesitate before accepting the Duke's pretensions: "Un petit s'en excusa / Mais ne le me refusa" [She demurred a bit but didn't refuse me in the end] (779–80). Like the prologue's author-narrator, this lady signs on to helping the Duke behind the scenes: "Car feroye / Plus pour vous, et toutevoye / Ne vueil je que nul le sache" [For I would do more for you; I nevertheless don't want anyone to know it] (897–99). Like the author-narrator, this lady even appears to exist to better the Duke, asking only "que je puisse estre cause de vostre exaulcement en vaillance" [that I may be the cause of your rise in valor] (II.278). "Car je ne vouldroie mie / Que tu deisses qu'a demie / Je me fusse a toy donnee" [For I do not wish that you could say that I gave myself only half-heartedly to you] (2748–50), the Lady says, and the author-narrator similarly appears to give herself almost entirely to her Lord.

As in both de Libera's and Butler's thinking, reflexivity therefore troubles the opposition of *je* to *tu,* since it makes Christine both *je* and *tu* in the Duke's story. It troubles the opposition of first- and third-person pronouns, too, because another figure equally hearkens back to the prologue: the Duke's cousin, the *tiers* to whom he unburdens his heavy heart. "Ne me devez receler / Vo courage ne vostre estre" [You ought not keep your feelings or state from me] (1678–79), says the cousin, who purports to be entirely at his relative's service. For some scholars, this cousin recalls Ami from Jean de Meun's *Rose*.[8] Yet, he also undoubtedly recalls the author, as his role might be described as an almost rosy recasting of the prologue, where taking the lover's confession is willed rather than compulsory—and where the confessor wishes to abet this affair.

And abet he does. The cousin concocts a plan for the lovers' sole rendezvous in the text, in a scene brimming with ambivalent reflexivity. The lady

---

8. Brownlee, "Rewriting Romance" 177; Kelly, *Christine de Pizan's* 134.

accepts that, "Avec mon cousin je voyse / Vestu com s'un varlet fusse" [I may go with my cousin (to her), disguised as if I were a servant] (2481–82). Over the course of this sequence, the Duke continues to insist on his disguise: for example, he says, "Lors ma robe desvesti / Et une autre revesti," [then I took off my robes and donned others] (2536–37), adding, "D'estre congneu me garday" [I made sure not to be recognized] (2541). The Duke's donning the robes of another recalls Christine's behavior in the prologue, *a fortiori* because it invokes the master-servant dynamic. Indeed, the *je* exclaims,

> Si voiez comment mestier
> Est aucuneffois au maistre
> Qu'il soit varlet, et puet estre
> Que souvent ainsi advient,
> A qui a s'entente avient. (2905–9)

Now you see how it is sometimes necessary for the master to become the servant, and maybe it often occurs in this way for he who realizes his intentions.

Since the Duke is pretending to be a servant, although he is really in charge, this passage may suggest that by initially presenting as servant, Christine was but pretending to submit to her Lord, although she always knew she was running the show. There is nonetheless an important difference between the Duke's and Christine's disguises. It is clear enough why the Duke dresses up as a servant; he wants his audience with his lady. What, though, is Christine's "entente" in representing herself as a "varlet"? Not love, in any straightforward sense, and obviously not sex. Rather, because reflexivity is so persistently ambivalent in this *livre,* I would suggest that it is to think through the complexity of the condition of the reflexive subject.

The plot's next movement, Sébille's dramatic intervention, supports this hypothesis. Granted, critics have never found Sébille's message to be too ambivalent (see note 7). Yet, like the preceding narrative, this letter is persistently, and elusively, glancing back to the prologue. Back, for example, is the motif of interpellation, as the Duke's lady hails her former governess: come to me, she says, "le plus hastivement que vous pourrez" [as quickly as you can] (IV.330). Sébille responds by claiming that she must instead attend to her ailing daughter—and so return the motifs of hesitating or even inventing pretexts.[9] Sébille then chides her former charge at length. This lady, Sébille claims, has betrayed the fact that she is in love by speaking in "paroles couvertes" [covert

---

9. *Le Livre des Trois Vertus,* where this letter is reproduced (I.xxvii, pp. 109–20), holds this up as the ideal excuse for a governess who does not wish to abet the princess's illicit affair.

language] (V.336). Yet, the author-narrator also speaks through "paroles couvertes," as we have seen. The behavior that threatens to undo the Duke's lady is, therefore, curiously similar to that through which Christine resists her own erasure. Reflexivity renders equally slippery Sébille's ensuing insistence that "courtly love" is predicated on a lie, according to which men claim that women make them valiant, while men really just destroy their reputations: "Et a dire, 'Je feray un homme vaillant,' certes je dis que c'est trop grant folie de soy destruire pour acroistre un autre" [And to say, "I'll make a man valiant," truly I declare it is too great a folly to destroy oneself to raise another] (V.342). While Sébille offers an important argument against the misogyny of *fin'amor*, it is not one that this text necessarily supports; for Christine makes the Duke into a valiant (enough) character without entirely destroying herself—and certainly without destroying her reputation. In fact, contrary to Sébille's notion that, though purporting to serve women, men "servent eulx mesmes quant l'onneur et le preu leur en demeure et non mie a la dame" [serve themselves when the honor and glory belong to them, not the lady] (V.342), Christine might be said to "serve" her own reputation in this *livre* despite purporting to serve the Duke. For while the Duke has been relegated to anonymity, this text, which only names Sébille (Brownlee, "Rewriting Romance" 181), would circulate with Christine's other works. "Glory and honor" seem, then, finally to belong to women here.

Reflexivity continues to foster ambivalence. Men, Sébille claims, are all too frequently insincere: "Pour les dames decepvoir dient ce qu'ilz ne pensent mie ne vouldroient faire" [In order to deceive ladies, they say what they neither think nor count on doing] (V.346). Yet, this is a text written by a woman who undertakes something she doesn't wish to do and says what she doesn't think. It also appears to be penned by a woman who chooses servitude, which is something Sébille cannot understand (V.346). Sébille frets, moreover, that adulterous affairs have the unfortunate effect of empowering the lady's actual servants: "Quel servitude a une dame . . . qui n'osera reprendre ne blasmer son servant ou sa servante . . . quant elle se sent en leur dongier" [What servitude for a lady who dares not correct or blame her servants, when she feels that they have something on her] (V.348). This is, however, not a text that frowns on dependence on servants, but rather one that exists because of the servant's skillfulness.

My goal is not merely to deconstruct this letter. Of course, "courtly love" is a misogynist construct, which Sébille calls out in new and important ways. In the context of this text, reflexivity nonetheless complicates things. It even troubles Sébille's basic message: as regards *fin'amor*, for women, "le plus seur est du tout l'eschiver et fouir" [the safest thing is to steer completely clear of it and flee it] (V.340). The letter is ill-positioned to argue that women should simply renounce the patriarchic trap of "courtly love," because it is persistently glancing back to the problem of the author-narrator's subjection to patriarchy, which it does not neatly renounce. Like the preceding narrative, it develops, instead, the notion that renunciation is no straightforward affair.

Sébille's letter nonetheless adds an important twist to the text's reflections on the ambivalence of subjection, which recourse to Butler again helps illuminate. Butler is fascinated by what happens to the bondsman once he realizes the value of his labors:

> The bondsman takes the place of the lord by recognizing his own formative capacity, but once the lord is displaced, the bondsman becomes lord over himself, more specifically, lord over his own body; this form of reflexivity signals the passage from bondage to unhappy consciousness. It involves splitting the psyche into two parts, a lordship and a bondage internal to a single consciousness, whereby the body is again dissimulated as an alterity, but where this alterity is now interior to the psyche itself. No longer subjected as an external instrument of labor, the body is still split off from consciousness. (*Psychic Life* 42)

Sébille's letter reflects a similar trajectory. The lord appears "displaced," with the bondsman (Sébille) now speaking for herself. Yet, argues Butler, even when the bondsman takes charge, the mode of subjection persists, although its object changes; the bondsman attempts to subject his body. Not dissimilarly, the subaltern attempts here to instill an "unhappy consciousness" in the lady, which would manifest itself as the repression of her bodily desires. The concept of the "unhappy consciousness" is also pertinent to the subjectivity of this subaltern, Sébille. Butler writes of the subject, "Every effort to . . . subordinate or to mortify its own body, culminates inadvertently in the *production* of self-consciousness as a pleasure-seeking and self-aggrandizing agent" (*Psychic Life* 53; original emphasis). In a similar vein, Sébille seems to take pleasure from refusing pleasure to the lady, in a self-aggrandizing gesture that comes to constitute her very identity. Sébille's identity is defined by her position against eroticism. It is also undeniably self-aggrandizing; witness the magnificent name, Sébille de Monthault de la Tour, which couldn't be loftier (Brownlee, "Rewriting Romance" 181). As mentioned, critics routinely stress, moreover, Christine's connections not only to Sébille's name but also to the position she advocates. In later texts—namely the *Livre des Trois Vertus,* where this letter is reproduced almost verbatim—Christine seems to adopt similar positions. Perhaps, then, Christine might be understood, like

Sébille, not as a self-conscious author who happens to take a negative view of the politics of "courtly love," but rather as self-conscious author *because* she takes a form of ambivalent pleasure from policing bodies: her own, and those of other women.

The letter's intradiegetic reception supports this quite heterodox reading of it; for the text could hardly react more ambivalently to Sébille's intervention. While the lady momentarily heeds her advice, the Duke, once he gets his hands on it, proclaims, "La voulsisse avoir noyee" [I wished that I had drowned her] (3236). By electing not to celebrate the letter, the text is turning against this turn against itself. It also turns against Sébille's letter more subtly, by inviting comparison between the Duke's and Sébille's pretensions, since the lady is equally passive before both. Indeed, whether acquiescing to the Duke or to Sébille, she hardly speaks for herself. The Duke's and Sébille's interests are, of course, diametrically opposed; yet the text elects to present both as dueling forces, each seeking to overcome the lady. In so doing, it represents the subjection of the (female) body by the lord and by the bondsman as eerily interrelated.

The *Duc* also chooses to have Sébille's intervention be ineffective. In the *livre*, it is but a temporary roadblock, overcome easily enough once the Duke demands one final audience with his lady: "Ainçois que du tout soye congeiez, que une fois puisse parler a vous affin que je prengne congié et die adieu . . ." [Before I am entirely dismissed, may I speak to you once more, so that I can take my leave and say farewell] (VII.360). Rather than prompting the definitive end of the relationship, the letter therefore becomes the occasion for more play about the motif of renunciation. It is an *adieu* to which the text itself seems to attempt to say *adieu*, after the Duke demands an "adieu sans adieu." It is a twist in this cycle of unresolved renunciations.

This motif of *adieu sans adieu* also permeates the final component of "the text's elaborate paratextual frame" (McGrady, "Patron" 210): the *Ballades de plusieurs façons*. A series of lyrics exchanged between the lovers that describes their suffering as their relationship "wears away over time" (Demartini 101), the *Ballades* are quite literally about the difficulty of renunciation. They also speak to the author's difficulties in renouncing this text, which seemingly will not end: even after the narrative proper has concluded and the author produced an epilogue. In such contexts, it is perhaps unsurprising that the final piece—the lady's *complainte*—invokes a sort of "adieu sans adieu." The *je* says of the Duke,

> Et au moins se congié pris
> Eust de moy, estre repris

N'en deust tant. Si a mespris
 Puis qu'il dessemble
De moy en qui avoit pris
Honneur, valeur et tout pris,
Dont ne me deust en depris
 Avoir, me semble. (129–36, p. 420)

And if he had, at the very least, taken leave of me, he shouldn't be reproached to such an extent. But he did wrong, since he abandons me through whom he had acquired honor, glory, and all renown. Thus he shouldn't hold me in disdain, I should think.

It makes sense that the text concludes by fretting over a (non)*adieu*. From one end to the other, it is self-consciously reflecting on the complexity of renunciation, which, it shows, is never satisfactory or complete. The *Duc* mobilizes reflexivity to think through the political, psychic, and philosophic ambiguity of renunciation; and this, no doubt, is because it understands how crucial it is to the condition of the subject.

We might even go further. If the *Duc* is about troubling renunciation, should we assume, as critics have (e.g., Brownlee, "Widowhood"; Altmann, esp. 221), that Christine renounces her interest in courtly themes as her career proceeds, coming to favor more didactic works? It is tempting to read the *Duc* as a sort of *mise en abyme* of Christine's literary trajectory. In her *oeuvre*, there is a "tension between courtly, relatively conventional themes" in texts written prior to c. 1404 and the "more purely didactic and political material" in the ensuing works, for which Christine is best known today (Altmann 242). This tension appears analogous to that within the *Duc*, between the verse narrative and lyrics, on the one hand, and Sébille's letter, on the other. When it comes to Christine's *oeuvre*, "the tendency is . . . to place more value on the latter than the former" (Altmann 242). Many critics seem to have taken Part III of the 1405 *Advision-Cristine* at its word, conceiving of the "courtly period" of Christine's career as "nothing more than a necessary first step in the establishment of her literary career as a woman writer" (Brownlee, "Widowhood" 347). As regards courtly love, so the story goes, "her own *vray sentement* changes" (Kelly, *Christine de Pizan's* 124), and Christine will "carefully and programmatically detac[h] her female-gendered authorial persona from the economy of sexual desire, normally associated with courtly discourse" (Brownlee, "Widowhood" 340).

Conceiving of the *Duc* as a *mise en abyme* for Christine's literary trajectory serves as a strong word of caution against this received narrative. It suggests that the renunciation of desire is not so straightforward. Instead, the turn against eroticism is a gesture characteristic of the ambivalence of the reflexive subject. Yet, rather than developing this thesis only in relation to Christine's *oeuvre*, I wish to look not forward but further backward, using the *Duc* to reconsider the representation of subjectivity in the vast literary traditions to which it responds.

LA FONTEINNE AMOUREUSE

The *Duc*'s juxtaposition of narrative verse, *forme fixe* lyrics, and prose epistolaries is an unmistakable nod to Machaut's legacy. Its self-reflexivity also smacks of earlier *dits*. Yet, for some critics, Christine uses reflexivity differently from her predecessors. J. Earl Richards contends, for instance, that Jean de Meun taught male authors to seek "refuge in . . . an indeterminacy deployed to reinforce the solipsism of the poet" (99). Christine disdained such navel-gazing, "because it turned" gender "into a matter of unresolved play" and "because historically misogynists had employed indeterminacy against women, as in the *Rose*" (112). I have argued that the *Duc* mobilizes reflexivity and indeterminacy in ways indeed not simply "solipsistic" or "playful." Yet, in this section, I explore how male-authored *dits* also self-consciously put reflexivity and indeterminacy to the purpose of thinking through philosophic, political, and psychic issues related to the condition of the subject.

In advancing this argument, it makes sense to look to the best-known author of *dits*: Machaut, whose "poetic I" has "exercised perhaps more fascination" over scholars than any other element of his work (Swift, "Poetic 'I'" 15). The *Fonteinne amoureuse* (c. 1360) is by all accounts one of Machaut's most self-reflexive texts. "Regularly fêted . . . as a quintessential portrait of medieval poet-patron relations" (McGrady, "Machaut" 364), it also depicts this relationship in a manner which, at instances, recalls the *Duc*. For example, the *Fonteinne* equally foregrounds interpellation. As it opens, the narrator finds himself alone in a creepy castle, where he is stunned by a voice: "Une creature / Oÿ, qui trop fort se plaignoit" [I heard a creature, who was very loudly lamenting] (70–71). Guillaume (as critics call the *je*-protagonist) then transcribes the intricate amorous *complainte* that this "creature," who turns out to be the Prince, delivers. As in the *Duc*, the poet therefore purports to "record the thoughts and sentiments" of the patron (Kelly, "Genius" 77); yet, also like in Christine's text, "technical virtuosity" and "exclamations over the poetic complexity of the poem" (Huot, "Reading" 33) prevent the reader from falling for the gimmick. The *Fonteinne* also calls attention to the poet's role when, the next morning, Guillaume meets the Prince as he prepares for exile.[10] The Prince requests that Guillaume "de m'amour et de ma plainte / Me faciés ou lay ou complainte" [make me a *lai* or *complainte* about my love and my plight] (1503–4), and Guillaume responds by pulling out a transcription of the lyric the Prince ostensibly recited the night before: "Sire, vostre requeste, / Tenez; vesla ci toute preste" [Sire, here's your request: it's all ready] (1519–20). The Prince is stunned. How could Guillaume have accessed his innermost thoughts? The remainder of the *dit* is also concerned with Guillaume and the Prince's "union of heads, hearts, and minds" (Kelly, "Genius" 79). The two fall asleep in a mythical garden. In a dream, Venus tells Guillaume the story of the Judgment of Paris, and the Prince's lady delivers a *confort* to her downtrodden lover. Upon waking, Guillaume and the Prince are astonished to have shared this dream. Finally, the Prince must depart. He bids *adieu* to his kingdom—but not before leaving everything in Guillaume's hands (see McGrady, "Tout son païs").

The *Fonteinne* and the *Duc* are therefore both interested in poet-patron relations; yet this cursory summary also points to differences in how they represent them. In particular, Machaut seems keener to embrace his lord's plight than Christine does—perhaps because his *dit* has no overt bone to pick with "courtly love." The *Fonteinne* nonetheless equally lends itself to the Butlerian framework I used to think about the *Duc*. As we saw, Butler focuses on how tensions between the bondsman and the lord emerge in the bondsman's work product, which "becomes the site for the redoubling of ownership and, hence, sets the stage for a scene of contestation" (*Psychic Life* 38). Critical responses to the *complainte* in particular and the *Fonteinne* more generally reflect how the text "designates a domain of contested ownership" (*Psychic Life* 38), since some scholars have stressed the patron's role "as a source and model," others have focused on the poet's agency.[11] It is more common, though, to emphasize the poet's "desire to call attention to his role in the production of love poetry," what Palmer terms Machaut's "metafictional impulse" ("Metafictional" 27). Like Christine, this bondsman appears to have awoken to the value of his craftsmanship.

Yet, rather than merely corroborating what we already know about the *Fonteinne*, recourse to Butler also encourages us to revisit its representation of subjectivity. Indeed, I shall argue that like the *Duc,* the *Fonteinne* treats the

---

10. The Prince is modeled on Jean de Berry. See e.g., Ehrhart "Only Connect" and "Machaut's."

11. Kelly, "Genius" 78. For the patron's importance, see esp. this piece. For the poet's agency, see McGrady's response, "Tout son païs," as well as Huot, "Reading" and de Looze, "Guillaume de Machaut."

notion of the subject with ambivalence, self-consciously probing the indeterminacy both of the Prince's *je* and of Machaut's. Resisting a tendency to understand the text as about literature not love, I also contend that it highlights the role of "passionate attachments" in the emergence and being of the subject.

Yet, before grappling with Venus, it is worth quickly locating the *Fonteinne* in relation to late medieval thinking on subjectivity and personhood, as this casts its philosophical stakes in an important new light. As noted, late medieval thinkers were fascinated by the question of what it means to be "numerically one," asking such questions as, "How many souls" are there "in a body? How many persons in a person?" (de Libera, *Quête* 246). In responding to such questions, philosophers would foreground the intellect, defining personhood more in terms of thought than bodily integrity. Any notion that we don't possess our thoughts was, accordingly, not taken lightly. Indeed, such issues were at the heart of the Averroes crisis, where Latin thinkers understood Averroism to be claiming that our thoughts, rather than being inherent in us, exist in a relation of "intimacy" to our minds, which serve as thought's suppoist (de Libera, *Quête* 427). The *Fonteinne* lends itself to these huge questions. When the two protagonists share one dream, the oneness of consciousness is at stake. As the text recognizes, this is a marvel that necessitates explanation (2641–98). The *dit* also troubles the relation of the Prince's thoughts to himself. After Guillaume pulls out "his transcription" of the *complainte*, the Prince exclaims,

> Mes cuers trop se merveille
> Et esbahist de ceste chose,
> Car je la tenoie si close
> Que penser ne puis ne savoir
> Que homs mortels la puist avoir. (1528–32)

> My heart marvels and is very stunned by this; for I had kept it so hidden that I cannot imagine or know how another mortal could possess it.

To what extent, this scene goads us into asking, are the Prince's thoughts actually his? To adopt a more philosophic lingo (see de Libera, *Naissance* 63–69), do they *inhere* in him or are they *attributed* to him by another? Aquinas and others attack Averroes for (ostensibly) claiming that "l'homme n'est pas le sujet de la pensée" [man is not the subject of (his) thoughts] (*Quête* 62), and it is tempting to conceive of the *Fonteinne* as staging something not dissimilar: a "creature" not really the subject of what "he" expresses.

Recourse to an unlikely place points to how seriously the *Fonteinne* is engaging with the problem of how we define the subject: Locke's *Essay Concerning Human Understanding*. De Libera emphasizes how, in Book 2, Chapter 27, Locke tests his famous notion that "personal identity" is defined by the "sameness of consciousness" by musing on several hypotheticals (de Libera, *Quête* 146). He wonders, for instance, whether Socrates and the Mayor of Queensborough would be the same person if they could somehow share all their thoughts. And furthermore, if sleeping Socrates and waking Socrates do not share one consciousness, are they therefore not the same person (*Quête* 146)? The *Fonteinne* tackles similar problems, both by staging two protagonists who "almost telepathically" (Lechat 145–46) share thoughts and by focusing on the limits of wakefulness from one end of the *dit* to the other. Some three centuries before Locke, the *dit* even seems to have found a way for these two scenarios to converge, as the vision raises the problem of a shared consciousness between separate sleeping bodies.

Critics have tended, however, to stress not the philosophical but the literary implications of the issues I am discussing. We suspect that the Prince is not the subject of "his" thoughts, because the *dit* thematizes its own craftsmanship. We can tell prince and poet apart, because the latter is interested in the condition of the poet (Huot, "Reading"). Focalizing on the "metafictional Machaut" risks, though, obfuscating the *Fonteinne*'s engagement with what is beyond or behind these literary issues.

Consider, even, the figure of Morpheus, who is so central to the *dit* that, according to Machaut, it was also known as "*Morpheüs*" (*Voir Dit* IV.126, X.186). In the initial *complainte*, the *je* frets, "Je m'en vois, et si n'est creature / Qui ma dolour doie a ma dame pure / Ramentevoir" [I am departing, and yet there is no creature who might relay my pain to my pure lady] (284–86). The *je* then comes up with a solution. He implores Morpheus to assume his form and to appear before her:

> Aussi de fait
> Elle verra les maus qu'elle me fait,
> Se Morpheüs a droit me contrefait,
> Et que je l'aim de loial cuer parfait,
>   Ferme et estable . . . (786–90)

Therefore, in actuality, she will see the pain she causes me if Morpheus accurately impersonates me—and that I love her with a loyal, perfect heart: solid and unwavering.

Morpheus, critics agree, resembles the poet. Like the poet, he is an "intermediary" (Brownlee, *Poetic Identity* 200), and stressing the importance of the intermediary "implies that the poet is the artisan, or at least the necessary catalyst, for the dream" (Lechat 149). Yet, the *je*'s recourse to Morpheus also resonates with more philosophical and psycho-political questions, such as those which, for Butler, result from the lord's reliance on the bondsman. According to her, that is, the lord formulates to the bondsman the imperative to "*be* [his] body," but this "projection" proves problematic, both because the bondsman will realize he's getting a raw deal—we'll come back to this—and because dependence on the bondsman's labors exposes the lord's limitations (*Psychic Life* 35). Similarly, in the *complainte*, the *je*'s recourse to Morpheus reflects his powerlessness before the necessity of exile. It also shows how his identity can be crafted or donned: how rather than being an essence, identity becomes a "deed" whose aim is "to create the continuity" of the self (*Psychic Life* 75). Indeed, Morpheus is a production destined to ensure the "continuity" of the *je*'s presence before his lady; yet by virtue of being a performance, Morpheus calls attention to the *je*'s instability, even to the paradoxes at the heart of his basic claims, which are here amorous. In the above-cited passage, for example, it is ironic that the Prince calls upon Morpheus to prove that his love is "ferme, estable," since Morpheus, by virtue of being ready to take on any form imaginable, seems ill-positioned to assert the "firmness" or "stability" of anything. The formula that, in the *complainte*, the *je* twice employs to insist on his constancy—"en ceste pel morray" [I will die in this skin/state] (361, 1013)—seems similarly ironic, because Morpheus, by impersonating the *je*, shows "skin" to be illusive. It is also striking that the *je* is so worried that his lady will find someone else (e.g., 301–6), as in this lyric, the *je* is arguably doing something similar: turning to, even embracing, a *tiers*.

Other seemingly metaliterary elements may be playing for higher stakes, too. As we have seen, Butler and de Libera stress the paradoxical temporality of the always-already reflexive subject. It would be difficult to imagine a text more invested in the always-already than the *Fonteinne*, which so memorably showcases Guillaume already possessing his patron's commission. This wonderful moment may therefore allude not only to Machaut's role in authoring his patron's thoughts but also to the temporality of the reflexive subject, which has always-already looked back on himself as if from beyond himself. Indeed, as the figure of Morpheus also suggests, when the bondsman is called upon to be the lord, he then exposes the lord's subjectivity to penetrating critical analysis, such as Butler's.

Like Butler, the *Fonteinne* also brings desire into the fold, exploring how it relates to reflexivity and subjection. Consider the opening stanza of the *complainte*:

> Douce dame, vueilliez oïr la vois
> De ma clamour, qu'en soupirant m'en vois,
> Tristes, dolens, dolereus et destrois,
>   Ne dou retour
> Ne say dire ne les ans ne les mois.
> Las! einsi pers les gracieus convois
> De vos dous yeus qui ont par meintes fois,
>   De leur douçour,
> Tres doucement adouci ma dolour,
> Joieusement fait joie de mon plour
> Et m'ont rendu scens, maniere et vigour,
>   Car de ces trois
> Estoie nus, quant vëoie l'atour
> Cointe et joli et vo corps fait a tour
> Qui passe tous en grace et en valour
>   En tous endrois. (235–50)

> Sweet lady, listen to the voice of my suffering, as sighing, I depart: sad, upset, pained and distraught. Nor can I foresee my return, whether years or months from now. Alas! Thus I am losing the gracious accompaniment of your sweet eyes that, many times, have in their sweetness sweetly calmed my pain, joyously turned my tears into joy, and restored my mind, spirits, and vigor. For I was without these three qualities, when I saw your gay and pretty attire and your perfectly formed body, which, in every place, surpasses all others in grace and valor.

"The lover's regrets initially seem . . . rather conventional," comments Lechat (144). Yet, as in the *Duc,* the poet's circumstances pierce through the clichéd rhetoric. The *complainte*, for example, opens with, "vueilliez oïr la vois," and Guillaume is also (ostensibly) listening to a voice. The *je* frets that he has lost the "convois" of his lady's eyes, and Guillaume is worried that he cannot see the "creature" he hears. As this majestic voice calms Guillaume's fears and brings him joy, so too the lady assuages the *je*'s pain. Machaut, *qua* poet, also seems to be morphing the Prince's sorrow into something more joyous— almost as if he were the *je*'s lady. If, that is, the lady's eyes "m'ont rendu scens, maniere et vigour," so too has Machaut, by authoring the *complainte*, provided "sense, elegance, and vigor" to the Prince's moaning, which is no doubt "without these three qualities" before it comes into contact with Machaut's poetic skills.

We don't, therefore, need to wait for Morpheus for reflexivity to rear its head. Rather, it infests the lover-lady dynamic, even down to the most run-of-the-mill courtly clichés. The *je*, for example, reflects, "Einsi en li mes cuers toudis prenoit / Tous ses ressors" [Thus in her, my heart always took all its strength] (265–66). In this *complainte*, his "cuers" is drawing all its "ressors" from a "li," although this "li" is Machaut. The *je* also insists, "Car je la ser et aim sans decevoir" [that I serve and love her, without deception] (293), and Machaut, by writing this *complainte*, is loyally serving his patron—and perhaps even loving him. For "no subject emerges without a passionate attachment to those on whom he or she is fundamentally dependent," as Butler writes (*Psychic Life* 7); and the *Fonteinne*, by interlacing the poet-patron relationship with the *je*'s amorous rhetoric, encourages us similarly to conceive of subjection as implicating passion.

Butler, as we have also seen, particularly stresses the ambivalence at the core of the desiring subject. The *Fonteinne* is about ambivalence, too, and Machaut's relations with himself are perhaps more demonstrably ambivalent than his ties to the Prince, to which I shall return. In the *Fonteinne* (as elsewhere), Machaut elects to present the *je*-protagonist Guillaume as "cowardly" and "inept" (Calin 151). Indeed, Guillaume quickly announces that he is "Rudes, nices et malapers" [brutish, foolish, and oafish] (140). He persistently advertises his weaknesses, such as when he embraces cowardice as the natural state for clerks (132–38). Critics have understood Machaut's use of Guillaume as a way to "deflect his responsibility for the significance of his material" (Ehrhart, "Only Connect" 142) or to "offer good examples of how *not* to" act (Armstrong and Kay 174; original emphasis). Recourse to Butler suggests, however, that it may be less a tactical decision than an important element in the text's reflections on subjection. As we saw in relation to Sébille, when the bondsman attempts to free himself of the lord, the mode of subjection persists, but the bondsman turns on facets of himself. He berates himself, as Machaut seems to be doing, for instance, when discussing his fear of sleeping alone:

> La gisoie en si petit point
> Que, s'aucuns preïst mon pourpoint
> Ou ma sainture ou ma chemise,
> Pour moy n'i fust deffense mise,

Non, par Dieu, qui mon corps preïst,
Ja remuer ne m'en veïst.
Et s'on dit que c'est couardie
Ou aucune merencolie,
Je n'en donroie pas deus pommes
Car je vi des plus vaillans hommes
Qu'on peüst vëoir ne nommer,
—Fust deça mer, fust dela mer—
Que, qui leur donnast de fin ambre
Reins et Paris, en une chambre
Sans compaignie ne geüssent
Pour neccessité qu'il heüssent. (95–110)

There I was lying in such a sorry state that, if someone took my doublet, belt, or shirt, I wouldn't put up any resistance: no, by God, even if someone made off with my body, I wouldn't lift a finger. And if people say that this is cowardliness or because of melancholy, I wouldn't give two apples [hoots], as I've seen some of the most valiant men that one can see or name, on this side or the other of the sea, who, if someone gave them fine amber from Reims or Paris, would not sleep in a room without company, however pressing their necessity.

Yet, Machaut is not simply berating himself. For just as he turns the prince's "inchoate gibberish" (McGrady, "Tout son païs" 24) into polished poetry, so too does the text morph Guillaume's childish reflections into something craftier—since despite himself, Guillaume announces many of the text's crucial terms here. "I wouldn't give two apples" alludes, for example, to Venus's recounting of the Judgment of Paris, which is also emphasized by the word "Paris." The seemingly superfluous "on this side or the other of the sea" announces the Prince's exile. If Guillaume feels himself unable to react, even if someone were to make off with his clothing, so too will the dreaming Prince not react, when his lady exchanges rings with him (2495–2510). Similarly, Guillaume frets that someone could "steal his body," and Morpheus will be implored to become the *je*'s body. Troubling the prospect of sleeping without another is, furthermore, the mirror-image of the more serious issue raised by the *dit*: how two people, sleeping together, might dream together.

The action of turning "gibberish" into something more meaningful therefore describes not only what the poet does for his patron but also what he does for himself. As in Butlerian thought, subjection, which initially characterizes the relationship with the lord, is also "internal" to the bondsman's "consciousness," which is "spli[t] . . . into two parts" (*Psychic Life* 42). One facet of his self—the intellectual, even authorial self—persecutes the "bodily self," the "actual individual in the animal functions" (*Psychic Life* 50, quoting Hegel) or Guillaume. Yet if, as in Butler's reading of Hegel, there is an important analogy to be made between how Machaut relates to his bodily self and how Prince and Poet relate to each other—as Machaut uses his keen intellect to translate the predicaments of each into something nobler and craftier—this would suggest that Machaut is not merely berating his bodily "alter ego." Rather, the *dit* may be more interested and invested in—even dependent on—the bodily than it appears. In concluding analysis of the *Duc*, I focused on how reflexivity troubles Sébille's political message. In concluding my reading of the *Fonteinne*, I shall do the opposite, thinking more about how bodies and sexual politics bear on the *dit*'s oft-remarked reflexivity.

One way of conceiving of the *dit*'s engagement with sexual politics would be in terms of the trajectory of *The Psychic Life of Power*. In this volume, Butler begins with fairly abstract philosophic analysis of reflexivity, looking not only to Hegel and Althusser but also to Nietzsche and Foucault. In readings of Freud, she then focuses on the interplay of reflexivity, melancholy, and desire. She hypothesizes that gender identity may result from the melancholic incorporation of foreclosed same-sex desires. I consider myself a man, because I have become the men I couldn't love. (I note in passing that this resonates with the oft-discussed prologue to Christine's *Mutacion de Fortune*, where she becomes a man after losing the man she loved).

In the *Fonteinne*, there are perhaps hints of the specter of sexual deviancy. The text, for instance, "eroticizes" the relations between Guillaume and the Prince, as Cerquiglini-Toulet has shown by observing how the Prince falling asleep in Guillaume's "giron" [lap] (1545) announces how Toute Belle will do the same thing during the lovers' first meeting in the *Voir Dit* (*Engin* 117–18). The *Fonteinne* also more subtly evokes the possibility of illicit desire. The final myth to which the *dit* looks is, for example, that of Zeus and Danaë. Here, the King of Olympus morphs into a golden shower, which streams through Danaë's prison window; he then has his way with her. In her *confort*, the lady argues that this myth demonstrates "how love conquers all" (2399). Yet, rather than pertaining to the lady's relation with the Prince, the myth more closely, and oddly, recalls Guillaume's relations with his patron, insofar as the Prince's wonderous poetry has streamed through the window as a golden shower, interpellating and enthralling Guillaume. This echo may point to the erotic implications of Machaut's poetic fantasy. Certainly, it suggests that this fantasy, like Zeus's behavior, plays on themes of interdiction, transgression, and impossibility.

We might, then, understand same-sex desire as potentially implicated in the interplay—as central to the *Fonteinne* as to *The Psychic Life of Power*—of such issues as melancholy, foreclosure, performance, and reflexivity. Such a reading nonetheless gives me pause. The text even seems to pre-empt it in its extensive treatment of the Judgment of Paris (1599–2144). In an account significantly indebted to the *Ovide moralisé* (see Lechat 155–63), Venus, who is "loved and served by lovers" (1708), describes her dispute with Pallas, "Goddess of Wisdom" (1705), and Juno, "Goddess of Wealth" (1706). She claims that her power is superior to those of the other goddesses, and Paris of course agrees, granting her the apple. Yet, if Venus's narrative is predictable, the *Fonteinne*'s decision to devote so much attention to it is less so. For if critics tend to stress how, in this *dit*, Machaut vaunts his own artistry before making off with the Prince's possessions, they would seem to be allotting the *pomme* to Pallas and then to Juno, rather than Venus. Why, if the *Fonteinne* is really about Pallas and perhaps Juno, but not Venus, would it foreground this myth where love triumphs over learning and wealth? Perhaps because it is deconstructing Paris's choice. Huot ("Reading"), in particular, emphasizes how Venus is both speaking as a clerk and addressing the poet rather than the lover. Pallas would therefore be effectively impersonating Venus (to play on the terms of Morpheus's behavior). A reading that suggests that the text is about desire would, it follows, have the problematic effect of granting Venus the *pomme* after all, when the point is that it is really for Pallas.

Yet, to read Venus as Pallas also strikes me as problematic. Such a reading does little to account for the text's decision (ostensibly) to embrace Venus. It also cannot account for the elements of the Goddess's representation that seem less clerkly, less Pallas-like, such as her "bawdy sense of humor" (Huot, "Reading" 42), which is particularly prominent when Venus is insisting on the pleasure she took in staring at "Jovis Preapus o sa perche" [Priapus with his rod] (1675). Insofar as fascination with the *bas corporel* distinguishes Venus from Pallas, the bodily appears, then, as a problem. Or, put differently, Desire emerges as a critical problem—if, as critics have argued (e.g., Kelly, *Machaut*), Desir represents for Machaut the physical, libidinal elements of eros. Certainly, Desir, who is generally figured as waging battle (e.g., 805) against the *je*, is conceived of as threatening in the *Fonteinne*. For example, Desir "m'art et m'assaut et tourmente" [burns, assaults, and torments me] (368); Desir "pique et boute" [jabs and pushes] (2314) and "maint outrage / Fait aus amans et mainte rage" [commits unto lovers many affronts and much violence] (2246–47). Yet, if the text "berates" Desir, the preceding analysis would suggest that its attitude toward Desir is not simply dismissive. Rather, the *Fonteinne* turns against Desir in a manner similar to how the bondsman turns against both his lord and his bodily self. This would imply that the text cannot neatly renounce Desir; it needs it, as its ambivalent relationship to Desir is crucial to its emergence as a reflexive text.

Put otherwise, Butler conceives of the story of the subject in terms of "dialectic reversals," which is similar to de Libera's notion that the history of subjectivity is one of "chiasms." Such "reversals" easily lend themselves to misinterpretation, as one can observe a certain state of affairs without comprehending that it is a response to a previous situation that has not been resolved so much as it is being continuously (although never successfully) worked through. Thus I have argued that it would be misleading to understand the *Duc* as "against courtly love," since such a view fails to account for Christine's deeply ambivalent ties to it, which reflexivity brings to the fore. Similarly, the *Fonteinne* appears to stage a dialectic reversal, whereby rather than writing about love, it loves writing. This does not, however, mean that the text is uninterested in eros. Rather, it is a turn characteristic of the emerging subject, who "cling[s]" to "thought" (*Psychic Life* 43) and attempts to subject the bodily but finds that he cannot actually renounce it. The genius of the *Fonteinne*'s critical analysis of the reflexive subject, I would therefore suggest, is twofold. One, the *dit* shows how the emergence of the subject is a shifty story, where (as we have seen) things are persistently switching places, inverting roles, and contaminating each other; contours are porous and unstable. And two, the *dit* suggests that the relationship between—to borrow some of Butler's terms—physical or erotic "desire" and "passionate attachments," on the one hand, and "reflection" or "reflexivity," on the other, is particularly crucial to the emerging subject but also both slippery and messy: even deeply ambivalent.

LE CHEVALIER DE LA CHARRETTE

In terms of subjectivity, is the *Duc* therefore a *dit*? Alas, things are not so clear-cut, because its critical analysis of the subject also hearkens back to verse romance, the other genre with which it is associated. And as with the *dits*, we can use the *Duc* to revisit representations of subjectivity in earlier, male-authored romances.

The *Charrette* (1176–81) is the logical place to turn, because its infamous prologue raises similar issues to that of the *Duc*, which may even be responding to it (Krueger, *Women Readers* 227). Chrétien initially claims to write this romance at Marie de Champagne's behest, "Come cil qui est suens antiers" [as he who is entirely hers] (4). After struggling to distinguish himself from the *losengiers* who flatter the Countess—their flattery is "voirs maleoit gré mien" [true, in spite of my best wishes] (20)—Chrétien says more about what he and Marie each bring to the text. Marie's "comandemanz" (22), he insists, "mialz oevre" [do more] (21) for the romance than his "sans" [wisdom] (23) or "painne" [labor] (23). While she provides the text's "matiere" [subject] (26) and "san" [main idea] (26), Chrétien contributes his "panser" [thinking] (28), "painne" [labor] (29), and "antancïon" [willpower] (29).

Scholars have understandably focused on the literary significance of these elusive terms. Yet the *Charrette*'s prologue, like the *Duc*'s, also speaks to the political, psychological, and philosophical complexity of subjection. It illustrates Chrétien's "dependency on a discourse" he "never chose but that, paradoxically, initiates and sustains [his] agency" (Butler, *Psychic Life* 2). "To persist in one's being means to be given over from the start to social terms that are never fully one's own," writes Butler (*Psychic Life* 197), and Chrétien does not choose his "matiere," while also struggling to accept the "terms" of the *losengiers*' flattery as his own. Their flattery suggests, too, a passionate component to subjection.

The prologue also resonates with the philosophic problem of how we define "what is mine" or the "entity/being," here the text (see de Libera, *Naissance* 190–99 for these terms). At stake, more precisely, is whether the romance is best described as the joint product of two beings or whether one figure is the "best part" ("le meilleur de moi" or "en lui") (de Libera, *Naissance* 195–96), with the other then being secondary, an attribute. At one level, the issue is whether the romance is defined by material or form. If Marie provides the *matiere*, to which Chrétien gives form, the text may be principally Chrétien's, if we follow Aristotle's reasoning whereby "the substance is the form" (see de Libera, *Naissance* 166). We might, however, also advance the opposite argument, as Aristotle famously claims in *De anima* that the soul is like the pilot of a ship, where the ship is the body (see de Libera, *Naissance* 175). If Marie's *san* functions as the soul of the romance, which is executed by Chrétien's *painne*, she would furnish its essential elements (as Chrétien claims). Such opposite interpretations are possible, because one casts the *Charrette* as primarily the product of Chrétien's crafty mind, the other as the product of Marie's genius and Chrétien's physical and intellectual labor. Things only get messier if we attempt to conceive of the romance as more genuinely the joint product of two minds, which nonetheless occupy different functions. Marie's and Chrétien's respective contributions seem, in particular, to resonate with an important distinction in noetics: that between the "intellect in potential" (en puissance) and "the intellect in act" (en acte) (see de Libera, *Naissance* 194–95). Marie would figure the former, Chrétien the latter. Yet, the relationship of these two elements to "what is mine" or "the entity" is no easy nut to crack. Ancient, medieval, and modern philosophers have had recourse to all sorts of acrobatics, whereby, for instance, the "entity" or "being" would correspond to the intellect both in potential and in act, whereas "my own" would refer principally to the intellect in act (de Libera, *Naissance* 195). Following this logic, the *Charrette qua* romance might be said to be both Marie's and Chrétien's, while the words on the parchment would be Chrétien's.

As this is a twisted distinction, I would suggest that Chrétien's prologue, like Machaut's *dit,* is exploring the problem of what defines the subject— or her/his text—in a manner that suggestively resonates with philosophic debates. In Chrétien's case, this argument is, however, more tenuous, since many of the philosophic issues I have been discussing came to the fore following the rediscovery of Aristotle's corpus primarily in the thirteenth century. Unlike with Machaut, we cannot posit a clear chronology, whereby literature wades into philosophy's waters. Yet if the *Charrette* appears to be engaging with issues that announce philosophy's difficulty in defining the subject, this is—like Guillaume's already possessing his patron's exact thoughts—a remarkable "coincidence" worth attending to.

What's more, the epilogue appears to support this counterintuitive idea that the *Charrette* is raising issues that, in philosophy, largely burst onto the scene later. In it, "Godefroiz de Leigni" suddenly emerges to inform us that "par le boen gré / Crestïen" [in accordance with Chrétien's wishes] (7106–7) he has taken over the final segment of the romance "des lors an ça / Ou Lanceloz fu anmurez" [from the moment when Lancelot was immured] (7108–9). The epilogue poses the opposite philosophical problem to the prologue. At stake is not how two minds might bear on a text composed by one body, but how one entity might be composed of two "numerically distinct bodies" that are, for us, "indiscernible in appearance" (de Libera, *Quête* 159). Similar to such theo-philosophic conundrums as two-headed monsters or Siamese twins, the epilogue raises the problem of whether the "entity" *qua* the *Charrette* denotes "one" or "two" persons. Medieval philosophy would later hold that "a two-headed . . . monster doesn't necessarily imply two persons; there needs to be two wills" (de Libera, *Quête* 239). Yet, while the theme of agency is pertinent to the epilogue, it does not serve neatly to distinguish Chrétien from Godefroi, since the latter insists that he works "par le boen gré / Crestïen." There is also the problem of where, precisely, the transition from "one" to "two" occurs, as the precise referent for "anmurez" is "uncertain" (Bruckner, *Shaping Romance* 88). If the text is (however deliberately) foraying into murky philosophic terrain, the ambiguity of the referent for "immured" may reflect the impossibility of identifying the exact point where "one" gives way to "two" in heterogeneous creations like Siamese twins or two-headed monsters. The ambiguity of "anmurez" may also comport a more figurative aspect. As we have seen, Butler is interested in how, in emancipating himself from the lord, the bondsman's psyche is "spli[t] . . . into two parts"; yet the "imprisoning frame" persists (*Psychic Life* 42, 86). The transition from prologue to epilogue may be understood in similar terms. The *Charrette* is born through Chrétien's subjection to Marie, but over the course of his labors, Chrétien's psyche splits into two.[12] He comes to identify with the reflexive element, which casts the labors of the bodily as other; and the motif of imprisonment furnishes the link between the bondsman's initial predicament and his later one.

Should this seem a bit speculative or neat, the *Charrette* is demonstrably concerned with questions about subjection, since, like the *Duc*, it keeps returning to them. Taking their cue from the repetition of the verse, "Come cil qui est suens antiers" [as he who is entirely hers] (4, 5656), which is employed to describe both Chrétien's subjection to Marie and Lancelot's to Guinevere, critics have studied how "the literary service of the poet mirrors and glosses Lancelot's knightly service—and vice versa" (Bruckner, *"Chevalier"* [1985] 141). This reflexivity tells us nothing definitive about the biographical Chrétien (Bruckner, *Shaping Romance* 84–86). It may, however, be telling us something about reflexivity's role in the emergence of the subject. According to Butler, "the story by which subjection is told is, inevitably, circular":

> On the one hand, the subject can refer to its own genesis only by taking a third-person perspective on itself, that is, by dispossessing its own perspective in the act of narrating its genesis. On the other hand, the narration of how the subject is constituted presupposes that the constitution has already taken place, and thus arrives after the fact. (*Psychic Life* 11)

Reflexivity fosters a similar "circularity" in the *Charrette*. If Lancelot's service to Guinevere mirrors Chrétien's to Marie, Chrétien is mobilizing a "third-person perspective" to think through the text's "genesis." Yet, if Lancelot's relationship to Guinevere somehow "glosses" Chrétien's to Marie, this is also "circular," since Lancelot's story "arrives after the fact," presupposing the "constitution" of the text, the emergence of which it is, theoretically, helping to explain.

If the *Charrette* is tackling the complexity of the condition of the subject, does it follow, as recourse to Butler would also suggest, that it treats it with ambivalence? Ever since scholars began to debunk the "fiction" (Bruckner, *"Chevalier"* [2005] 141) according to which Chrétien did not want to write this

---

12. For Godefroi as fiction of Chrétien's, see Dragonetti, *Vie* 13–15 and Hult.

romance because he did not approve of adultery, the idea of an underlying ambivalence has gone out of fashion. It has notably given way to emphasis on "inner poetic effect" (Hult 84), whereby Chrétien is "credit[ed] with certain attributes," such as "irony, cleverness, even craftiness, a taste for the enigmatic, a desire to exploit ambiguity" (Bruckner, *Shaping Romance* 89). This critical turn has produced spectacular results. It nonetheless risks foreclosing the text's critical analysis of the psychic, political, and philosophic subject by putting the emphasis so squarely on the literary.

Consider, even, the most contentious issue in critical debate over the prologue's meaning: what to make of the distinction between *san*, which Marie provides, and *sans*, which Chrétien does. Scholars have delved into etymology in attempting to clarify these uncomfortably proximate terms.[13] Yet, I would suggest that the text self-consciously but elusively evokes the messiness of this distinction within the narrative, where there is a crucial confusion not of *san* and *sans*, but of *sanc* or blood (which, in the Guiot manuscript, can be transcribed *sans* [e.g., 1160, 3630]). During Lancelot and Guinevere's only sexual encounter, he bleeds all over her sheets, while Kay, also in the room, sullies his sheets with the blood of his wounds. The next morning, everyone gets it wrong. Méléagant thinks the bloody sheets are proof that Guinevere and Kay have slept together (4748–67). Even Guinevere wonders if she had a nosebleed (4782–83). The confusion between Guinevere's, Lancelot's, and Kay's *sanc* may reflect that between Marie's *san* and Chrétien's *sans*; and this would suggest that these putatively literary issues are more eroticized, more ethically charged, and generally messier than scholars tend to presume.

It is, though, Lancelot's story that best corroborates the hypothesis that the *Charrette* is about the interplay of ambivalence, reflexivity, and subjectivity. For Butler, that is, the lord formulates the following "imperative to the bondsman": "you be my body for me, but do not let me know the body you are is my body" (*Psychic Life* 35). Similarly, in this romance, Lancelot "becomes" Arthur's body, by fighting his battles for him. Yet, in "becoming" the lord's body, the bondsman goes too far, setting up "a domain of contested ownership," which, in the *Charrette,* has a name: Guinevere. By fighting for Arthur while lying with his wife, Lancelot speaks to power's propensity simultaneously to work for and against itself. The romance seems, however, more interested in this bondsman's "resolution of freedom into self-enslavement" (*Psychic Life* 31). For Lancelot, the great liberator of the captives of Gorre, is of course "possessed" (Lazar 245) by his love for Guinevere. As in Butler's

---

13. Rychner, "Prologue" and "Encore le prologue"; Frappier; Bruckner "*Chevalier*" [1985] 136–37.

reading of Hegel, the bondsman's attachment to his lord morphs into a more internalized and psychically dense version of subjection.

Lancelot certainly suffers from an "unhappy consciousness." "His own severest critic" (Bruckner, "*Chevalier*" [1985] 150), he exemplifies the "turning of a subject against itself that takes place in acts of self-reproach, conscience, and melancholia that work in tandem with processes of social regulation" (Butler, *Psychic Life* 18–19). The infamous episode with the cart, where Reison induces Lancelot to hesitate before he heeds Amors's injunction to hop aboard (360–77), is the most dramatic instance of Lancelot's pausing to reflect or "turn" on his actions. It shows how this subject has a "split" consciousness (*Psychic Life* 42), which judges his behaviors and engenders "reproach," or both public and private forms of shaming. This is, moreover, hardly the only instance where Lancelot pauses to take stock of his behaviors, as critics have observed (e.g., Lacy, "Thematic Structure"; Bruckner, *Shaping Romance* 77–84). During his first combat with a knight, he will, for example, feel "honte" [shame] (866) because he takes too long to triumph—and this reflexive moment inspires his victory immediately thereafter (864–80). In the following sequence, Lancelot encounters a maiden being assaulted, and he knows he must rescue her; yet he hesitates, because he does not wish to be distracted from his quest for Guinevere (1097–125). These different instances speak not only to the persistence of the motif of reflexivity in the *Charrette* but also to its ambivalence, as reflexivity for Lancelot seems synonymous with self-beratement. It also leads others to berate him, most notably Guinevere (4484–89). And if Lancelot's hesitation before aiding the Demoiselle Entreprenante plays on his hesitation before jumping onto the cart, we might also advance that the text treats Lancelot's reflexivity critically—or even ambivalently.

Lancelot's ambivalent reflexivity reflects, moreover, a twisted relationship between his body and mind. Like Butler's split subject, Lancelot can seem intent on "vacating the body and clinging to what appears to be most disembodied: thought" (*Psychic Life* 43). For example,

>   Et cil de la charrete panse
>   Con cil qui force ne desfanse
>   N'a vers Amors qui le justise,
>   Et ses pansers est de tel guise
>   Qui lui meïsmes en oblie,
>   Ne set s'il est ou s'il n'est mie . . .
>   De rien nule ne li sovient
>   Fors d'une seule, et por celi
>   A mis les autres en obli,

A cele seule panse tant
Qu'il n'ot ne voit ne rien n'antant.
Et ses chevax molt tost l'enporte,
Ne ne vet mie voie torte,
Mes la meillor et la plus droite . . . (711–16, 720–27)

And he of the cart, as if he had no strength or resistance against Love who controls him, was pondering; and his thoughts are of such a sort that he forgets himself. He knows not if he exists or if he doesn't. He can remember nothing at all—except one thing, and for her, he has forgotten all others. So much is he focused on his thoughts of her that he hears, sees, and takes in nothing. And his horse very swiftly carries him along, not taking a twisted path but the best and straightest one.

Our hero fervently clings to his *pansers*, where he seems paradoxically most and least himself. He can be defined purely by his love for Guinevere, but his body, in instances such as this, appears no more "his" than his horse. Throughout the romance, Lancelot continues to subordinate the "bodily condition of his own life" (Butler, *Psychic Life* 32) to his amorous thoughts. Here, for instance, is him crossing the perilous Sword Bridge:

A la grant dolor con li sist
S'an passe outre et a grant destrece,
Mains et genolz et piez se blece,
Mes tot le rasoage et sainne
Amors qui le conduist et mainne,
Si li estoit a sofrir dolz. (3110–15)

With great pain, he crossed the bridge as he wished—and in great distress.[14] He wounds his hands, knees, and feet, but Love, who drives and leads him, also entirely calms and heals him. Thus his suffering felt sweet to him.

Lancelot's subordination of his "bodily condition" to his amorous *pansers* allows him to advance on his quest. Throughout the romance, he even proves that he is Guinevere's "suens antiers" [entirely hers] (5656), by repeatedly putting himself in predicaments where his body "N'iert mie toz antiers ne sains" [was neither intact nor healthy] (3098). Lancelot's neglect of "the bodily con-

---

14. Note that this could also be translated, "with the great pain that pleased him, he crossed the bridge . . ."

dition of his own life" is nonetheless paradoxical. At one level, because it must be performed in episode after episode; it is therefore never complete. Like Butler's unhappy subject, Lancelot illustrates how "there can be no final leave-taking of the body within life" (*Psychic Life* 48)—perhaps most dramatically during his failed suicide attempt (4257–399). At another level, Lancelot's self-beratement is also ironically "self-aggrandiz[ing]" (*Psychic Life* 49). The prioritization of his amorous *panser* over his bodily condition routinely leads to great chivalric feats, for which he earns unparalleled renown. Because it is perpetually incomplete and ironically self-aggrandizing, the subjection of the bodily functions as a sort of "performance." This is notably the case at the Tournament at Noauz, where Guinevere twice instructs Lancelot to do his worst [au noauz] (5654), and he spectacularly fails: "Por a morir rien ne feïst / Se sa grant honte n'i veïst, / Et son leit et sa desenor" [Come death, he would do nothing, unless it brought him great shame, harm, and dishonor] (5669–71). As we have seen, in Butler's retelling of Hegel,

> The self becomes an incessant performer of renunciation, whereby the performance, as an action, contradicts the postulation of *in*action that it is meant to signify. Paradoxically, performance becomes the *occasion* for a grand and endless action that effectively augments and individuates the self it seeks to deny. (*Psychic Life* 49, original emphases)

Lancelot is, similarly, performing the renunciation of his chivalric prowess. Yet, as a lover and as a knight, this performance "effectively augments and individuates the self it seeks to deny." Indeed, Guinevere, the damsels, and the other knights are captivated, amused, and moved by Lancelot's contradictory performance (5952–6022).

If Guinevere—and Chrétien—seem to delight in "catch[ing] Lancelot" in "foolish postures" (Bruckner, "*Chevalier*" [1985] 151), we might, then, conceive of their behavior not as opposed to Lancelot's best interests, but rather as exploiting the reflexive subject's twisted penchant for self-aggrandizing self-beratement. I will return to Guinevere momentarily. First, I wish to emphasize how the romance is also structurally complicit in what Haidu has called Lancelot's "identity problem" (*Subject Medieval/Modern* 101). The *Charrette*, it should be recalled, was long considered to be "poorly conceived" and "badly constructed" (Kelly, *Sens* 1). In the wake of Kelly's pioneering work, scholars have shown how "analogues multiply through the romance and connect its episodes" (Bruckner, "*Chevalier*" [2005] 144), with "meaning aris[ing] out of the play between . . . repetitions and variations of typical events and figures" (Bruckner, "Interpreter's Dilemma" 164). In a classic article, Bruckner concentrates, for instance, on the episode with the Demoiselle Entreprenante, "the meaning" of which "can be fully understood only when ... parallels" to Lancelot's quest "are superimposed" ("Interpreter's Dilemma" 164). This provocative scene—where a maiden offers Lancelot lodging in exchange for his sleeping with her, before staging her own rape but failing to seduce him—encourages us to think more about such themes as female agency and the relationship between force, volition, and desire (164).

There is more to be said about this episode. Yet, rather than continuing to explore issues it raises, it may be worth asking why the romance raises issues in this way. While the *Charrette*'s recourse to *aventures* seems to be principally conceived of as an aesthetic technique, recourse to Butler suggests that it also partakes in its critical analysis of subjection. According to Butler, that is, the "'becoming'" of the subject takes the form of "an uneasy practice of repetition and its risks, compelled yet incomplete" (*Psychic Life* 30). This repetition is always ambivalent, since it both constitutes and contests the subject(ion) it nominally reaffirms. The *Charrette* seems, therefore, to be structured in a manner similar to how the subject functions. Like Lancelot, we repeatedly perform our subjection, but each episode of repetition exceeds any neat narrative of the cohesive self, a sort of "quest" for identity into which it is folded.

Perhaps at this juncture it would make sense to show how another *aventure* refuses nicely to be fitted into Lancelot's quest. Yet, following Lancelot's lead, I wish to take a leap of sorts, by bringing Chrétien back into the equation. For just as critics have studied how adventures trouble the terms of Lancelot's quest, so too does the romance mobilize reflexivity to trouble the terms of what we might call Chrétien's "implicit quest" to be a great romancer, which has been subjected to less scrutiny than Lancelot's quest for Guinevere.

More concretely, while critics have tended to stress Chrétien's relationship with his protagonist (e.g., Bruckner, "*Chevalier*" [1985] 177), I would observe how the *Charrette,* like the *Duc,* is also ripe with more confusing instances of reflexivity. In the initial sequence, for instance, Kay tells Arthur, "Je n'ai volenté ne talant / De toi servir d'ore en avant" [I do not wish or desire to serve you any longer] (91–92). Guinevere then begs him to remain at court. It is intriguing that the romance opens with a woman instructed to beg a courtier to remain at his functions, as this rubs up against the "fiction," whereby Marie requests that Chrétien write the romance, although he demurs. Coming on the heels of the prologue, this may suggest that the author, like Kay, reckons that making a show of hesitating will profit him. Kay asks, however, for more than he can handle; he later complains to Lancelot that "tu as a chief treite / La chose que ge n'i poi treire" [you have completed what I couldn't pull off] (4010–11). As this sounds like something Chrétien could say to Godefroi, who ostensibly completes the romance he didn't, it may point to a certain complicity between the infamous *losengier* and Chrétien (cf. Laranjinha 181–82). In any case, this motif of being unable to *parfaire* recurs repeatedly in the text. A proud knight, for example, says to Lancelot:

> Einz te deüsses apanser
> Que tu anpreïsses tel chose
> A quel fin et a quel parclose
> Tu an porroies parvenir ... (2590–93)

Before beginning this endeavor, you should have thought about the end and resolution to which you would bring it.

Lancelot pays no attention to this taunt. Yet, it points to a real issue for Chrétien, who seems not to have foreseen the romance's *fin* or *parclose*. Rather, he hands things over to Godefroi—who, for that matter, does not (and cannot) bring about resolution in the love story (see Hult 86; Prior).

The *Charrette* mobilizes reflexivity to trouble the terms of Chrétien's literary project in other ways, too. Chrétien's ties to Guinevere are worth rehearsing. Both manipulate the protagonist (Bruckner, *Shaping Romance* 82ff.). Both are, albeit in different ways, the raison d'être for his behaviors. If Lancelot is persistently trying to read Guinevere's cues, so too have critics been on the hunt for Chrétien's; indeed, as Lancelot is desperate to locate and behold Guinevere, scholars have attempted to locate and behold "Chrétien." "Je serai anz et vos defors" [I will be inside and you outside] (4514), says Guinevere to her beloved, before he pries open the bars on the window behind which she awaits him. Chrétien also seems trapped within, behind, or above this text, and countless critics have tried to pry open the bars of its language.

Quasi-exclusive emphasis on Chrétien's ties to Lancelot risks, therefore, precluding what we might call reflexive "loose ends," or parallels linking the author figure with other characters.[15] It is as if Chrétien had been put on an "implicit quest" to become a great author, which he attains via Lancelot's prowess. Yet, while Lancelot experiences *aventures*, which are challenging for him (and for us), this sort of adventure has largely been denied to Chrétien. Not attending to reflexive "loose ends" has, in turn, the effect of foreclosing ethical questions (for instance, could Chrétien be like the insincere Kay or the somewhat sadistic Guinevere?) as well as erotic ones (does Chrétien's inter-

---

15. For "loose ends" in the text, see Bruckner, "*Chevalier*" [1985] 163 and *Shaping Romance* 89.

est in Lancelot mirror Guinevere's?). It also presupposes an exclusivity—and by extension, a gendering—of identification, as this author will identify with this knight.

Godefroi picks up on the notion of reflexive "loose ends" and their relation to gender and sexual politics. Yet, before turning to "his" section, it is worth spending a moment more with Guinevere, who up until the last few paragraphs has been largely absent from my analysis, as if "the problem of woman ha[d] been subsumed under the dilemma of the hero's identity" (Krueger, *Women Readers* 54). Such an approach to her character would not be odds with scholarship, which routinely stresses her "passivity," sometimes her inscrutability.[16] Yet, rather than signaling the romance's lack of interest in her, these factors, which seem equally pertinent to Lancelot's predicament, may allow us to conceive of Guinevere as supplementing (in the Derridean sense of serving both to confirm or complete and to replace or undermine) the foregoing analysis of Lancelot's subjectivity. Consider, for instance, the theme of displacement. The romance is not only about Lancelot's figurative displacement of Arthur and the psychic prison he forges for himself but also about the queen's displacement and imprisonment, both literal and more figurative (cf. Krueger, *Women Readers* 37–39, 61–67). Guinevere's displacement would, therefore, serve both to confirm the centrality of the motif of displacement to the romance and to challenge how important Lancelot's psychic displacements are, as she seems more removed or displaced within—and from—the romance than he. Similarly, as regards the renunciation of the body, Lancelot's body is repeatedly neglected (by him) only so to be praised (by others), while Guinevere's body is worshipped by Lancelot only to be "renounced" by the text, largely relegated to its margins. She thus confirms the pertinence of the theme of the renunciation of the bodily to the text, while being more "renounced" than he ever is. Like Lancelot, moreover, Guinevere seems to have an "unhappy consciousness," which is particularly manifest when she berates herself for her icy reception of Lancelot (4180–247). This "unhappy consciousness" appears, for her as for him, to reflect confusion of notions of self and other, inside and outside. Indeed, if Guinevere refuses to speak to Lancelot when he has rescued her, this is perhaps less the sign of her ambivalence toward Lancelot than a twisted reflection of how *she* is not actually allowed to speak much in the romance, which is then projected onto him (cf. Krueger, *Women Readers* 60–61). This sense that Guinevere supplements analysis of Lancelot's subjectivity is particularly strong when, in the

---

16. For her passivity, see e.g., Bruckner, "*Chevalier*" [1985] 153; "Interpreter's Dilemma," 167; Brownlee, "Transformations" 167. For female desire as "enigma," see Krueger, *Women Readers* 55–66.

romance's final sequence, Lancelot returns to Arthur's court, and Guinevere wishes that her "heart" could "embrace" (6831) him. Yet, "li cors . . . se celot" [the body held back] (6832):

> Et se Reisons ne li tolsist
> Ce fol panser et cele rage,
> Si veïssent tot son corage,
> Lors si fust trop granz la folie.
> Por ce Reisons anferme et lie
> Son fol cuer et son fol pansé,
> Si l'a un petit racenssé
> Et a mis la chose an respit . . . (6842–49)

> And if Reason didn't remove this reckless thought and her fury, everyone would have seen her all true feelings, and this would have been too great a folly. Thus Reason imprisons and binds her mad heart and crazy thoughts, calming her a bit and putting this off for now.

This sequence plays on "Lancelot's first inner debate between Reason and Love," as Bruckner has shown (*Shaping Romance* 80). According to her, "The comparison at once brings the lovers together and reveals how different is the lesson each of them has to learn" (80): Lancelot has learned not to obey Reisons, while Guinevere must heed him. Yet, the lesson each learns is also curiously similar, as Guinevere, like Lancelot, moves from external subjection to a more internalized form of imprisonment, which requires the renunciation of bodily impulse. It is also important that this is the queen's only mention in the romance's final sequence (Hult 93); for the text is renouncing Guinevere as she attempts to renounce her impulses. This is, however, paradoxical, as by looking to Guinevere, the text is not perfectly renouncing her—or her body. Rather, Guinevere appears to have become something like "the bodily remainder" that, as we saw in analysis of Lancelot, cannot be neatly suppressed.

As we also saw in passing, Butler argues against a tendency to oppose "identification" and "desire," notably by hypothesizing that gender identity may be the result of foreclosed desires. Similarly, I am suggesting that Lancelot's desire for Guinevere does not function in opposition to identification. Sure, he is on a quest to rescue the lady he loves; yet, reflexivity also morphs this straight trajectory into something messier, whereby Guinevere reflects (on) his predicament.

If this sounds abstract, there are various ways to demonstrate how the romance does not oppose identification and desire. One, to which I merely glance, is to remark how it does not oppose identification to hate (rather than love). For while it is generally accepted that Méléagant "stands as the antitype to Lancelot, isolated and hateful, completely lacking in courtly virtues" (Klassen 9), the two are also curiously—even uncomfortably—similar. One of the narrator's initial observations about Méléagant might as well, for instance, be a description of Lancelot: "Nus ne fust miaudres chevaliers, / Se fel et deslëaus ne fust" [no one could be a better knight, were he not reckless and disloyal] (3164–65). And if the text hints at important similarities between Lancelot and Méléagant, this would suggest that rather than simply being diabolic, Méléagant is despised by Lancelot and vilified by the romance so as not to reckon with the similarities or "identification" between these men.

Yet, it is Godefroi's section that more explicitly brings together the motifs of supplemental logic and curious—often cross-gender—identification. Indeed, Godefroi completes, transforms, and subverts the preceding narrative, as Brownlee argues ("Transformations" 163–64). He also appears to identify with Méléagant's sister, whom he introduces as follows:

> Cele estoit suer Meleagant,
> Don bien vos dirai ça avant
> Mon pansser et m'antencion,
> Mes n'an vuel feire mancion,
> Car n'afiert pas a ma matire
> Que ci androit an doie dire,
> Ne je ne la vuel boceier
> Ne corronpre ne forceier,
> Mes mener boen chemin et droit. (6243–51)

> She was Méléagant's sister. I will later tell you my plan and intentions for her. But here I don't want to mention it, since it isn't fitting to my material that I should discuss it now; and I don't want to twist, corrupt or force the tale, but rather to carry it on its rightful, straight path.

As this superfluous passage bombards us with literary terms that recall the prologue, Godefroi seems to be calling attention to himself—and, so doing, to allude to his similarities to Méléagant's sister (Hult 88–91). Indeed, in the romance's final segment, the imprisoned Lancelot appears to "pla[y] the role of Chrétien's Guinevere," while this "female character," "a locus of efficacious activity," gets Lancelot out of a jam—as Godefroi does Chrétien (Brownlee, "Transformations" 164, 167). Critics have not, however, sufficiently asked why Godefroi would associate himself with Méléagant's sister. Because Méléagant's sister fleetingly appeared earlier in the text, Godefroi is perhaps picking up on the possibility of mining reflexive "loose ends." He is also picking up on the relation of dialectic reversals to the modalities of the gendered and desiring subject; for what, in the prologue, was an endeavor desired by a woman but executed by a man becomes that of another man who executes his endeavor as a woman. Godefroi's segment also raises issues related to desire. For Brownlee, the erotic is "visibly . . . suppressed" ("Transformations" 168) in it, notably when Méléagant's sister attends to an injured Lancelot:

> Soef le menoie et atire
> Si com ele feïst son pere,
> Tot le renovele et repere,
> Tot le remue, tot le change. (6666–69)

Carefully she oversaw his progress and cares for him, as she would her father; she revives and fully heals him, she treats him and entirely transforms him.

This mention of Méléagant's sister behaving unto Lancelot as she would her father seems, however, both jarring and unnecessary. To my ears, it suggests that rather than having suppressed desire, Godefroi's segment is calling attention to its suppression. Other instances corroborate this notion that—as in Sébille's letter or Machaut's *dit*—the renunciation of desire is not simple or straightforward. For example, just before taking care of Lancelot, Méléagant's sister must free him from the tower. She says,

> Me covient porquerre
> Ou que soit ci an ceste terre
> Aucun engin, se je le truis,
> C'om puisse croistre cest pertuis
> Tant que vos issir an puissiez. (6607–11)

I need to find, somewhere in this land, some way—if I can find it—by which one can expand this hole/opening so you can get out.

The act of liberating the great knight is curiously eroticized; Lancelot's "hole" must be widened for him to be saved. Rather than having moved beyond the erotic, this sequence seems to me to be picking up on Lancelot's sexual passivity, which was latent earlier in the text: when, for example, Lancelot is nearly raped by the Demoiselle Entreprenante, or when he, not Guinevere, bleeds during sex (cf. Samuelson, "Affirming Absence" 101). Instead of reading Godefroi's segment in terms of the renunciation of desire, we might therefore see it as interrogating the motif of renunciation. Chrétien's (ostensible) renunciation of the text furnishes the space for Godefroi's intervention, but Godefroi's intervention is also *about* renunciation, as it troubles the male subject's renunciation of femininity and grapples with the problem of renouncing desire.

With Christine, Machaut, and Chrétien—and de Libera and Butler—I have argued that the story of the subject is no *droite voie*. At the level of the individual, the subject is not accurately described either as someone who does in the mode of subjectivity or as someone onto whom something is done in the mode of subjection. Rather, the subject is an indeterminate but highly charged—ambivalent—amalgamation of inside and outside, "self" and others.

At the macrolevel, the story of the subject isn't much straighter. This chapter has resisted the narrative, often implicit in scholarship, whereby the medieval subject was making amazing breakthroughs that gesture toward the modern "I." Granted, stressing the part played by the Middle Ages in the rise of the individual or the evolution of the self-conscious author has been important, since contributions of the medieval period to these notions have been unfairly neglected. Yet, there is equally urgent work to do in resisting this narrative—even when it makes space for the Middle Ages.

Indeed, as the always-already reflexive subject resists grammatical and narrative paradigms or logic, so too might we try to imagine a relation between (at one level) verse romances and *dits* and (at another level) courtly literature and queer theory that better reflects the challenging modalities of this paradoxical, ambivalent subject. What does this mean? As regards the first relationship, I have suggested that the reflexive subject in verse romances and *dits* is always-already looking both back at itself and beyond itself. It follows that *dits* may be understood as (paradoxically) only developing the earlier genre's examination of the subject by regressing more—and/or differently—back into examination of the ambivalent reflexivity already characteristic of the subject. Rather than celebrating new developments that announce a more modern subject in the mode of progress, critics of *dits* might, then, reckon with how the fervent reflection on subjectivity in these late medieval works is often (and genuinely) new paradoxically because it mines the problem of what is already there and won't go away, including, in particular, what *dits* glean from verse romance.

It is perhaps a greater problem how receptive these medieval texts are to being queered in the manner of this chapter. To turn to the infamous Althusserian image on which Butler draws, verse romances and *dits,* such as those studied here, can seem to lend themselves to interpellation by poststructuralist theory like Butler's. And as Butler interrogates the "readiness to turn" (*Psychic Life* 107) of the addressee being hailed, so too can we reflect on the ramifications of courtly literature's propensity to turn toward queer theory's call and beckoning. At one level, there are historical reasons for this, and queer theory could surely do a better job looking backward (I note in passing that there seems to have been one full-length article on the medieval period in *GLQ* in the last decade). Yet, rather than adopting a sort of narrative logic that beats the refrain that queerness could be more convincingly historicized, I am more drawn to how, like the always-already reflexive subject, the always-already queer aspects of the medieval subject shouldn't fully add up or make sense. Indeed, if the relationship between the medieval subject and the postmodern queer one is certainly not one of total alterity—as I (following others) have argued—it is also not one of pure identity. Rather, it is paradoxically fitting and logical that the medieval courtly subject and the modern queer one would have a messy and illogical relationship, because courtly literary and queer theory both focus on the illogical nature of the reflexive subject. What's more, as this subject is defined by her/his ambivalence toward him/herself and what lies beyond him/herself, so too can the relationship between courtly texts and queer theory usefully reflect and generate ambivalence. Indeed, in my view, it would not necessarily be a bad thing if this chapter generates some mixed feelings: perhaps for the medievalist not comfortable reading these canonical works as queering the subject, or for the queer theorist who, for instance, feels that bringing Butler to these medieval texts implies significant torsion. If my goal is to confront and reflect critically on the unflagging ambivalence of the subject within texts, it is imperative to write in a way that fosters ambivalence, rather than flattening it out.

The next chapter is also about charged but illogical and messy relationships. It focuses, however, not on the condition of the subject but on the relations between putatively heterogenous narrative levels and segments.

CHAPTER 2

Medieval Metalepsis
Queering Narrative Poetics

Gérard Genette defines metalepsis as "any intrusion of the extradiegetic narrator or narratee into the diegetic universe . . . or vice versa" (244). The epilogue to the *Bel Inconnu* (c. 1200) is medieval French literature's best-known instance of "metaleptic writing" (Perret 139). The author, Renaud de Beaujeu, interrupts his protagonist's story to implore his own lady to give him a sign of encouragement. Initially referring to himself in the third person, he writes,

> Quant vos plaira, dira avant,
> U il se taira ore a tant.
> Mais por un biau sanblant mostrer
> Vos feroit Guinglain retrover
> S'amie, que il a perdue,
> Qu'entre ses bras le tenroit nue.
> Se de çou li faites delai,
> Si ert Guinglains en tel esmai
> Que ja mais n'avera s'amie.
> D'autre vengeance n'a il mie,
> Mais por la soie grant grevance
> Ert sor Guinglain ceste vengance,
> Que ja mais jor n'en parlerai
> Tant que le bel sanblant avrai. (6253–66)

When it should please you, he'll say more; otherwise, he will stop speaking for the time being. But given an encouraging glance ["un biau sanblant"], he would—for you—have Guinglain reunite with his lover, whom he had lost, and he would hold her naked in his arms. If you hold out on this, Guinglain will be in such trouble that he'll never recover his lover. He has no other possibility of revenge, but for his great grievance, he will enact his vengeance upon Guinglain, as I will never say any more about him, until I have received an encouraging glance.

Scholars have often understood this epilogue in terms of a "generic clash" at play throughout the romance.[1] Like Renaud's earlier intrusions into Guinglain's story, this epilogue gestures toward lyric poetry, which characteristically leaves desire suspended. Such suspension is welcome here, because Guinglain is juggling two irreconcilable claims: a socially sanctioned marriage with la Blonde Esmeree in the tradition of Arthurian romance, and a more private affair with the mysterious Pucelle aux Blanches Mains that recalls Celtic *lais*. As the text cannot reconcile the competing generic demands embodied by these two women, it turns to lyric convention for poetic resolution, even if the resolution works precisely because it doesn't resolve anything.

Yet, as critics have suggested in different ways, Renaud's intervention also intersects more complexly with the protagonist's storyline. Guinglain's major mistake in his relationship with la Pucelle aux Blanches Mains is that of absconding, and it seems to me that Renaud may even be echoing this grave error; for the text's premature conclusion also represents a dishonorable leave-taking, yet one of Guinglain, not by him. Renaud's infidelity toward his protagonist would therefore be paradoxically indistinguishable from his fidelity to him, as he both abandons his protagonist and mirrors his behavior. Troubling notions of fidelity resonates, moreover, with the romance's plotline. Similar to how Guinglain cannot be faithful to one woman without being unfaithful to another, the reader is here torn between two competing amorous claims: those of Renaud and Guinglain. And if this intrusion seems to look both forward and backward, inside and outside, we might wonder whether Renaud is best described as intruding into the protagonist's story or whether Guinglain's predicament somehow dictates the terms of (or intrudes on) this intrusion (cf. Haidu, "Realism" 50). The epilogue explicitly addresses such issues of control and domination, by claiming it is up to Renaud's lady whether he shall continue. Again, though, this turn outside the text also

---

1. De Looze, "Generic Clash." See e.g., Haidu, "Realism" 59–60; Colby-Hall; Gaunt, *Gender* 103–15.

loops back into it, since within the diegesis, the Pucelle aux Blanches Mains explains how she has manipulated Guinglain since his childhood (3212–42, 4974–94). Recourse to an all-powerful woman therefore marks the abrupt end to the romance and its return to the theme of a woman pulling the strings behind the stage (cf. Perret 145–47; Gaunt, *Gender* 111–12).

For the narratologist Debra Malina, "the metaleptic cycle forces us to read deconstructively: we must refrain from shutting down meaning, re-containing narrative and its subjects within our usual frames, and instead remain open to unresolvable ambiguities" (19). The epilogue to the *Bel Inconnu* similarly confuses our "usual frames," entangling inside and outside, resolution and irresolution, fidelity and infidelity, power and powerlessness.

This chapter contends that metalepsis is often pushing us "to read deconstructively" in verse romances and *dits*. Yet, before continuing, it is necessary to better "frame" the term, which I do somewhat differently than structuralist narratology has (cf. Prince 50–51). I shall define metalepsis as the interpenetration, which generally "operate[s] through *repetition*," of ostensibly discrete narrative levels or textual elements.[2] This broad definition is able to account for the knotty ways in which narrative levels intersect in the epilogue to the *Bel Inconnu*. In its emphasis on repetition across narrative levels, it also resembles definitions of metalepsis's cousin, *mise en abyme*. Indeed, though clearly indebted to lyric tradition, Renaud's epilogue exemplifies the four features that Lucien Dällenbach considers to be characteristic of the "reflexive metanarrative" (*méta-récit réflexif*); it reflects, halts, and interrupts the diegesis, while introducing "a factor of diversification" (71). Narratologists have long noted the proximity of *mise en abyme* and metalepsis (Cohn). Metalepsis may even have been on André Gide's mind when he coined the term *mise en abyme* in 1893. "No action on something without retroaction on the subject performing the action," writes Gide (40), whose focus is less on doubling *per se* than on the "mutual construction of the writer and the text," as Dällenbach insists (25). Gide is drawn to how writer and text "through the[ir] juxtaposition, lose their internal stability and distinctness from each other" (Butler, *Gender Trouble* 167); he is fascinated by their metaleptic interplay.

This chapter thus adopts a broad conception of metalepsis, which infringes on that of *mise en abyme*; I prefer the former term because it emphasizes disruption.[3] Metalepsis also has a longer history, and my understanding of it shares something with its medieval usage. Introduced but derided by Quintilian, metalepsis (and/or its Latin equivalent, *transsumptio*) was present in

---

2. Butler, *Gender Trouble* 198; original emphases. See below for why I am using Butler in these contexts.

3. See, however, Uhlig, for an opposing take on metalepsis and disruption.

twelfth-century rhetoric and rose to prominence in the following century (Purcell). For William Purcell, it refers to "a syllogistic pattern which connects unrelated expressions through intermediate terms" (374). At the crossroads of logic and rhetoric, metalepsis is a figure of style that refers to an invisible logical jump; as Purcell maps it, it generally takes the form of "AB, BC, AC," where what we see is "AC," when we would expect either "AB" or "BC." The reader must then re-construct in her mind the logical move. How, for example, did we get to snowy teeth?[4] Because snow is white, and whiteness describes teeth, so snowy teeth. This operation is similar to what I have done in relation to the *Bel Inconnu* and will do with *Partonopeu de Blois, Silence,* and the *Prison amoureuse*. The question will be what invisible and logical—or, more often than not, *illogical*—connections tie together heterogeneous narrative levels or segments. While the previous chapter considered the authorial/narratorial *je* in terms of subjectivity, this chapter will, then, focus on more local relations between this *je* and the diegesis: on something like what Spearing calls the "deictic" function of the textual "I" (*Textual Subjectivity*).

In the boundary-crossing spirit of metalepsis, I am, moreover, particularly concerned with how, in texts about *fin'amor*, unruly narrative poetics map onto unruly gender and sexual politics. I have begun to set the stage for this move, by inappropriately—or metaleptically, as Michael Lucey would have it (esp. 808–10)—using quotes from Judith Butler to describe narrative metalepsis. This is because Butlerian queer theory and narrative metalepsis seem to me to intersect in important ways. At the most basic level, both are focused on "inappropriate ways" of acting and relating (Lucey 808–9). Both more precisely challenge notions of "fixed sites of . . . permeability and impermeability," whether of bodily surfaces or of narrative levels or units (*Gender Trouble* 180). And because both Buterlian queer theory and metalepsis engage with abjection, they destabilize the binary opposition of inside to outside. Indeed, among Butler's most important contentions is the idea that, as regards gender and sexual politics, "the construction of an 'outside'" is always-already "fully 'inside,' not a possibility beyond culture, but a concrete cultural possibility that is refused and redescribed as impossible" (*Gender Trouble* 105). Metalepsis similarly functions by bringing "inside" what conventionally lies "outside" the diegesis (and/or vice versa), in a theoretically "impossible" move. And in narrative metalepsis as in Butler's work, the effect is generally one of making it "unclear how to distinguish the real from the unreal" (*Gender Trouble* xxiv). Or, put somewhat differently, metalepsis and Butlerian queer

---

4. Purcell 378–89 takes this example from Geoffrey of Vinsauf. See Purcell 378ff. for the relationship of metalepsis to metaphor.

theory each destabilize the ground on which conventional narratives stand, by taking aim at the opposition of cause and effect. In fact, rhetoric often describes metalepsis as the confusion of cause and effect, and narrative metalepsis troubles the (generally implicit) assumption whereby the extra-diegetic world is the absent cause of the diegetic, which cannot touch it or be touched by it (this is what interests Gide). For her part, Butler, who occasionally uses the term metalepsis in this rhetorical sense (e.g., *Gender Trouble* 202; also Freccero 2–9), argues that gender identity is an effect of behavior that is only masquerading as its cause.

Both narrative metalepsis and Butlerian queer theory therefore put pressure on such charged oppositions as those of cause and effect, inside and outside, natural and unnatural, and true and false or real and fictive. Inspired by these resonances between the two, this chapter looks to three quite different texts—*Partonopeu de Blois, Silence,* and *la Prison amoureuse*—to study the relation of disruptive narrative poetics to disruptive sexual politics in each. More precisely, I explore how, in *Partonopeu,* two facets of the romance's narrative poetics—its very verbose narrator and the romance's continuations—deconstruct, both in literary and more politicized terms, such oppositions as those of inside to outside, the legible to the illegible, and the legitimate to the illegitimate. Afterward, I suggest that *Silence*'s author-narrator Heldris de Cornuälle, whose "basic conservatism" (Jewers, "Non-Existent Knight" 96) has gone largely unquestioned, more curiously relates to the protagonist's performance of her/his gender than it would seem, making this already slippery romance even slipperier. I then argue that Froissart's *Prison amoureuse,* which is generally read as barely concerned with amorous issues, instead explores possibilities for confusing and denaturalizing the relation between discourse and desire. Finally, in the conclusion, I reflect on the pertinence of the concept of metalepsis for theorizing the relationships both between verse romances and *dits* and between courtly literature and queer theory.

PARTONOPEU DE BLOIS

The modern reception of *Partonopeu de Blois* pales in comparison to its medieval one. Few medievalists would spontaneously rank this late twelfth-century "best-seller" (Bruckner, *Shaping Romance* 109) alongside the *Tristan* and *Graal* material as the "third chef d'oeuvre" of medieval French letters, as Anthime Fourrier once did (*Courant réaliste* 315). Perhaps, as Penny Eley suggests, the extreme *mouvance* characteristic of *Partonopeu*'s manuscript tradition has rendered it all but illegible to the modern reader (1). This *mou-*

vance, which we will look at more closely, seems, however, not to be purely accidental; rather, it reflects the superlatively "Protean" (Bruckner, *Shaping Romance* 109) character of this vast, heterogeneous romance. A cursory summary of the text gives a taste of how it brings together a wide-ranging array of different elements. The prologue introduces the author-narrator's "double stance" as both clerk and lyric lover (Bruckner, *Shaping Romance* 110–13). It is followed by a genealogy of the Kings of France that recalls *romans antiques* (Simons and Eley, "Prologue"). The story then begins. The young hero, Partonopeu, is lured away by a fairy-like woman, who grants him every favor but one: he is forbidden from seeing her. This initial segment recalls both the myth of Psyche and Cupid and *lais* such as *Lanval*.[5] Partonopeu's time in the opulent Eastern kingdom of the Empress Melior is interrupted by two returns to France, one of which, detailing the conflict between the French crown and Pagan intruders, reads rather like a *chanson de geste*. Partonopeu then sneaks a peek at Melior. This is not well advised, as over the course of thousands of lines, he must work his way back into her good graces and secure her court's approval for their marriage. Complete with a crucial tournament followed by triumphant wedding celebrations, this segment seems more "romance-like," even if a very chatty narrator keeps interrupting things. Finally, formal experimentation becomes even more explicit in the continuations. Describing the aftermath of Partonopeu and Melior's marriage, the continuations notably alternate between octosyllabic and decasyllabic couplets and alexandrines arranged in *laisses*.

Critics have been particularly drawn to *Partonopeu*'s narrator. Dubbed the "romance's most remarkable feature" (Krueger, "Textuality" 58), this anonymous *je* intervenes at length some sixteen times in the romance proper.[6] If one includes the prologue, his intrusions total well over 1000 lines (cf. Krueger, "Author's Voice" 127). Critics (e.g., Bruckner, *Shaping Romance* 144–45; Eley 200) have sometimes divided his interventions into two categories: one, more "subjective," where he compares the struggles of the characters to his own unhappy love story; and another, more "didactic," where he focuses on the issue of chastity—of which he is no fan—and on the treatment of women by "clergastes" [bad clerks] (5497). Uniting these intrusions is his persistent focus on desire. This raises the question: do seemingly unruly narrative poetics correspond to unruly gender and/or sexual politics?

---

5. For *Partonopeu* and Psyche, see T. Brown and Bruckner, *Shaping Romance* 122–23. For *Partonopeu* and *lais*, see e.g., Bruckner, *Shaping Romance*, 123–25.

6. See also Fourrier, *Courant réaliste* 428 and Eley 199. My count, defining at length as over three verses of commentary.

This narrator, as has been amply remarked, does have a tendency to empathize with women, which he advertises; for example, "J'aim totes dames comme moi" [I love all women as myself] (5507). Indeed, he is more likely to underscore parallels between his predicament and those of various women than he is to insist on similarities between himself and Partonopeu.[7] He particularly stresses his proximity to Melior, claiming, for instance,

> Tant reconnois son estre en moi
> C'or m'est avis que jo le voi
> Et que je part a son deshait,
> Car en merci sui de tel plait. (8583–86)

> I so recognize her predicament in my own that it seems to me that I see her now, and that I partake of her plight, as I, too, am at the mercy of a similar struggle.

These explicit identifications with Melior herald more substantial parallels between her and the narratorial *je*. As Bruckner has observed, both Melior and the poet manipulate the protagonist while remaining invisible to him (cf. *Shaping Romance* 133–38). What's more, after Partonopeu peeks at Melior and her magic powers fade away, her proximity to the poet becomes even more pronounced. Melior describes her clerical formation and capacities to Partonopeu, explaining how she would conjure vast illusions of knightly jousts and animal combats for her father's court—or, as Bruckner suggests, how she would spawn literary fiction (*Shaping Romance* 112).

For Bruckner, the two sorts of spectacles that Melior puts on—a private, erotic show just for Partonopeu and these larger public performances—correspond to the narrator's two types of interventions; both the *je* and Melior have public and private modes (*Shaping Romance* 112). Yet, we never witness Melior's public performances. There are, however, numerous instances where other characters must formulate more impartial, detached judgments. In the climactic tournament scene, for example, Melior discovers that Partonopeu is among the fighters. She struggles to conceal her burning desire for him. She must defer to eight judges, four Christian and four Muslim, who more stoically debate the merits of the different pretenders to her hand, finally selecting Partonopeu because of his exceptional beauty. The interplay of subjective and objective judgment that characterizes the narrator's interventions

---

7. For comparisons to women: 7581–88, 8443–47, 8583–86, 8982–9004, 10073–92. For comparisons to Partonopeu: 1866–80, 4038–42, 4529–34, 7517–24.

is thus mirrored within this scene, as Melior's judgment is more partial, the judges' more removed. Play on the inside/outside binary also manifests itself in another way here, as the narrator exhibits a curious willingness to sympathize with Partonopeu's opponents—such as his principal foe, the Sultan Margaris, who "cuide a tos estre nonpers" [believed himself superior to all others] (7979). According to the narrator, Margaris is quite correct (7981); he even embodies the former glory of love, which is—alas—now extinct (7961–8038). Margaris is, moreover, prepared to convert to Christianity in order to marry Melior, as are all her other Muslim suitors—"Chascuns d'[ic]els sa loi lairoit / Por Melior s'ele voloit" [Each of them would abandon his faith for Melior, should she so desire] (9781–82)—and it is striking that the narrator seems to echo this sentiment, since he twice insists that his desire for his lady is greater than his wish for Salvation (7111–12, 7518–22).

It is, though, a servant girl who furnishes the strongest, and strangest, example of how the narrator can place his sympathies in unexpected locations. At least four times, the *je* compares his plight to that of Persewis, who, though of noble extraction, is the servant to Melior's sister Urraque.[8] Both he and Persewis, who has fallen head-over-heals for Partonopeu, are victims of unrequited love:

> Et Persewis od els i est
> Qui don ne puet avoir ne prest
> De ço qu'ele aime, ains li vait si
> Qu'ele aime et si n'a point d'ami.
> Si faç jo, caitis, tot adés . . . (7581–85)

> And Persewis is with them, who can have no gift or loan from him whom she loves. Rather, it is her fate to be in love but yet to have no lover. Such is also the case for poor me, without interruption.

Persewis is here standing beside Melior and Urraque, as they nervously watch Partonopeu battle. The odd thing, however, is that she doesn't need to be there—or in the romance at all, as her actions never advance the plot. For Bruckner, Persewis "seems to have been invented chiefly to demonstrate . . . the power of Partonopeu's beauty to inspire love in any susceptible female who sees him" (*Shaping Romance* 130). Compelling, such a reading nonetheless ascribes a clear point to Persewis's character, whereas Persewis is arguably like the narrator precisely because their love has no point, as it seemingly

---

8. See 6303–6, 8443–48, 8997–9004, and below.

cannot come to be. To understand Persewis as primarily serving to reinforce Partonopeu's beauty forecloses, moreover, the possibility that the romance may be experimenting with "the extension of . . . legitimacy" to perspectives traditionally cast as "false, unreal, and unintelligible" in courtly literature, to borrow from Butler's description of her goals in the 1999 "Preface" to *Gender Trouble* (xxv).

Or, put differently, it raises an important question: how subversive is the inversion of the male gaze that the romance—aided by narratorial intrusions such as these—effects by positioning "Partonopeu, not Melior, as the primary object of our agreeable contemplation" (Bruckner, *Shaping Romance* 129)? Sure, it may seem unusual when, for instance, just before being chosen to wed Melior, Partonopeu finds himself stripped nearly naked—"en corte chemise" [in short undergarments] (b10429)—for all to judge.[9] Yet, the protagonist's objectification appears generally in keeping with his interests and those of both the French and Byzantine courts—and would thus seem not too subversive. Indeed, Partonopeu's beauty even functions similarly to chivalric might in other romances, as it serves as proof of the righteous protagonist's worth and gets him out of trouble time and again. And if the protagonist's beauty is his not-so-secret weapon for advancing his—and patriarchy's—ambitions, the romance's "practice of 'inversion'" may be "committed to the very model of normalization" it would appear to disrupt.[10] In a similar vein, we might argue that the narratorial intrusions, which scream the *je*'s love for his lady, do not morph into something queerer by virtue of often intervening in the contexts of characters' fawning over the beauty of a boy. Rather, they reflect and promote a certain sexual normativity that would overpower any oddity in what the romance is getting up to with the protagonist.

Such a view could account for various seemingly more reactionary positions that the narrator appears to hold. Chimène Bateman notes, for example, how his "espousal of tolerance and *folie* . . . translates into an attitude of extreme rigidity toward women. The narrator's frequent condemnations of women who say no leave little or no space for the consideration of female desire" (174). For her part, Eley has called attention to how the romance obsessively denounces the *fils a vilain*, "a low born individual who has been raised to a position of influence at court" and "threatens to blur class distinctions" (51). Neither the narrator's hatred of chastity nor his obsession with the *fils a vilain* seems to me, however, straightforward. As regards the latter, for example, certain statements that appear to denounce this usurper—such

---

9. See Simons and Eley, "Male Beauty" 51–52 and Bruckner, *Shaping Romance* 129.
10. Cf. *Gender Trouble* 37, discussing Wittig's *Corps lesbien*.

as the narrator's contention that noble women married to bad men should be unfaithful so that the child's blood is not tainted (307–12)—seem too far-fetched, straining credulity. It is noteworthy, too, that in the initial genealogy of the French crown, there is a perfect alternation between good and bad kings, in an "ABAB" pattern (399–448). Blood does not predict *cortoisie* when it comes to the Kings of France. The romance also contains multiple *éloges* of low-born but invaluable advisors, such as Melior's principal counselor Ernoul: "S'il ert molt bas enparentés / N'i doit il estre refusés" [Though he was very low-born, he shouldn't be ignored there] (a10419–20). Equally striking is the dearth of information provided about Partonopeu's father, about whom we learn nothing—except that he quickly dies when Partonopeu is first at Chef d'Oire (2047–48). If the romance wished unequivocally to promote the importance of patrilineal blood, surely it could have come up with something more about the hero's lineage.

As the continuations take up the theme of the *fils a vilain*, I will return to it in discussion of them. For now, I am suggesting that the romance's preoccupation with the *fils a vilain* is not simply a reactionary reflex that points to the narrator's rather closeted conservatism. Instead, something messier is afoot, as the assertion that blood is legible and confers legitimacy is obfuscated by a presentation of the theme that is not very legible and possibly illegitimate. Perhaps counterintuitively, the rhetoric ostensibly pitted against the *fils a vilain* even pushes us more rigorously to locate the queerness of the romance's narrative poetics, by situating it less in terms of stances that the narrator adopts (however progressive or reactionary they appear) and more in terms of the effects of destabilization and dissonance, which should neither be presumed nor excluded, that his intrusions may produce. As Butler suggests, subversiveness is less a matter of the content of one's beliefs—since what is considered subversive both evolves and depends, and the most radical ideas can be uncritically regurgitated—than of the modalities by which one throws a wrench in patriarchy's cogs (see *Gender Trouble* xxii–iii).

For Butler, that is, there can be no formula for "subversiveness," since "subversiveness is the kind of effect that *resists calculation*" ("Critically Queer" 29; original emphasis). She nonetheless sketches out strategies for effecting disruption that are deconstructive, as the goal is not to invert or transcend binaries but rather to disarm them by denaturalizing them. Patient analysis of some of the narrator's more elaborate intrusions suggest that they function to similar effect. His second extended intervention, for instance, occurs during Partonopeu's first return to France. Partonopeu is engaged in one-to-one combat with the Danish Sornegur, on which hinges the fate of France. Neither has the upper hand, until Partonopeu "drece l'espee / Que Melior li ot donee" [raises the sword that Melior had given him] (3393–94). "Dont li est menbré de s'amie" [He then recalls his lover] (3396), which propels him to up his game and the *je* to intervene:

> A Sornegur rest bien avis
> Que de l'estor li estoit pis
> Et que ses compains s'est molt fains
> De quanqu'il se conbati ains.
> Ensi set amors ensegnier   3415
> Cascun home de son mestier,
> Cevalier de cevalerie
> Et clerc d'amender se clergie.
> Vilonie tolt et perece,
> Cortesie done et largece.   3420
> Dame qui n'aime tienç a fole;
> Poi pris son fait et se parole.
> Mais s'ele est bele u de l'endroit
> C'on l'en quiere, si l'otroit.
> La moie amie en fin m'ocit,   3425
> Tant se desfent et escondit.
> Escondire afiert a laron.
> Ja s'el me croit ne dira non.
> Siens sui liges et ses feels,
> Bien se doit metre en mes consels.   3430
> Segnor, ne vos anuit, por Deu,
> Se j'entrelais Partonopeu
> Et paroil de ço dont plus pens,
> Car u soit folie u soit sens,
> U as dolor, la est tes dois;   3435
> U as amor, cele part vois.
> Li dois siolt estre a le dolor
> Et li iols tos jors a l'amor.
> Partonopeus le fait si bien,
> Li rois le crient sor tote rien.   3440

Sornegur had the impression that he was losing the battle and that his adversary had hardly been giving it his all when fighting before. Thus love knows how to teach each man his trade: the knight, chivalry; and the clerk, to better his *clergie*. Love removes vileness and sloth and bestows courtliness and generosity. I consider that any lady who doesn't love is mad; I hardly value her actions or her words. But if she is beautiful and of the sort that her love is besought, she should grant it. My beloved is, finally, killing me, so much does she resist and deny me. To deny belongs to the thief. If she believes me, she will no longer say no; I am her subject and servant, and she should take my advice into account. My Lords, may it not bother you, by God, if I abandon Partonopeu, and speak about what occupies my mind more. For whether it is folly or good sense, where you feel pain, you place your fingers, and where there is love, you glance. The fingers should belong to pain, while the eyes should always be love's. Partonopeu fights so well that the King fears him more than all else.

This intrusion (which is similar in each of the seven manuscripts of the romance that contain this scene) does not initially seem metaleptic or subversive, as the narrator appears to "abandon" his protagonist in order to assert that women should acquiesce to whatever men require.[11] Yet, not unlike how Butler argues that certain of Monique Wittig's works mobilize "an internal subversion in which the [gender] binary is both presupposed and proliferated to the point where it no longer makes sense," so too does this intrusion presuppose, proliferate, and confuse the binary opposition of inside to outside (*Gender Trouble* 173).

We begin to sense metaleptic overlap between the narrator's rhetoric and the protagonist's predicament when he claims that fingers are for pain, eyes for love (cf. Bateman 168). Clearly, this does not describe Partonopeu's relationship with Melior. The narrator is also more generally echoing his protagonist's behavior, since Partonopeu succeeds in combat because he recalls his absent lady at this moment in time, and the narrator is similarly recalling his beloved. As in the epilogue to the *Bel Inconnu*, the ostensible turn away from the protagonist is also a turn toward him. The narrator is paradoxically "within" the diegesis, by virtue of contemplating his private "without."

Play on the inside/outside binary then proliferates. The narrator acknowledges that his intrusion may seem inappropriate—"My Lords, may it not bother you"—and this sequence announces another inappropriate intervention; in the immediately following lines, Marés, a *fils a vilain*, breaks the pact according to which only Partonopeu and Sornegur will duel it out. Nearly at the same time as Marés "S'enseigne escrie et el camp entre" [cries out his slogan and enters onto the battlefield] (3449), the narrator is also calling attention to himself, intruding into the diegesis and even breaking the implicit "pact" to relay Partonopeu's story.

---

11. See manuscript B 3305-34; G 3406-30; L 3219-42; P 3400-23; T 3305-32; and V 3361-88. All transcriptions are from the electronic edition: https://www.dhi.ac.uk/partonopeus/.

Play on the inside/outside binary also bleeds into more secondary characters. Mortified, the Danish emperor will, for example, permeate the French lines so as to offer himself up as compensation for Marés's treason: "Entr'als se met con uns des lor" [He infiltrates their ranks as if he were one of them] (a3509). Like our narrator, Sornegur exposes the fluidity of categories of inside and outside. Yet, when he finally surrenders to the French, the soldiers are not very interested, because they are so distressed over having lost Partonopeu: "Car comment puet joïr altrui / Qui son cuer a tot plain d'anui?" [For how can one delight another, when one's own heart is so full of trouble?] (3639–40). As this is the very sentiment the narrator has just expressed—his own pain prevents him from celebrating Partonopeu's feats—the narrator is again behaving like characters in the diegesis, by virtue of focusing on his own problems, not those of others.

The opposition of inside and outside therefore falters here, as these categories become confused. A digression that initially seems superfluous and reactionary potentially morphs, then, into something quite different: into "an experience . . . mobile and complex," even "subversive of all fixed positionings," to borrow Spearing's description of the play of perspectives in the Middle English romance's initial segment (*Medieval Poet* 154).

The narrator's first major intrusion, which occurs during this sequence, more forcefully brings these deconstructive tactics to bear on issues of gender and sexuality. Coming at "a conspicuously idyllic point in the narrative" (Grossweiner 399), it describes what Partonopeu and Melior get up to in the bedroom.

> Puis que li mangiers fu finés,   1855
> En le cambre est al lit alés.
> Od Melior a son delit;
> Assés i jue, assés i rit,
> Et n'est mervelle s'il a joie,
> Car tant li seit conter la bloie   1860
> Et de deduit et de grant sens
> Et des fais de l'ancien tens
> Que nus ne set tant bien entendre
> Qui ne peüst de lui aprendre.
> Douce et soef a le parole,   1865
> C'est une riens qui molt m'afole;
> Ço ai de m'amie et nient plus,
> Par tant m'i tieng et pens et mus,
> Et Dameldex, qui ne menti,

Me doinst qu'el m'aint si con j'aim li   1870
Et qu'a moi pere se francise,
Car ce n'ert ja que autre eslise.
Partonopeus a son delit,
Li parlers de lui molt m'ocit,
Car il a tos biens de s'amie;   1875
Jo n'en ai riens qui ne m'ocie.
Il ne le voit, mais a loisir
Le sent et en fait son plaisir.
Je voi la moie et n'en faç rien;
J'en ai le mal et il le bien.   1880

After the meal was finished, he went to the bedroom. With Melior he has his delights. He plays and laughs plenty, and it is no marvel if he finds joy; for his blond beauty knows how to narrate things amusing and very wise, even feats of ancient times, such that no one could be so clever that he couldn't learn from her. She speaks to him sweetly and softly—and this drives me crazy, as I get this and no more from my lady. For this reason, I remain pensive and mute. And may God, who has never lied, grant that she should love me as I do her, and that her generosity be expressed to me, as I will never choose anyone else. Partonopeu has his pleasure; talking about him is utterly killing me, as he gets all good things from his beloved, while I have nothing that doesn't destroy me. He doesn't see her but can touch her at will and have his pleasure with her. I see my lady but get to do nothing. I get only the bad and he the good.

During sex scenes, romance narrators often pipe up to say what they cannot or will not say (Samuelson, "Affirming Absence" 92–96). *Partonopeu*'s narrator is, however, preoccupied with what he cannot experience. This peculiar twist then gives way to an even more surprising one, since, as Bateman keenly observes, "all of the terms used to describe Melior's storytelling in this passage can be found in the prologue" (166). Indeed, if Melior here recounts "fais de l'ancien tens" [feats of ancient times], the *je* has claimed to write an "estoire d'antif tens" [story of ancient times] (78). And while Melior's storytelling is pleasing and instructive, *dulce et utile,* so too, according to the prologue, "nus escris n'est tant frarins ... Dont on ne puisse exemple traire" [No writing is so worthless that one cannot learn from it] (103–5).[12]

---

12. This paragraph and the next draw on Samuelson, "Affirming Absence" 98–99.

It is, however, odd to cast Melior "as a double of the narrator" (Bateman 166) here, both because Melior and Partonopeu are engaging in sexual activity and because the narrator so emphatically opposes his situation to theirs. At one level, the effect of this metalepsis is to erotize the *je*'s relationship with his protagonists, by implicating him in this sex scene through a backdoor of sorts. At another level, metalepsis serves to trouble—or deconstruct—the privative opposition that ostensibly underpins this intrusion. Indeed, while the narrator stresses that "I get only the bad and [Partonopeu] the good," things are not so clear-cut, if we look more closely (or dive under the covers); for the narrator is also subtly inserting himself, and his craft, into this sex scene. This intrusion therefore scrambles the opposition between "having" and "not having"—which, for psychoanalysis, is so charged in relation to gender and sexuality—and the pleasure becomes the confusion generated by the interpenetration of narrative levels as these characters copulate.

"Faire en porroie .j. autre livre" [I could write another book about it] (t14584), declares the narrator—perhaps alarmingly—about his love toward the end of the lengthiest continuation of the romance, T. One could similarly spend more time "extracting the honey" (120), to borrow the narrator's earlier expression, from other metaleptic moments. I wish, however, to turn to the "continuation(s)," where narrative poetics and sexual politics continue suggestively to intersect. In six out of the seven manuscripts (all but A), what scholars refer to as the "romance proper" in fact culminates in an instance of metalepsis (which prefigures the epilogue to the *Bel Inconnu*).[13] Although Partonopeu and Melior are married, the narrator informs us that he has more to tell: about Anselot, Partonopeu's faithful servant, whom he abandoned in the Ardennes; Gaudin, his former comrade-in-arms; and the Sultan, who still loves Melior. Yet, he will only continue "if his lady winks at him": "s'ele me gignot de l'uel" (b10622).

Unlike in the *Bel Inconnu,* in five of the six *Partonopeu* manuscripts that contain this passage, the Lady apparently "Velt que plus die" [wishes that I say more] (b10659). The narrator picks up the protagonist's story, warning us, "Se Parthonopex a sa pes, / Guerres et mal li sunt molt pres" [If Partonopeu is at peace, war and woes are in the making] (b10677–78). Yet he decides not to tell us immediately about the Sultan's invasion: "Mais cest conte met en respit / Tant qu'un altre vos aie dit" [But I will put this tale off until I've told you another] (b10703–4). The suspension of the romance thus immediately gives way to an instance of suspension within the continued narrative.

---

13. See Eley 162–63 and for Manuscript A, Simons and Eley, "Subtext."

In the first segment of the "continuations," Anselot's story, this motif of deferral then proliferates. When Partonopeu stumbles on Anselot, he hesitates before approaching him (b10748-776). Anselot and Partonopeu then "Ont . . . mis le conte en respit / Duque devant l'empereris" [put off telling the tale, until they come before the Empress] (11088-89). *Respit* colors Anselot's telling of his tale, too. He defers explanation of key elements, such as why he dwells on his dog: "Assez orés al conte avant / Por coi je parol de lui tant" [You'll hear plenty later in the tale about why I am saying so much about him] (b11163-64). His story is also about deferral. The niece of the Emperor of Rome falls in love with him, but he keeps delaying any rendezvous with her: "Terme li mis de jor en jor / De parler i priveement, / Mais onques ne li ting couvent" [I said each day I would speak privately with her, but I never held up my end of the bargain] (b11274-76). Because he incessantly "forgets" to come together with Euglar, Anselot is nicknamed "[Ansiaus] Oublieus" [Anselot the forgetful] (b11286). Since a secondary character who has been forgotten by the main narrative becomes "the forgetter," and since this segment that exists after the main events so thematizes deferral, it may be self-consciously reflecting on its status as what has been forgotten and/or deferred by the main narrative.

Scholars have, however, understood Anselot's section in terms of another kind of *différance*: its "mixture of closeness and distancing" in relation to the preceding tale, which manifests itself as the "systematic doubling" of elements from the romance proper (Eley 142, 141). Among the elements from the earlier text on which Anselot's section draws, one is most prominent: the motif of the *fils a vilain*. When Partonopeu stumbles on Anselot, he is cursing—vulgarly, and at length—*fils a vilain* (b10777-836). He and Partonopeu then debate whether there are fundamental differences between the *cortois* and the *vilain*. After Anselot tells his tale, "N'a chevalier en la maison . . . qui vilain n'ait en despit" [there is no knight in the household who doesn't despise *vilains*] (t11684-86). Yet, if Anselot's obsession with the *fils a vilain* recalls the preceding romance, it seems to go too far; it may, as Eley observes, become "overkill," pushing us "to look beyond the obvious—perhaps *too* obvious—message" (137; original emphasis). I would suggest that it comports a self-reflexive aspect. When debating with Anselot, that is, Partonopeu asserts,

> Que trestuit li home del mont
> D'un pere et d'une mere sunt.
> Trestuit sunt d'Adan et d'Evain
> Et li cortois et li vilain
> Et tuit li sot et tuit li saige.
> Quel devise a en lor parage? (b10943-48)

that all the men in the world are from one father and one mother. All are from Adam and Eve, both the courtly and the uncourtly and all the stupid and all the wise. What distinction is there in their extraction?

Partonopeu's question is similar to that which scholars have asked of this continuation. Is it from the same "pere" as the original romance? Where exactly is the "devise" [division] between the two, and does their "parage" seem fundamentally different? Not only, then, is Anselot's narrative looping back to a theme in the preceding narrative but it is also alluding to the issue of its own status in relation to the romance proper. This is, however, paradoxical; for the Anselot section would be legitimate because, like the earlier romance, it is about legitimacy, but it is leveraging the legitimacy conferred by treating the question of illegitimacy to call into question its own legitimacy. As Butler invites us to do, it delegitimizes stable notions of legitimacy by proliferating and confusing them.

One manuscript breaks off during Anselot's section (B), another after it (L). Yet, three trudge on, recounting the Sultan's attack against Melior's forces. The Sultan thinks that Melior has, against her wishes, been stolen from him by the faulty ruling of the judges. He attempts to rectify their error on the battlefield. Like Anselot's section, the ensuing continuation(s) implicate deferral; Melior, for example, begs Partonopeu to obtain a cease-fire, "Mais por delai, non por la pais" [just to buy time, not for everlasting peace] (t12014). The text performs *delai*, too, as over the course of thousands of lines, Melior and Partonopeu fade from view, giving way to lengthy debates and battle sequences between different characters, many of whom we have not previously encountered. Only one manuscript, T, appears to bring things to a close. A messenger flatly informs the Sultan that Melior does not love him, so he gives up his claims:

Quant li soudans l'a entendu,
Sachiés que moult fu esperdu.
Ne vos voil faire lonc sermon:
Ci finerons nostre leçon.
Je ne vos puis mie conter
Les dolors qu'il prist a mener;
Puis s'en ala en son païs. (t14559–65)

When the Sultan heard this, know that he was very devastated. I do not want to go on for too long. Here, we will end our tale. I cannot even tell you the pain that overcame him. Afterward, he left for his native land.

Some twenty lines later, this massive romance is done. For Fourrier (*Courant réaliste* 383 n.141), Bruckner (*Shaping Romance* 155), and Eley (165–77), this conclusion feels abrupt; it may even be illegitimate. I would respond that its genius lies in how it troubles legitimacy. For not only is it about the legitimacy of claims—the Sultan's claims, he learns, are illegitimate, so it is time to bow out—but it also more seductively deconstructs notions of poetic legitimacy, as the fact that the Sultan withdraws when he no longer views his lady as encouraging him recalls how, thousands of lines previously, the poet declared he would not persist without encouragement from his lady. This is, however, paradoxical; for the continuation(s) ostensibly exist because the lady winked, but they tell a tale where it seems that a woman should not have pretended to encourage her desperate suitor, as it leads to utterly needless trouble. As with Anselot's section, the remaining continuation(s) are thus legitimate insofar as they are self-consciously about legitimacy—poetic and sexual—but this comes at the price of their calling attention to their own potential illegitimacy. And insofar as they make "distinguishing . . . the legitimate from the illegitimate" so difficult, *Partonopeu*'s narrative poetics powerfully intersect with Butler's strategies for queer subversion (*Gender Trouble* 89). In other words, this is not a romance that is queer simply because it inverts the male gaze or because the narrator makes uncouth remarks about desire, but one which more profoundly mobilizes narrative poetics to destabilize binaries fundamental to the workings of patriarchy.

SILENCE

Various scholars have studied the influence of *Partonopeu*'s narrative poetics on later texts.[14] I wish, however, more generally to explore how unruly narrative poetics and sexual politics would continue to intersect, even when, as is far more frequently the case in romance, the *je* is less colorful and insistent than here. In the *Roman de Silence,* for example, the author-narrator Heldris de Cornuälle is generally read as attempting to slap order onto potentially corrosive material. This romance's plotline may be more provocative than *Partonopeu*'s, but its narrative poetics seem more conservative. This text from the second half of the thirteenth century is about a "vallet ki est mescine" [lad who is a maiden] (3954). Faced with a prohibition on female inheritance, Cador and Eufemie choose to raise their daughter as their son, with Silence then excelling at traditionally male pursuits. Over the past decades, critics

---

14. Simons and Eley, "*Partonopeus*"; Reydners; Grigsby; Krueger, "Author's Voice" 129.

have shown how this romance problematizes the legibility, and legitimacy, of sex. Because nobody realizes that Silence was not born male and because this girl shines as a boy, gender may be a construct rather than an essence, the domain of Noreture (Nurture) rather than Nature. The romance, it is argued, also troubles legibility *tout court,* by emphasizing "linguistic play" and "the indeterminacy of signifiers" (Gaunt, "Significance" 202).

Yet, while Nature apparently had to find an entirely new mold (1900–1) for Silence, the encasing of this tale does not seem nearly as radical. "How," Elizabeth Waters asks, "do we account for this incongruity between the traditional frame and the subversive center of the story?" (37). Indeed, while the romance has generated a "spread of interpretations" (Haidu, *Subject Medieval/ Modern* 240), critics have largely read with, against, or through the author-narrator's "basic conservatism" (Jewers, "Non-Existent Knight" 96), which has gone unchallenged. Yet, similar to how Robert Clark has called on scholars to "set aside assumptions about the main character's identity as female" (54), I would caution against assuming that Heldris is simply reactionary.[15] For Butler, drag exposes how gender "is neither a purely psychic truth, conceived as 'internal' and 'hidden,' nor is it reducible to a surface appearance; on the contrary, its undecidability is to be traced as the play *between* psyche and appearance" ("Critically Queer" 24; original emphasis). Similarly, I shall argue that metalepsis in *Silence* fosters a confusing "play" between the inside and outside of the story, which has important consequences for how we understand Silence's crossdressing as well as the romance's gender and sexual politics more generally.[16]

At one level, the romance is quite explicit that Silence's performance of gender and Heldris's performance of the romance overlap, since while disguised as a boy, Silence temporarily dons another disguise: that of a *jongleur.* Perhaps Silence's success as *jongleur* points to how "the public voice of the *trouvère* is . . . a neutral space where masculine and feminine voices blend" (Jewers, "Non-Existent Knight" 103; also Callahan). This notion of "blending" seems to me, however, more generally and subtly to pertain to how Heldris's narration relates to Silence's transvestism. Consider, for example, how Heldris introduces the story of Silence, after having recounted the courtship of her/his parents:

---

15. It is also in keeping with Clark's argument that I use both male and female pronouns to refer to Silence. I employ "s/he" rather than "they" to reflect how, in my view, *Silence* is struggling with the gender binary; Silence is more torn apart by it than s/he is transcending it.

16. Of course, drag and crossdressing are not the same thing. Drag has no necessary relation to sex, gender identification, or sexual orientation. I turn to drag as theorized by Butler because it is associated with performance and performativity—as are gender and sexuality in (the performance of) this romance. See also Waters for *Silence* and Butler's work on drag.

Huimais orrés conte aviver,
Sans noise faire et estriver.
De Cador, de s'engendreüre
Comence chi tels aventure
C'ainques n'oïstes tele en livre.
Si com l'estorie le nos livre,
Qu'en latin escrite lizons,
En romans si le vos disons./
Jo ne di pas que n'i ajoigne
Avoic le voir sovent mençoigne
Por le conte miols acesmer:
Mais se jel puis a droit esmer
N'i metrai rien qui m'uevre enpire
Ne del voir nen iert mos a dire
Car la verté ne doi taisir.
Avint si par le Deu plaisir
Que Eufemie ot conceü. (1655–71)

Today you will hear a tale brought to life, without fuss or resistance: of Cador, of his progeny, begins here such an adventure that you have never before heard the likes told in a book. As the story recounts it, which we read written in Latin, we render it in French for you. I am not saying that I don't often add lies amidst the truth in order better to adorn the tale, but if I can judge fairly, I will not include anything that lessens the quality of my work. Nor will there be any avoiding the true, because I ought not to silence the truth. It came about by God's will that Eufemie conceived a child.

This passage recalls other romance prologues that claim to be faithfully translating from a Latin original (which may well never have existed). It is also not unusual to add a few "lies" to "ornament" the story, or to supplement one's source with "aucun buen dit" [some good writing] (142), as Benoît de Sainte-Maure puts it in the *Roman de Troie*.

Yet, this passage is also slyly glancing toward Silence's unconventional upbringing. Zan Kocher has remarked how the phrase "conte aviver," which seems to mean "to bring a tale to life," could also mean "to bring up a count," and Silence is a count (355–56). "Por le conte miols acesmer" might also mean "to dress up the count better" (see Kocher 355), and Silence spends most of the text "dressed" in a role s/he considers "better": for example, s/he reflects, "miols valt li us d'ome / Que l'us de feme" [male roles are better than female ones] (2637–38). When, moreover, Heldris proposes to tell this story "sans noise faire" [without making a fuss] and when he claims that "la verté ne doi taisir" [I should not be silent about the truth], he is alluding to the motif of silence, which proliferates in the romance—and, by virtue of being so loud, is disnatured (cf. Gaunt, "Significance" 202). Silence is notably named Silence because s/he must "celer et taisir" [hide and not speak of] (2071) "her" sex. The phrase "la verté ne doi taisir" thus appears at odds with Silence's injunction to silence. Yet, Heldris may be like Silence, or like her/his parents, insofar as he slips in some important "lies." He is nonetheless quick to add, "n'i metrai rien qui m'uevre enpire" [I will not include anything that worsens my work]. This formulation soon intersects with the plotline, as roughly a hundred lines later, Heldris describes how Nature crafts Silence as follows: "Mais Nature garda si bien / En s'uevre n'a a blasmer rien" [But Nature made very sure there is nothing blameworthy in her work] (1893-94). The romance will also continue to fret that Noreture "empire" [worsens] (2326) Nature's best piece of craftsmanship.

This passage thus initially seems to constrain Heldris to what, following Butler, we might call "regulatory norms" ("Critically Queer" 22); Heldris will be faithful to his source, and this sounds like many a romance prologue. Yet, as in Butler's conception of drag, there is also an "undecidability" between the inside and the outside of the story, which sows confusion.

Metalepsis is just as disruptive in the prologue that, coming nearly 2000 verses earlier, introduces the larger romance. Here, Heldris informs us that he needs to say his piece so that "quant venra al conte dire / N'ait en moi rien qui m'uevre enpire" [when it comes to telling the tale, there won't be anything in me that detracts from my work] (81-82). Because the plotline, as we just saw, raises the issue of "detracting from the work," Heldris is paradoxically glancing toward his upcoming *matière* by virtue of insisting that he is not yet talking about it. The "before" is uncomfortably implicated in the "after."

In fact, this prologue, despite seeming only "indirectly" (Akbari 41) linked to the upcoming narrative, even offers a quite disruptive reading of it. Heldris violently denounces how "Li avoirs fait l'ome lanier . . . Il ne fait el fors soi sollier" [wealth makes man craven; he does nothing but defile himself] (57-59). Yet, in the ensuing story, Silence is compelled to compromise her/himself for material gain. S/he will, for example, wonder, "Fu ainc mais feme si tanee / De vil barat, ne enganee / Que cho fesist par covoitise?" [Was there ever a woman so overcome by vile deceit, so tricked, that she would do this for greed?] (2583-85). The prologue therefore stands in a troublesome relation to the diegesis; it even brings to the fore issues of legitimacy. On its surface, that is, it raises such questions as whether *jongleurs* are legitimately compensated or whether avarice leads to shameful, illegitimate behavior. At another level, we can ask whether this screed is legitimate or unbecoming of a serious romancer (cf. Psaki 84–85; Kocher 353); whether there is a legitimate connection between the prologue and the ensuing tale; and even whether the prologue delegitimizes the protagonists' ensuing behaviors.

It might, however, be objected that *Silence* is less about avarice than the "feudal politics of lineage," which do legitimate the recourse of Silence's parents and their progeny to such extremes (Kinoshita, "Heldris" and "Male-Order Brides"). Yet, the romance seems to me to undercut any neat notion of the politics of lineage, by mobilizing repetitions that function like the metaleptic interplay we have been analyzing, insofar as they cast the relationship of parents to progeny more as a confusing "blending" than a legitimate, straightforward affair. Consider, for instance, Heldris's description of Cador's frenzied, amorous state, as he pines after Silence's future mother during their initial courtship:

> Oïstes vos ainc mais conter
> De calt, de froit, qui sunt contrarie,
> Que en un cors peüscent faire?
> S'en moi peüst valoir Nature,
> Ja voir si estrange aventure
> A mon las cors n'en avenist;
> L'uns viers l'altre ne se tenist.
> Mais jo sui tols desnaturés
> Et si cuic estre enfaiturés. (1024–32)

> Have you ever before heard said that hot and cold, which are contraries, could coexist in one body? If Nature could assert herself in me, then never would such a strange adventure befall my weary body. Hot and cold could not coexist. But I am completely denatured and thus believe myself bewitched.

True lovers, we know, experience love as "courtly contradictions" (Kay). Yet, in an "estrange aventure" or "strange twist," this description of Cador's amorous experience also announces Silence's transvestism. In Silence, two contraries—male and female—come together, and while Nature struggles to assert her rights, Noreture threatens to "denature" (2595) and possess Silence. The progeny appears, therefore, as "a repetition" of the terms of the father's erotic predicament: yet one "which is not its consolidation, but its displacement," insofar as it is unclear why a description of courtly desire should prefigure Silence's transvestism (*Gender Trouble* 42).

Other similarly confusing repetitions link the two *volets* of the romance. At one point, Cador reasons that he should not confess his love to Eufemie, since,

> Et feme rest de tel afaire,
> Ne fait pas al miols que puet faire,
> Sa volenté tient por raison,
> De soi honir quiert oquoison,
> Son voloir trait contre nature,
> Contre raison, contre droiture:
> Ne prent garde u s'amor desploie
> Et puet sel estre se desroie
> Que mariër puet a plaisir.
> Mais mioldres pooirs est taisir. (667–76)

And woman is of such a sort that she does not do what is best for herself. She considers her impulses reasonable and seeks out occasions to shame herself; her will goes against nature, against reason, against rectitude. She isn't careful where she places her love, and it might be the case that she errs if she might marry for pleasure. But the best thing to do is to be silent.

The father's misogynistic rant plays on the terms of Silence's future crossdressing. It introduces the notion of veering "contre nature," as well as the imperative to be silent ("mioldres pooirs est taisir"). And by doing this, it brings to the fore a contradiction. As a "lad who is a maiden," Silence excels in all but one domain, sexuality, where it seems that s/he cannot succeed; yet sexuality is not evacuated from this romance, because the parents' desire is persistently imbricated in Silence's ensuing transvestism. The romance seems even to be leaving the door open to a sort of "non-causal and non-reductive connection between sexuality and gender," which is what Butler invites theorists to do ("Critically Queer" 27).

It is, though, the strange echoes linking the parents' courtship to the deviant Queen Eufeme's attempts to seduce an entirely recalcitrant Silence that best get at the slipperiness of the romance's representation of courtly desire. When, for example, Cador's and Eufemie's mouths first come together, they share "one of the longest kisses in medieval literature" (Jewers, "Non-Existent Knight" 100). At one point, Heldris observes,

> Sans dire font, si com moi sanble,
> De fine amor moult bone ensegne,

> Car li baisiers bien lor ensegne,/
> Et li qu'il trait paine et martire,
> Et lui qu'ele l'aime et desire,
> Car n'est pas baisier de conpere,
> De mere a fil, de fil a pere:
> Ainz est baisiers de tel savor
> Que bien savore fine amor. (1094–102)

> Without speaking, it seems to me, they amply demonstrate the signs of true love. For the kiss teaches them much: her, that he suffers and martyrs himself for her; him, that she loves and desires him. Indeed, it is not a familial kiss, like that of a mother to her son or the son to his father. Rather, it is a kiss with the savor that true love savors.

It is hard, however, to imagine anyone being confused about the nature of this kiss, thinking it was of the familial sort. Why, then, Heldris's superfluous remarks? No doubt because, later in the romance, someone will indeed be confused about the line between erotic and platonic *bisous*: Silence, who fails to recognize the nature of the kisses Eufeme desires from her/him.

> Joste la face, sos sa guinple
> Li dona cil [Silence] .i. baisier sinple,
> Car il n'entent pas, al voir dire,
> Con fait baisier ele desire.
> Et la dame, qui nen a cure
> D'estre baisie en tel mesure,
> Li done .v. baisiers traitis,
> Bien amorols et bien faitis . . . (3765–72)

> Beside her face, under her wimple, Silence gave her a simple kiss—because, to tell the truth, he doesn't understand what kind of kiss she wants. And the lady, who does not wish to be kissed in such a way, gives him five agreeable kisses, very amorous and very lovely.

In this instance as in others, the licit encounters of the parents and the illicit encounters between the queen and Silence seem to be confusingly linked. The queen's advances on Silence even appear as the disruptive repetition of the courtly codes embodied by Silence's parents; they expose how, as Butler puts it, "the law turns against itself and spawns unexpected permutations of itself" (*Gender Trouble* 127). Such an interpretation is all the likelier, because the motif of "turn[ing] against oneself" haunts the scenes where the queen makes advances on Silence, particularly when she convinces herself that Silence must be a sodomite:

> Ainc nel lassça por parenté,
> Mais el a en sa volenté.
> As vallés fait moult bele chiere
> Et a lor compagnie chiere.
> Herites est, gel sai de fi,
> Et jo de m'amor le deffi.
> Honte li volrai porcacier. (3943–49)

> He is not refusing because of familial ties, but rather because he desires something else. With other lads he seems in particularly good spirits and he values their company. He is a heretic, I am sure of it, and I withdraw my love from him. I wish to cause him shame.

Yet, the queen is the one who seeks out this "something else," as she attempts to engage in same-sex behavior (Blumreich) and ends up procuring her own shame. And if the queen's language "turn[s] against" itself here, we may read her deviant behavior as demonstrating courtliness's propensity to do the same. Indeed, in this romance so obsessed with the difference one letter can make—Silence is Silentia or Silentius; Eufeme and Eufemie are separated by a measly "i"—there seems to be a troublesome slippage possible between "ireté" (e.g., 3874, 4007), the word used for heritage or for licit filiation, and "erite," the term used for sodomy or for the mis-repeating and disruptive unraveling of social order.

Granted, we are not meant to sympathize with Eufeme. She meets justice when Silence succeeds at capturing Merlin, who, legend has it, can only be captured by a woman. Merlin then exposes all—including how the queen has taken a male lover, disguised as a nun—and the queen is executed. Yet, while this final section is usually read as "predetermined, traditional, and even doctrinal" (Bolduc 110) or as "reiterat[ing] hegemonic norms" (Waters 45), I would counter that it also foments a more disruptive indeterminacy. For McCracken, "The story's neatly sewn-up ending leaves gaps and dangling threads that dispute the 'naturalness' of Silence's reclaimed female gender" ("Boy" 523). The ending, where Silence's "natural" sex is restored, does seem "neatly sewn-up," but if this romance teaches us anything, it is that being "neatly sewn-up" and "genuine" or "natural" are quite different things. Indeed, similar to how Silence seems "trestolt malles" [entirely male] (2478) but has something else going on "under the garments," so too would I extend McCracken's notion to suggest that this sequence, which appears "trestot" reactionary, may be a parody of a straight conclusion: a performance that, like Butler's understanding of drag, is so valuable because it sows confusion. Put differently, Merlin's uncontrollable hysterics, which are about to erupt, are not necessarily "normalising laughter" (Pratt 100) that "does not disrupt patriarchy and hierarchy but reaffirms them" (Kinoshita, "Heldris" 405). Rather, this sounds to me more like the "laughter" that "emerges in the realization" that everything is "derived" (*Gender Trouble* 189).

More concretely, the sequence kicks off when Silence leaves to pursue Merlin. S/he wanders forlorn in the forest until an anonymous old man, perhaps Merlin himself, "literally gives Silence the edible props which will allow her to capture" Arthur's uncle (Stock 25). Some of the first words this old man speaks to Silence are striking:

> Amis, lasscier le dementer.
> Jo ai veü jadis enter
> Sovent sor sur estoc dolce ente,
> Par tel engien et tele entente
> Que li estos et li surece
> Escrut trestolt puis en haltece. (5915–20)

> Friend, let be your torment. Previously I have often seen successful grafting performed on a lifeless stock with a nice graft, done so cleverly and purposefully that the stock and the addition grew together in height.

"Grafting," as Gloria Gilmore observes in relation to this sequence, is "the superimposing of an unnatural order, and in Alain de Lille's thinking, highly improper" (113). It is ironic that the "natural" conclusion opens with a gratuitous image of unnatural propagation. Things become even more confused when Nature and Nurture return to debate. Nurture bemoans how it is in Merlin's nature to be attracted to the odors of cooked food, by which Silence will lure Merlin; yet, as critics have remarked (e.g., Pratt 93–94; Akbari 44), Merlin's nature is thus figured by what doesn't exist naturally in the forest. We might even say of Merlin's "nature" what Butler says of "sex": "that designation supposed to be most in the raw, proves to be always already 'cooked'" (*Gender Trouble* 51). Nature and Nurture also get side-tracked by a debate about Adam and Eve, where they take up the weighty question of how Evil comes to be, if God creates everything but cannot be *in malo*. Yet, as Haidu remarks, both Nature and Nurture presume that Adam, not Eve, is lured by the devil. As earlier in *Silence,* this myth so often used to "reinscrib[e] female secondariness" (Haidu, *Subject Medieval/Modern* 252) is emphatically, and curiously, not put to this purpose here.

Once Silence captures Merlin, things remain just as convoluted. Merlin asks him/her why s/he is out to get him, and Silence responds:

> Mes ancestres fu mors par toi,
> Gorlains, li dus de Cornuälle.
> Tu en morras, comment qu'il alle.
> Merlin, assés le me tuas
> Quant Uterpandragon muas
> En le forme al duc mon a[n]cestre
> Et toi fesis altretel estre
> Com fu ses senescals avoec.
> Uter en menas droit illuec
> U il o la feme al duc giut,
> Quant a Artu le preu conciut. (6144–54)

> My ancestor was killed by you: Gorlain, duke of Cornwall. You shall die for it, whatever happens. Merlin, you as good as killed him, when you transformed Uther Pendragon into the likeness of my ancestor the duke, and you made yourself look like you were his seneschal accompanying him. You led Uther right to the spot where he lay with the duke's wife, and she conceived the noble Arthur.

Because Silence hunts Merlin on the orders of the king, and because we have not previously heard anything about this illustrious ancestor, this response is jarring. Silence's genealogy is not integrated into the romance in a graceful, seemingly natural way. Rather, this seems to be another instance of "unnatural" grafting. This summary of Merlin's machinations hardly serves as a description of "natural" filiation either, as Uther Pendragon is morphed into Gorlain and lies with his wife. The romance might also be understood as grafted onto the Arthurian world (or vice versa), since before Silence is tasked with capturing Merlin, the sole mention of Arthurian landmarks comes at the very beginning of the text, when Ebain is identified as the greatest king in England "besides . . . King Arthur" (109; Pratt 88). The protagonist's, Arthur's, and the romance's genealogy therefore each fail at doing what genealogy theoretically should: anchoring things in a natural, legitimate sequence. It follows that this sequence's embrace of the "feudal politics of lineage" may not be as genuine as it would appear.

When Merlin arrives at court, irony becomes even louder—and not only because Merlin sees through deceptions that no one else can. Consider, for example, the king's response to the increasingly worried queen's request that Merlin be killed:

> Moi lasciés convenir et dire,
> Faire mon bon et mon plasir.
> Sens de feme gist en taisir.
> Si m'aït Dex, si com jo pens,
> Uns muials puet conter lor sens.
> Car femes n'ont sens que mais un,
> C'est taisirs. (6396–402)

> Let me decide and speak; let me do as I wish and please. For women, wisdom lies in not speaking. God help me, according to me, a mute could proclaim their wisdom. For women there is only one wise thing to do: to shut up.

Excerpted as such, this passage is appalling. In the context of this romance, though, it is paradoxical; for by having kept silent about her secret, Silence would appear to be the perfect woman, the incarnation of "sens de feme." Yet Silence is only "silent," because she is raised as a boy. It is thus ironically by being raised male that Silence behaves as the ideal woman. The gender binary does not make sense here.

According to Butler, drag "fully subverts the distinction between inner and outer psychic space and effectively mocks both the expressive model of gender and the notion of a true gender identity" (*Gender Trouble* 186). Capping this sequence that explores the possibility of recovering "a true gender identity," Heldris's epilogue also subverts—even mocks—this distinction between inside and outside:

> Maistre Heldris dist chi endroit
> C'on doit plus bone feme amer
> Que haïr malvaise u blasmer.
> Si mosterroie bien raison:
> Car feme a menor oquoison,
> Por que ele ait le liu ne l'aise,
> De l'estre bone que malvaise,
> S'ele ouevre bien contre nature,
> Bien mosterroie par droiture

C'on en doit faire gregnor plait
Que de celi qui le mal fait. (6684–94)

Master Heldris says here and now that we should love the good woman more than we hate or blame the bad one. I will explain my logic: a woman has less reason, provided she has the time and opportunity, to be good than bad; if she acts well, (she goes/it is) against nature. I can rightly show that we should make a bigger fuss about her than a woman who does evil.

Another misogynistic outburst. Heldris claims that women are naturally evil, and by being a virtuous woman, Silence is combatting her feminine nature. Yet, this is also deeply ironic; for Silence, who was a man in name or shell only, concludes the romance as woman in name or shell only, as she is *still* acting against her female nature. The *décalage* between interior and exterior is not resolved but inverted. This is not a romance that straightens things out; and its queerness is, to an important extent, performed by narrative poetics that are so persistently "making trouble," using metalepsis to extend the confusion between insides and outsides thematized at the level of the plot.

LA PRISON AMOUREUSE

I began analysis of *Silence* by claiming that its plotline seems more provocative than *Partonopeu*'s, while its narrative poetics appear more conservative. Late medieval *dits* generally tug, though, in the opposite direction, as they self-consciously call attention to poetic innovations, while the love stories, which they never totally forego, can feel like they lose steam. If *dits* often effect a sort of metaleptic inversion whereby the "without" of the *narration* is brought "within," one often gets the impression, that is, that the love story nominally "within" is being ushered "without."

In Jean Froissart's 1372–73 *Prison amoureuse*, for example, "the plotline is very thin" (Thiry 15). The *je*, who adopts the pseudonym Flos, loves a lady who is unconvinced by him. "Pour moi esbaniier / Et ma dolour oubliier" [to enjoy myself and forget my pain] (3603–4), he becomes immersed in correspondence with a man who goes by Rose. Rose writes to Flos seeking advice in affairs of the heart. Flos encourages him in his endeavors, which prove more successful, as Rose is able to overcome his initial trepidations.

Because we learn little more about either love affair, Froissart would seem to be "barely bothering ... to maintain the fiction of a love story" (Lechat 293). Rather, the *dit* appears more interested in the relationship between Rose and Flos. This relationship has a historical dimension, since Rose's lengthy *songe* (2252–3420) alludes to the 1371–72 Battle of Baesweiler and the ensuing imprisonment of Froissart's patron Wencelas of Brabant.[17] Yet, it is principally a literary one in this *dit*, where, by all accounts, "the art of writing . . . itself" steals the show (Cerquiglini-Toulet, "Fullness" 225). Certainly, this collection of "lettres, epitles, escriptions [writings], traitiés amoureus [love treatises], balades, virelais, complaintes et toutes manieres de devises" [and all kinds of pieces] (XII.170–71) advertises its poetic virtuosity. It also flaunts its intertextuality. Most notably, a pseudo-Ovidian myth (Flos's *dit* [1316–2002]) and an allegorical dream-vision in the tradition of the *Rose* (Rose's *songe*) serve as its centerpieces (cf. Huot, *From Song* 312). The *Prison* might also be described as the "mixtion" [mixture] (1694) of various Machaldian *dits*, although Froissart does not fess up to his debt to the Master. From the *Voir Dit*, the *Prison* borrows the formal "mixtion" of lyrics, narrative verse, and prose letters, as well as the desire playfully to dramatize the process of creating the book we are reading.[18] The *Prison*'s interest in patronage relations and allusions to an actual patron's incarceration recall the *Fonteinne amoureuse* (Lechat 276–77), while the almost silly narrator is a staple of Machaut's *dits* more generally.

Because the *dit* is so patently interested in poetics, it is understandable that critics tend to view its engagement with *fin'amor* as secondary, even minimal. The *dit* begins, for example, with God's command to Moses: "De tout ton coer, de t'ame toute, / Ton signeur aimme et se le doubte" [with all your heart and all your soul, love and fear your lord] (11–12). Flos immediately glosses God's words in amorous terms: "L'amour pour le service glose" (14). Yet, scholarship has found this gloss no more convincing than Flos's later ones, which we shall examine in detail; rather than understanding "service" as standing for love, the *dit*'s seemingly meager and superficial amorous rhetoric is always glossed in terms of literary "service." I wish, however, to argue that the *Prison* represents a radical engagement with desire, not despite but because its treatment of love appears so unconvincing.

At one level, it is even fairly easy to indulge the queerness of the *Prison*, as an important element of it lies near the surface. The basic metaleptic inversion operated by the text—whereby the homosocial relations at the level of the *narration* take center stage while the heterosexual love stories that traditionally drive the diegesis fade into the background—allows the specter of "homosocial desire," and even of sexual deviancy, to rise to the fore. The

---

17. This was first uncovered by Auguste Scheler and Kervyn de Lettenhove. It was elaborated by Fourrier in his edition of Froissart's text ("Introduction" 20–28) and Thiry. See also Busby 91.

18. See e.g., de Looze, "From Text" 88–90; Lechat 273–74; Findley 13.

Prison acknowledges early on this possibility of a deviant lack of interest in women. Protesting the sincerity of his love, Flos writes,

> Car je seroie trop honteus
> S'on me comptoit avoec les deus
> Qui onques d'amer ne dagnierent
> Ne nulles dames n'adagnierent:
> Narcissus et Bellorophus. (159–63)

> For I would be too ashamed to be considered alongside these two who never were willing to love and who didn't cherish any women: Narcissus and Bellorophus.

Some twenty lines are then devoted to the transgressions of these mythological figures, with the latter being an invention of Froissart's, who refuses the advances of various women (Fourrier, "Introduction" 17–18 in Froissart, *Prison*). Yet Flos, who is perpetually lacking in self-awareness, seems to have the same issue, which suggests that his deviancy may also be at stake here.

Not long after this, Flos's lady calls him out, singing in a *virelay* that he wears melancholy so well that he must be relishing it (429–60). I am, similarly, suggesting that we are invited to call out Flos's (and the text's) lack of interest in loving women, while wondering what else is being relished. On closer inspection, certain lyrics that purport to be for women do, for instance, appear to be more concerned with men. In the *complainte de moralité* (3010–153) in Rose's *songe*, for example, the *je* calls for an eagle to liberate him, because "Tout roi doient l'un l'autre aidier" [all kings must aid each other] (3122). The lady, to whom the *complainte* is ostensibly sent, is not mentioned. And while a male interlocutor displaces any female *tu* in this *complainte*, Flos's *lai* (2142–93; 3515–674) illustrates this process unfolding. In this intricate piece, the *je* expresses little desire for his amorous sufferings to end. Rather, in nearly every stanza, he describes how, "s'un compagnon veïsse / A cui mon estat deïsse, / Moult me peuïst conforter" [if I encountered a companion to whom I could reveal my plight, he could greatly comfort me] (3544–46). Because the *Prison* is so focused on "homosocial desire," we might even wonder if some of the lyrics that do nominally invoke women are not actually about men. The repeated, and clichéd, protestations of total devotion—one *virelay*, for example, reads, "Quanque j'ai, sans remanant, / Jusques a l'ame, / Vous present, ma chiere dame" [whatever I possess, without holding anything back, down to my soul, I offer to you, my dear Lady] (935–37)—do seem, in the context of the *dit*, to pertain more to the mutual affection of the *compains* than to either love affair. It is also noteworthy how Flos composes particularly melancholic pieces when he is intensely fretting over Rose's silence (2021–204).

Yet, similar to how the inversion of the male gaze in *Partonopeu* is but the tip-of-the-iceberg for the romance's more rigorous deconstruction of charged binary oppositions, so too is this potentially deviant interest in homosocial literary relations but the first step in the *Prison*'s more complex interrogation of how poetics and desire intersect. It would, in other words, be as crude to argue that the *dit* simply transfers erotic desire from the lady to Rose (or from the *histoire* to the *narration*) as it would be to argue that the text is just uninterested in desire. Rather, the *Prison* is up to something messier—and more metaleptic, according to this chapter's conception of the term—as it casts sexual desire for a woman as an "outside," which the text nonetheless confusingly "maintains . . . within itself," to return to the terms of Butler's thinking.[19] This is particularly dazzling in Rose's *songe*, which has long been read as about Wencelas of Brabant's captivity at the hands of the Duke of Jülich between August 1371 and July 1372—and thus as the part of the text where the amorous rhetoric most transparently stands for something else. In this dream-vision, the *je* defends the righteous cause of Justice, Pité, and Raison by leading an army against Orgeuil [Pride]. Two things then go terribly wrong. First, Avis [Sensibility] requests that her mother Atemprance [Moderation] be included in the protagonist's army, but Desir and Hardement [Boldness] refuse, because she is a woman: "Tout y ariens honte et diffame, / Se par le consel d'une fame / Nous couvenoit user" [We would be quite ashamed and dishonored were we to need to proceed by heeding a woman's advice] (2494–96). Atemprance then goes on to lead Orgeuil's army, which nonetheless only emerges victorious because Desir, supposed to form the *je*'s rear-guard, is nowhere to be found at the crucial moment: "Ou est Desirs, di je, au besoing?" [Where is Desire, I say, when we need him] (2784). As mentioned, critics have mapped different aspects of this vision onto elements of the Battle of Baesweiler as described in the *Chroniques*: Orgeuil is probably William VI, Duke of Jülich; Desir may be Robert of Namur; Hardiment, Guy I of Luxembourg; and so forth (esp. Thiry 24). Yet, the vision can also be understood as illustrating the dangers of excluding women and of Desire's absence (cf. Nouvet, "Pour une économie" 347; Findley 10–11). If, that is, it unquestionably alludes to Wenceslas's plight, thus pushing us to look through the amorous rhetoric, the dream-vision also points to the danger of overlooking this rhetoric, as without the woman and desire, things turn to chaos. In a disorienting way, amorous issues are both superficial, unessential elements of this *songe* and (part of) the hidden meaning.

---

19. *Gender Trouble* 44. Cf. Nouvet, "Pour une économie" esp. 343–45; Findley.

Such features as the protagonists' flowery pseudonyms, ostensibly chosen to honor their ladies (691–96, 856–94), further suggest that the *dit* both effaces (desire for) women and, insofar as the men bear female pseudonyms to which much reflection is devoted, incorporates their effacement. Indeed, as Butler theorizes that gender identity may be the result of failing to grieve foreclosed desires, so too are identification and desire suggestively collapsed in these pseudonyms, where the men nominally become the women that the text will not show them loving. Yet, if the *dit* is not so much uninterested in women and desire as it is including their effacement, this makes for a fine line for the critic to walk, because it is difficult to understand the exclusion of love and women as consistently both reflecting and inviting critical reflection on gender and sexual politics. Consider, in this respect, Flos's myth of Pynoteüs, as well as the readings it has spawned. Pynoteüs and Neptisphelé are two young lovers modeled on Pyramus and Thisbé. Like in Ovid's myth, a lion devours Neptisphelé. Vengeful and grief-stricken, Pynoteüs will eventually set about reconstructing his *amie,* following in Pygmalion's footsteps by forging a statue into which Apollo breathes life—and which even passes for the true Neptisphelé. In this inserted *dit,* then, the "'real' woman" is replaced by a "crafted object" (de Looze, "From Text" 101). And for many critics, this corresponds to how the larger *dit* functions. Indeed, scholars often stress how the God of Poetry, Apollo, occupies in Pynoteüs's myth the role Venus plays in the myth of Pygmalion; the myth, and in turn the larger *dit,* are then read as "striking illustration[s] of poetic power."[20] Issues of gender and sexuality are thus sidelined.

Yet, Flos seems to resist such a reading in his elaborate gloss of this myth. In Letter IX, he notably contends that the young couple formed by Pynoteüs and Neptisphelé represents the "desir et plaisance qui sont encorporet en" Rose [desire and pleasure that are embodied in (Rose)] (IX.154). The lion who takes Neptisphelé from Pynoteüs represents, for Flos, Envie. The God of the Sun, who animates the sculpted but lifeless Neptisphelé, signifies the "dieu d'Amours," who resurrects Rose's amorous "joie" (IX.154–55). And with the help of this god, adds Flos, Rose need not fear anything, least of all "dreams, visions, or marvels," "car che ne sont que toutes coses vainnes et nulles" [as these are all but vain and irrelevant things] (IX.155).

By glossing Apollo as Love, this explanation reverses the substitution of Poetry for Love into which critics have read so much. Yet scholars have not placed much weight on this for a good reason: the gloss is extremely uncon-

---

20. Quote from Brownlee, "Ovide" 161, referring in particular to Pynoteüs's *orison*; see also Lechat 292. For Apollo in the myth, see e.g., Brownlee, "Ovide" 159–61; de Looze, "From Text" 101–2; Nouvet, "Pour une économie" 350–51; and Huot, *From Song* 314.

vincing. As Nouvet notes, it proceeds "by strict equivalences," by almost arbitrarily substituting one noun for another: say, Envy for the lion ("Pour une économie" 345–46). It can also feel uncomfortably acrobatic, namely when the couple formed by the two lovers comes to represent two emotions—Desire and Pleasure—that are both "embodied" in one lover, Rose. What's more, when it denies that "songes," "visions" or "mervelles" convey truth, the gloss seems to disqualify itself, as its raison d'être is to uncover the truth contained in Flos's marvelous *matière*. Despite Flos's best efforts, it also never becomes clear that the myth has much to do with Rose's amorous struggles. As Lechat puts it, "The story told doesn't seem . . . to contain as many analogies to [Rose's] predicament as one might expect" (284).

Yet, if Flos's reading has failed to convince critics, it is precisely because this gloss is unconvincing that it can be understood as powerfully intersecting with queer theory. According to Butler, "only when the mechanism of gender construction implies the *contingency* of that construction does 'constructedness' *per se* prove useful to the political project to enlarge the scope of possible gender configurations" (*Gender Trouble* 51; original emphases). This gloss about desire feels patently "constructed," and critical consensus according to which it is deeply unconvincing suggests that it "implies" the "contingency" of positing Rose's amorous predicament as the meaning behind Flos's myth. In a quite Butlerian vein, the effect of this gloss is, then, to expose how sexual feelings, though pitted as cause, are rather an effect of discourse, which is only afterward—and arbitrarily—cast as its cause.

I am therefore suggesting something paradoxical: that this extremely metaliterary *dit*'s seemingly contingent relationship with desire betokens an important engagement with desire's contingency. But what's to say that this is true—and that my gloss is not as wobbly as poor Flos's? To some extent, to make this analogy is both to authorize and to caution against my reading. As critics have long argued, the *Prison* is about generating interpretations; in it, literature emerges as "a *productive* dialogue with its audience" (McGrady, *Controlling Readers* 186; original emphasis). If the text "depicts literary interpretation as theoretically an endless cycle that continues the production of the narrative fiction" (de Looze, "From Text" 104), it would invite different readings, ranging from the more valid to the aberrant. Yet, rather than understanding a queer reading as authorized by the *Prison* in this manner, I would suggest that this allowance for different *and* aberrant readings partakes of the *dit*'s queerness. We have, that is, seen how Butler understands "proliferation" to the point of "confusion" as an important tactic for effecting subversion. The *Prison* seems to be up to something similar, as tenuous readings proliferate within—and perhaps beyond—the text. There is also, within the *dit*, a "superabundance of *coffrets,* folios, envelopes, sacks, and tomes into which letters, poems, and manuscripts are put," which equally generates a sense of confusion (de Looze, "From Text" 92). Indeed, not only will Flos have "grant painne" [great trouble] (3774) collecting these disparate elements together into a *livre* but these containers even multiply to such an extent that, as Fabienne Pomel observes, "the reader comes to confuse them" (123). Instead of protecting against dispersion and assuring cohesion, these containers create confusion and threaten cohesion by proliferating. And if the intradiegetic glosses and containers are like Butler's tactics for queer subversion insofar as they mobilize proliferation to foster confusion, it follows that a queer reading of the *Prison* may contain other readings, although it paradoxically only does so insofar as it insists on how the *dit* uses proliferation to resist the possibility of containing meaning.

As this is a complex—even convoluted—argument, it makes sense to look at another zany gloss in order to think more about the *Prison*'s engagement with proliferation, confusion, and containment, as well as its relation to Butlerian theory. In Flos's reading of Rose's *songe,* also included in Letter IX, he first suggests that the bed and room in which the *je* is initially approached by Justice, Pité, and Raison—who symbolize virtues in his lady—represent "la douce pensee, gaie et amoureuse, qui est dedens vous encorporee" [the sweet thoughts, gay and amorous, that are embodied in you] (IX.151). The allegories who then appear represent the "consel" (IX.151) no lover can do without. Avis's defection represents Rose's being dumbstruck in the presence of his lady. Then comes the battle:

> Par la quele guerre et bataille j'entens la vie amoureuse de vous et de vostre dame, les priieres, les responses, les refus et les escondis; et la desconfiture de vous et des vostres j'entens par la biauté et la douce phizonomie de son regart, qui vous prent et lace toutes fois et toutes heures que vous le veés. (IX.152)

> By which war and battle I understand the love of you and your lady: the requests, responses, refusals, and excuses. And by the defeat of you and your army I understand the beauty and the sweet physiognomy of her gaze, which takes hold of you and ensnares you each time and always when you see it.

Flos is not done. When the vanquished *je* is imprisoned, this symbolizes his amorous "langeur" (IX.152). Atemprance, Avis, and other (now) benign personifications keep him company while he awaits an eagle who will liberate him. The eagle signifies "francise" [nobility], who brings with him "humilité, pité, misericorde et debonnaireté" [humility, pity, mercy, and goodness] (IX.153). The lover is then just so "ravis en parfaite joie" [overcome with perfect joy] (IX.153) that he wakes up.

Like the preceding one, this gloss fosters a sense of *desconfiture,* which perhaps echoes the chaos resulting from the battle within the *songe.* Yet, this does not mean that the gloss is meaningless or inconsequential; rather, the confusion may be quite meaningful. As Butler explores "possibilities of doing gender [that] repeat and displace through hyperbole, dissonance, internal confusion, and proliferation the very constructs by which they are mobilized," so too is Flos's gloss "mobilized" by the terms of Rose's vision, which it then confusingly repeats and displaces (*Gender Trouble* 43). In fact, the gloss represents a series of displacements, as the circumstances of the Battle of Baesweiler seem translated into the dream-vision, which is then translated or recast in terms of Rose's amorous relations with his lady (cf. Nouvet, "Pour une économie," esp. 352–55). This series of displacements creates a sense of "dissonance," since the historical event comes awkwardly to rub shoulders with the amorous rhetoric. This has, too, the more specific effect of troubling the relationship between desire and the referent, because the dream-vision would seem to refer to the Battle rather than Love; Desire is again cast as cause, when it seems to be an effect only contingently related to the tale. Flos's gloss implicates "confusion" in other ways, too. As Nouvet observes,

> This gloss is founded on a strange inversion of the relation between container and contained, since it interprets Rose's presence in the room as the inclusion of amorous thoughts within him. The room (container) becomes the thoughts (contained) such that Rose contained by the room is transformed into a space containing thoughts. (346–47)

Flos's gloss is, then, confusing the inside/outside binary, and I call attention to Nouvet's gloss of it for two reasons. One, because this is a sort of *mise en abyme* for the larger *Prison,* which operates a "strange inversion" of the "container" (the *narration*) and the traditionally "contained" love story, which proves equally disorienting. Two, because it intriguingly intersects with the Butlerian gesture of suggesting that the *container qua* body generates the illusion of the *contained* interiority, which is similar in form to how Rose's containment in the vision becomes, in the gloss, the containment of love within him. For Butler and Flos, the inside is always-already the outside, and vice versa—and this is queer metalepsis at play.

It is not, moreover, only through these glosses that the *Prison* engages with what Butler calls "discursive resignification" ("Critically Queer" 21). For example, Rose repeatedly claims that his *songe* must have been inspired by Flos's tale of Pynoteüs: "Je n'en sçai qui encouper fors vostre livret de Pynoteüs et de Neptisphelé" [I don't know whom to blame except your little book about Pynoteüs and Neptisphelé] (VII.113; also VIII.149, IX.153). Fourrier once took Rose at his word, arguing that there is a "strict parallelism" between the two inserted pieces, since both "result in analysis of amorous behavior through examination of its cogs" and both contain further inserted pieces: in Flos's case the *orison de Pynoteüs*, in Rose's the *complainte de moralité* ("Introduction" in Froissart, *Prison* 20). More recent critics (e.g., de Medeiros 171) have accepted both Rose's statement and Fourrier's argument without developing either. Rose's vision functions, however, by twisting crucial terms from Flos's tale in quite ambiguous ways. For example, in Flos's *dit*, the lion devours Neptisphelé and is then dragged by Pynoteüs before an animal court, where he is devoured by the attendees; the devourer becomes the devoured within this myth. Rose's vision extends this dynamic of inversion, as the *je* declares himself, in the *complainte*, to be like an imprisoned lion who must rally the animal court over which he presides: "Oés, bestes, qui sui vos rois" [Listen, beasts, to me your King] (3042). The antagonist in Flos's myth has become the protagonist of Rose's dream-vision. In Rose's dream, this lion then calls for the eagle to liberate him, by "Jettans feu et flamme a tous les" [spewing fire and flames on all sides] (3359). Yet, in Pynoteüs's *orison*, when fire falls from the sky, it does not liberate but instead reflects the needless destruction caused by Phaeton's stubborn desire to drive Phebus's chariot. The problem in one instance has become the solution in the next.

The causal relationship between these pieces is not, therefore, as direct as Rose or Fourrier implies; rather, it takes the form of a more confusing interpenetration of narrative segments, what I have been calling metalepsis. This sense of disruptive crisscrossing can also more forcefully implicate gender and sexuality, such as when, early in the *dit*, Flos stumbles upon his lady and other *demoiselles* frolicking about. These ladies notice that Flos wears a "loiiere" [pouch] (1084) around his waist, and they make off with its contents: two letters from Rose, which contain a *balade* and a *virelay*. Flos struggles to regain possession of his beloved letters, which the women coquettishly hide in their clothes. An "estour" [battle] (1127) ensues, albeit "Sans mautalent et sans irour" [without ill-will or anger] (1128).

> La fui je boutés et saciés
> Et detirés et embraciés
> Par jambes, par corps et par bras,
> Sans noient espargnier mes draps. (1133–36)

There I was shoved, pulled at, grabbed and hugged—by my legs, body, and arms—without my clothing being spared at all.

The dueling parties finally come to an agreement. Flos's lady can cut the parchment with her ring, with Flos retaining the letters, the ladies taking the lyrics in order to copy them.

Critical responses to this "romp" (Findley 9) have proliferated. While Cerquiglini-Toulet ("Fullness" 236–37) stresses the materiality of the pouch and poetry's status as prized commodity, de Looze reads the scene as showcasing Flos's symbolic "castration" ("From Text" 93). For McGrady, it is about how, like Flos's spilling his "literary seed" (*Controlling Readers* 182), the *Prison* generates interpretations, while Pomel sees it as speaking to the uncomfortable proximity between raptus and literature in the *dit* (129–30). Brooke Heindrich Findley suggests that these women possess "creative powers" but may resemble the maenads who dismember Orpheus (1, 9–10). For my part, I see this scene as operating a series of curious inversions, where there is nonetheless a common denominator: erotic and meta-poetic issues are confusingly imbricated, an elusive metalepsis at play. For instance, whereas it would typically be others—especially *losengiers*—who wish to get their eyes on the lover's secrets, here it is the beloved herself who desires for them to be revealed. And while in other texts lovers can grasp their love letters to their breasts, here the women slide the letters in their bosoms in order to keep them away from the "lover" who grasps at them. It is also striking that the Lady uses the ring, symbol of amorous union, to sever lyrics from letters, thus bringing the lyrics into circulation without the particular contexts the letters provide—and where she should figure so prominently.

The various echoes linking this scene to others in the *Prison* reinforce the sense that this episode is about generating confusion between putatively heterogenous elements. This amorous "battle" announces, for instance, Rose's dream, although it is not otherwise clear what the two have in common—or why the text should wish to bring together these very different amorous struggles. When the ladies copy these lyrics, this foreshadows, moreover, how Rose's lady will insist on copying Rose and Flos's correspondence, which in turn prompts Flos's organizing of the *Prison* into a "livre" (XI). Yet it is also not clear what is similar—or being copied—among these two different instances of copying. Furthermore, when Flos's body and clothes are being pulled in all directions, and the letter cut, this seems to announce the hackneyed disorder of the *Prison* itself. As mentioned, Flos will struggle considerably to bring together disparate, often torn, materials: he declares, "Or en y a de pluiseurs tires, / Et de rompues et d'entires, / Dont c'est grant painne au rajouster" [There are many sorts (of writings), both torn and whole, which it is very difficult to reassemble] (3772–74). Yet, if Flos's body—and not the lady's, as is typically the case in lyrics—is *like* the larger *dit*, what does this portend? I confess that I find it difficult to bring together these different instances of tearing apart and reassembling.

One term seems best to describe the *Prison*'s poetics, both in this scene and elsewhere: "recreation." Recurring four times in the *dit* (254, II.62, VI.105, VII.112), this term directly refers to the pleasure afforded by distraction; it is where the frustrated Flos finds solace, primarily but not solely in his literary exchanges with Rose. Yet, "recreation" also has another implication in the *Prison,* since this is a *dit* about re-creations: whether that of Neptisphelé in Pynoteüs's myth (cf. Findley 14) or of the various disparate pieces and glosses brought together to make up the *Prison.* "Recreation" may, too, faintly recall "recreans," which in the *dit* (151, 2042) refers to baseness—and slightly smacks of deviance. And in the *Prison,* these different senses of recreation—(potentially deviant) pleasure and literary creation—are relentlessly intersecting, although (and indeed appropriately) in ever-indeterminate, even aberrant ways.

The *Prison* concludes with Flos's gloss of the myth of Phaeton, which capitalizes on this engagement with indeterminacy and aberrancy, both poetic and sexual. As mentioned, Flos had earlier inserted this story, which would be familiar to readers of the *Ovide moralisé,* into his pseudo-Ovidian myth, where Pynoteüs uses it to flatter Apollo. In Rose's final letter, he claims that his lady, who has now read through the correspondence between the companions, thinks this episode was unfairly neglected (as if she weren't more unjustly neglected by the text). Embarrassed by his forgetfulness—apparently, "a che jour j'avoie grant dolour ou chief" [on that day I had a bad headache] (XII.172)—Flos now happily glosses the episode. Like his earlier ones, his final reading teeters on incoherence. This time, Phaeton symbolizes Desir, the son of Ymagination (his mother) and Amour (his father). "Le kar dou Solel" [Apollo's chariot] that he insists on driving represents "la vie amoureuse" (XII.173). Desire/Phaeton is saddled on a horse that signifies Fole Emprise [Imprudent Undertaking]. The other horses are Jonece [Youth], Lie Pensee [Happy Thoughts], and Wiseuse [Futility], while the chariot represents Fole Plaisance [Imprudent Pleasure]. Phaeton attempts to steer the chariot with the whip of Atemprance, the bridles of Congnissance [Knowledge], and the words of Avis, but he can't keep it on the "chemin de Raison" [the path of Reason] (XII.173). "Ensi que li amans s'outrequide" [as the lover becomes overconfident] (XII.174) and loses all sense of moderation, and as rumors spread about the love affair, things spiral out of control. Fire—seemingly signifying excess passion, the indiscretion of the lover, and/or the destructiveness of the behavior of slanderers—is unleashed, until Pité and Francise [Nobility] set things straight.

This *glose* adds up no more than the others do. Yet, it no doubt gets pride of place in this *dit* for a reason: it functions performatively. Not only is the aberrancy of Apollo's chariot at stake but also that of this gloss, which similarly "pert la voie de Raison" [wanders from the path of Reason] (XII.174). Flos seems no more up to the task of steering the meaning of the tale than Phaeton his chariot; of both Pyntoeüs's struggle to control the horses and Flos's to master the threads of his text, we might say, "il ne les puet mestriier" [he can't control them] (XII.136). The irony, then, is that Flos's gloss works because it doesn't work; it treats aberrancy aberrantly. At another level, the "larger" irony is that, in so doing, he provides a sort of *mise en abyme* of the text that he narrates, as the *Prison* never seems able to keep its chariot on any remotely *droite voie*. And there is, too, the larger and perhaps more consequential irony, whereby the gloss signals how the chariot representing "la vie amoureuse" in courtly letters seems unsteady, prone to perpetual—and dangerous—deviance. In other words, not only is the instability of Pynoteüs's chariot at stake in this shifty *dit* but also that of Flos's gloss, the *Prison amoureuse*, and *fin'amor*, or desire as expressed in late medieval courtly letters.

While *Partonopeu*, *Silence*, and the *Prison amoureuse* are all quite different texts, I have argued that narrative poetics function, in a manner, to similar effect in each; they serve less to "bring out the intelligibility . . . of the text"— as *mise en abyme*, Dällenbach argues (16), should—than to foster a provocative sense of unintelligibility. Indeed, metalepsis has the effect of calling into question the legibility, and even the legitimacy, of narratives—and, because these are stories about desire, of their representations of gender and sexuality. The metaleptic crisscrossing of narrative levels and segments is a "site" for the "intervention, exposure, and displacement" of "reifications" (*Gender Trouble* 42).

This implies that, almost paradoxically, narrative poetics in these verse romances and *dits* are effectively antinarrative, as they disrupt the coherence of the ostensibly mimetic *histoires* that are relayed and of the texts that relay them. As we have seen, they also disrupt ways in which gender and sexual identity purport to fixity, determinacy, progress, and resolution. They trouble aspects of the narratives—and even of the narrativity—on which normative gender and sexual politics (whether medieval or modern) rely.

The next chapter considers this antinarrative impulse in verse narratives in terms of their relationship to lyric poetry. It emphasizes, too, how the insertion of lyrics into verse narratives inflects representations of gender and sexuality. Yet, before moving on from metalepsis, I wish to stress the figure's pertinence to theorizing the relationship between, on the one hand, verse romances and *dits,* and on the other hand, courtly verse narratives and queer theory. This chapter has defined metalepsis as the illogical points of convergence between ostensibly discrete narrative levels or segments: a messy, disruptive crisscrossing. Similarly, verse romances and *dits* might be understood as putatively (although imperfectly) distinct generic planes; yet their juxtaposition or crisscrossing is productive or—more accurately—disruptive in the mode of metalepsis, shaking up entrenched critical narratives about these genres and texts associated with them (such as the notion that late medieval *dits* have a distinctly secondary interest in gender and sexual politics). By the same token, we might attend to metaleptic intersections between the courtly and the queer, where the point would be that, like metalepsis, these repetitions make trouble and shake up assumptions of ours. Not only, that is, does the medieval "touch" the postmodern, as Dinshaw famously argues, but we also stand to be "de-invented" (Edmondson 144) by our interactions with it. Indeed, I have suggested that unexpected, elusive, and troublesome points of contact between narrative levels and segments *within* medieval French verse narratives reflect unexpected and underexplored points of contact *between* these medieval verse narratives and modern queer theory. In this respect, I see this chapter (and book) as working with the brilliant work that has explored, beyond the constraints of a more traditional historicism, new ways for pre- and postmodern sexualities to intersect—such as Dinshaw's *Getting Medieval* or Freccero's *Queer/Early/Modern.* And it is in the spirit of these works to imply that the relationship between premodern culture and postmodern queer theory is *queerer*—according to a certain conception of the term as endlessly disruptive—than any queer theory focused quasi-exclusively on the (post) modern could be. For it is this illogical and seemingly improper metaleptic crisscrossing between pre- and postmodern that stands to be most disruptive of (often un- or underexamined) narratives about what the modern and postmodern are.

CHAPTER 3

~

On Sameness, Difference, and Textualizing Desire
Queering Lyric Insertion

In Jean Renart's *Roman de la Rose ou de Guillaume de Dole* (c. 1208–10), a *jongleur* tells Conrad—Germany's emperor and most eligible bachelor—about the beautiful Lïenors and her magnificent brother Guillaume. Conrad instantly falls in love with Lïenors, so he invites Guillaume to court, where he makes a great impression. Conrad is even so taken by the brother that he decides to marry the sister. Yet, his jealous Seneschal is determined to stir up trouble. He learns from Lïenors and Guillaume's mother that she has a rose-shaped birthmark on her upper thigh, and he uses this inside knowledge to allege that he has taken Lïenors's virginity. Upon hearing this, Conrad and Guillaume are despondent. It falls to Lïenors to take initiative. She journeys to court, where she accuses the Seneschal of having raped her. In defending himself against these baseless allegations, the Seneschal unwittingly concedes that he has never met Lïenors. Having reestablished her virginity, Lïenors can now become Conrad's wife.

This romance has, then, a reasonably enticing plot. Yet, in its oft-commented-upon prologue, Renart almost completely ignores it, as he "promotes his poetic method and medium rather than the story to follow" (Butterfield, *Poetry* 19). He boasts, for instance, that

> aussi com l'en met la graine
> es dras por avoir los et pris,

> einsi a il chans et sons mis
> en cestui *Romans de la Rose*,
> qui est une novele chose
> et s'est des autres si divers
> et brodez, par lieus, de biaus vers
> que vilains nel porroit savoir.
> Ce sachiez de fi et de voir,
> bien a cist les autres passez. (8–17)

> just as one puts red dye on cloth so that it may merit praise and esteem, so too has he put songs and music in this *Romance of the Rose*, which is a new work. It is also so different from any other—and embroidered, in places, with beautiful lyrics—that no one uncourtly could grasp it. Know this by faith and in truth: this romance has far surpassed all others.

These lines are nonetheless crawling with metaleptic allusions like those we looked at in the previous chapter. The "red dye" ("graine") will, for example, reappear three times (512, 1816, 1827; see Jewers, "Fabric" 916). This notably draws our attention to the color red, which is the only detail we learn about Lïenors's rose (see Zink, *Roman rose* 62–63). The textile metaphor also announces the sequence where Lïenors and her mother embroider while singing *chansons de toile*.[1] The participle "brodez" [embroidered] recurs, however, only twice, each time to describe a piece of embroidery that Lïenors tricks the Seneschal into wearing, which is blotted red by his blood (4293, 4826). Other ostensibly literary claims also seem to bleed into the storyline. As this colorful romance "a . . . les autres passez" [has surpassed all others], so too does Lïenors; according to one admirer, "Aussi passe, ce m'est avis, / de beauté bele Lïenors / totes les autres" [thus the beautiful Lïenors surpasses, it seems to me, in beauty all other women] (1417–20). Like the romance, Lïenors may even be described as a "novele chose." For rather than seeing her, Conrad only interacts with her via "noveles" [reports] (e.g., 1759, 3708). The Seneschal's false allegations, which Conrad refers to as "la novele / de sa perte et de son domage" [the news of her loss and harm] (3606–7), then showcase the danger for her of depending on "noveles." Yet, in proving that she is a virgin, Lïenors makes herself "new again," which resonates, perhaps, with how this innovative romance will appear "nouviaus toz jors" [forever new] (23) to all.

On closer inspection, this prologue therefore both implies the priority of the romance's "hybrid form" over its "thematic content" (Ramm 402) and

---

1. See Boulton, *Song* 85–87; Zink, *Roman rose* 22–25; Solterer, "At the Bottom" 221–23.

deconstructs any such neat opposition. In fact, similar to how Renart brags that the songs will seem perfectly fitted to their new narrative context (26–29), so too is the prologue's larger strategy of only glancing to the ensuing storyline via the prism of literary issues nicely fitted to this story, where Conrad's interactions with Lïenors are so heavily mediated, both by others and by discourse itself. By not looking directly at the upcoming tale, the prologue is paradoxically looking right at the indirectness that characterizes Conrad and Lïenors's love.

In this chapter, I contend that the technique of lyric insertion, which Jean Renart boastfully inaugurates here, also functions deconstructively, both in this text and in later verse romances and *dits*. Bucking a critical tradition that has often understood the insertion of lyric pieces into narratives in strikingly binary terms—opposing, for example, orality to literacy, code to message, or diachronic to synchronic temporality—I am interested in how lyric insertion troubles the "complex exchange of inside and outside, self and other," "'pre' and 'post,' or before and behind," and "front and back, proper and improper."[2] Focusing on the interpenetration of lyrics and surrounding narratives, I suggest that the narratives supplement, in the Derridean sense, the inset lyrics. The insertion of lyrics into narrative functions, that is, both "as a re-appropriation of the presence" of the lyrics and as "un réquisitoire contre la négativité de la lettre" [an indictment of the negativity of writing"] (Derrida, *Grammatologie* 200–201). For both literally and more subtly, lyric insertion "fits into the same cloth" (*tissu*—and note the metaphor) lyrics and narrative in a gesture that proves "dangerous," since it troubles the terms, claims, and modalities of courtly lyrics (*Grammatologie* 208).

In *de la Grammatologie,* moreover, Derrida foregrounds the relationship between the supplement and sexuality, by holding up Rousseau's autoeroticism as prime example of "ce dangereux supplément." Onanism is not without relation to troubadour and trouvère lyrics, which both invoke and replace the Lady. Lyric insertion might, in turn, be understood as exaggerating the lyrics' affinities with masturbation, by emphasizing the mediation of love experiences by signs (or songs) and the self-reflexivity of literature. And as Derrida shows how Rousseau's onanism exposes the absences that always menace notions of presence, I shall explore how lyric insertion can subject the construct of *fin'amor* to a deep "hermeneutics of suspicion" (Edelman, *Homographesis* 7).

---

2. Cf. Cerquiglini-Toulet's opposition of *collage* to *montage* (*Engin* 23–32); Huot's contrast between song and book, performance and artifact, and orality and literacy in *From Song*; or Taylor's distinction, picked up by Boulton in *Song* (18–20), between code and message. The oppositions are quoted from Edelman, *Homographesis* 65, 191, 131. See below for explanation of recourse to Edelman here.

In considering the queerness of lyric insertion, my reflections are in dialogue with Edelman's essays in *Homographesis,* which stand out for their concern with the interplay between rhetoric, deconstruction, and sexuality. In this volume, Edelman explores how the "spectacle of sodomy" effects a "disorientation of positionality" for normative sexual identity and even meaning more generally (185, 183). Perhaps more modestly, I suggest that the insertion of lyrics into narratives can effect a "disorientation of positionality" in relation to the lyrics and the love they always champion. Somewhat more precisely, Edelman argues,

> The historical positing of the category of "the homosexual" textualizes male identity as such, subjecting it to the alienating requirement that it be "read," and threatening, in consequence, to strip "masculinity" of its privileged status as the self-authenticating paradigm of the natural or the self-evident itself. (*Homographesis* 12)

Being careful with the "category of 'the homosexual'" (as Edelman is), I will argue that the insertion of lyrics into narratives fosters a "invitation" to "read" courtly desire in an "alienating" way, troubling the lyrics' "privileged status" as the "paradigm" of "courtly love" and denaturalizing the desire they express. Romances and *dits* employing lyric insertion often have the effect of getting at "the constitutive incoherence that marks" the courtly lover (*Homographesis* 66).

It is, of course, not a straight path from lyric insertion to queer sexuality, but this is also the point. This chapter explores how the two rub up against each other in their mutual emphasis on indeterminacy. Renart's romance is an obvious place to begin. It is credited with having inaugurated the practice of inserting lyrics into narratives, and it has also proven receptive to queer readings. I am interested in how these seemingly unrelated elements intersect. I then turn to two roughly contemporaneous texts from around the turn of the fourteenth century—Jakemés's *Roman du Châtelain de Coucy et de la Dame de Fayel* and Nicole de Margival's *Dit de la Panthère*—for two reasons. One, because each text's obsession with one trouvère lends itself to queer readings, as these verse narratives uncomfortably juxtapose the *fin'amor* sung in the lyrics with the love expressed *au second degré* for the trouvère's lyrics. Two, because both have been tagged as "transitional" in a narrative of lyric insertion that moves from Renart through to Machaut.[3] They are thus well positioned

---

3. Boulton, *Song* 187, referring to the *Panthère*.

to challenge both the binaries that critics have used to frame this phenomenon and narratives of its evolution, such as one which moves from emphasis on "orality" in thirteenth-century romance to "literacy" in fourteenth-century *dits*. I explore, therefore, how lyric insertion can trouble the "straightness" of language, (verse) narratives, and desire within texts—as well as that of the critical narratives into which this literary phenomenon has been fitted.

LE ROMAN DE LA ROSE OU DE GUILLAUME DE DOLE

In Renart's *Rose,* the second song that Conrad sings is the first stanza from a famous *chanson* by the Châtelain de Couci:

> Li noviaus tens et mais [et violete]
> et roissignox me semont de chanter;
> et mes fins cuers me fet d'une amorete
> un doz present que ge n'os refuser.
> Or m'en doint Dex en tel honor monter,
> cele ou j'ai mis mon cuer et mon penser
> q'entre mes bras la tenisse nuete
>   ainz q'alasse outremer. (923–30)

> The new season and May and violets
> and the nightingale inspire me to sing,
> and my true heart gives me a little love
> as a sweet present that I dare not refuse.
> May God now let me so rise in honor
> that she in whom I've placed my heart and thoughts
> I should hold naked in my arms
>   before I go abroad.

Zink once remarked that Renart's romance is "comprised entirely of substitutions and displacements" (*Roman rose* 58). Here, Conrad's act of signing represents both. It reflects an *amor de lonh* born during literal deviations. As Conrad returns to court after assisting the Count of Guerre, he and the *jongleur* Jouglet "issent fors del chemin amdui" [go off the path together] (650). Only then does Jouglet tell Conrad about this mind-blowing brother and sister duo, prompting this flight of song the next morning. Conrad's singing also evokes more figurative, and important, "substitutions and displacements."

Given that he has not laid eyes on Liënors and knows little about her, Conrad seems, as Maureen Boulton puts it, to be "in love with love" (*Song* 28), which he expresses by superposing himself onto the lyric *je*. Rather than genuinely inhering in Conrad, love appears, then, as an external, discursive element that he misinterprets as expressing his true self; or, as Edelman writes of James Baldwin's *Just Above My Head*, "'passion' . . . designates the vast . . . complex of social forces that implants desire *in* us so that we misrecognize it *as* us" (*Homographesis* 61; original emphases).

As critics have observed (e.g., Boulton, *Song* 4, 35; Huot, *From Song* 111), there is an ironic distance between Conrad and this *je*, notably because the emperor is not off to the Crusades. Moreover, the remainder of the original song—not included in the sole extant *Rose* manuscript—describes a love affair menaced by "fausse amie" [False Lover] (18), "fausse amours" [False Love] (27), and "li felon" [the evildoers] (36), whereas Conrad has no reason either to doubt Liënors's fidelity or to fear the meddling of others at this stage ("Li nouviauz tanz" in Châtelain de Coucy, pp. 76–78; cf. Huot, *From Song* 111–12). This gap between Conrad and the lyric *je* may reflect the misrecognition paradoxically constitutive of sexual identity. The romance's distance from the terms of the song nonetheless shouldn't be presumed, as it might be understood as extending the themes of displacement and dispossession at stake in the lyric. If, that is, the lyric *je* is sent *outremer* in the Châtelain's song, so too does the displacement of the song into this romance force it elsewhere, even challenging the proximity of the lyric *je* to its desired object, by distancing the *je* from itself and from its original contexts. The Châtelain's song is, in other words, about dispossession. He says, for instance, of his enraptured heart, "Tant con fui mienz, ne me fist se bien non, / Mes or sui suenz, si m'ocit sanz raison" [as long as I was my own, it did me nothing but good, but now that I am hers, it destroys me without reason] (21–22). In its new context, the poem goes from being *mienz*, or the property of the *je*-singer, to *suenz*, that of Conrad. Lyric insertion may, then, be effecting an act of dispossession akin to that which the lyric describes. This insertion therefore functions queerly in two ways: on the hand, because it points to the discursivity of desire and the troublesome ties between misrecognition and sexual identity; and on the other, because it deconstructs notions of proximity and possession by implying that displacing and dispossessing the lyric is potentially in keeping with its terms.

But is the narrative so subtly engaging with the lyrics? Perhaps counterintuitively, the little *rondets* scattered throughout the romance corroborate this hypothesis. Here, for example, is the second chain of *rondets,* sung as Conrad presides over courtly festivities:

C'est tot la gieus, enmi les prez,	It's way over there, in the middle of the fields,
Vos ne sentez mie les maus d'amer!	You don't feel the pangs of love!
Dames i vont por caroler,	Ladies go there to dance—
remirez voz braz!	Watch your arms!
Vos ne sentez mie les maus d'amer	You don't feel the pangs of love
si com ge faz! (514–19)	As I do.
C'est la jus desoz l'olive,	It's over there under the olive tree
Robins enmaine s'amie.	That Robin brings his lover.
La fontaine i sort serie	The water flows clear from the
desouz l'olivete.	Fountain under the olive tree.
E non Deu! Robins enmaine	In God's name! Robin brings
bele Mariete. (522–27)	The beautiful Mariette.
Main se levoit Aaliz,	Alice got up early,
J'ai non Enmelot.	My name is Amelot.
Biau se para et vesti	She attired herself and dressed up prettily
soz la roche Guion.	Under the Guyon rock.
Cui lairai ge mes amors,	To whom will I leave my love,
amie, s'a vos non? (532–37)	But to you, my love?
Main se leva la bien fete Aeliz,	The noble Alice gets up early,
par ci passe li bruns, li biaus Robins.	By here passes the brunette, the handsome Robin.
Biau se para et plus biau se vesti.	She attires herself prettily and dresses up even better.
Marchiez la foille et ge qieudrai la flor.	Tread on the leaves, I'll pluck the flower;
Par ci passe Robins li amorous,	By here the amorous Robin passes,
Encor en est li herbages plus douz. (542–47)	And the grass is all the softer.

These *rondets* are composed of several different elements. As Butterfield remarks in her groundbreaking study, there is "a pastoral scene 'la gieus' ('over there')" and another "describing Bele Aeliz" (*Poetry* 46). These descriptions alternate with the "refrain," "a brief first-person exclamation of love," which was likely sung by a chorus or other singers (45). If, then, there is a tension in the romance between Conrad's particular desire for Lïenors and a more general, impersonal "love of love"; and if lyric insertion appears to dramatize the tension between narrative elements, relayed in the third person and the past, and the lyric *je* speaking in the present or the future, it is surely worth noting that these tensions are both already manifest within these songs. The romance mirrors the *rondets*, then, not by being identical to them, but by extending the tension between inside and outside and particular and general that they embody (cf. *Homographesis* 112).

Similar tensions play themselves out among these *rondets*. The substitution of various singers performing the songs echoes, for instance, the exchange of names and fragments among them; to give one minor example, "Mains se levoit Aeliz," from the third *rondet*, becomes, "Mains se leva *la bien fete* Aeliz" in the fourth.[4] Rather than presenting as hermetically closed, the *rondets* therefore participate in an economy based on "substitutions and displacements." And I use this term economy deliberately, since the above-cited chain of songs comes amid our introduction to the feudal economy over which Conrad presides. As critics have remarked, this economy relies on persistent gifting and the circulation of obligations rather than on direct imposition (e.g., Zink, *Roman rose* 12–20; Dragonetti, *Mirage* 167–70). For Jewers, Renart is calling our attention to "the kind of monetary reality rarely portrayed in medieval romances" ("Fabric" 917). Jewers also argues that this economy subsumes the lyrics, which "exist in an implied textual economy of exchange that mirrors that of an increasingly realistic society" (914). The perpetual circulation of goods and deferral of payment in the narrative may, however, represent less a turn from the lyrics toward "monetary reality" than the extension of the lyrics' emphasis on exchange. It is, in other words, fitting that these lyrics, which function via *différance*, circulate in a narrative economy where things are constantly being exchanged but never firmly possessed. In this sense, the romance is not "realistic," as some have suggested; yet, this is also not a misapprehension, as others have countered.[5] Rather, the romance is troubling the opposition of the "poetic" to the "real" or the "figural" to the "literal," by challenging us to glimpse the figural, rhetorical, or even lyric nature of "monetary reality" (cf. *Homographesis* 79).

This notion that the surrounding narrative is complexly engaging with the terms of the lyrics takes another turn in the only song attributed to Conrad. Our emperor sings,

---

4. For the "bele Aeliz" topos, see Butterfield, *Poetry* esp. 46–47, 107.

5. Zink cautions against overstating the realism of the romance (*Roman rose*, 12–20); Dragonetti agrees (*Mirage* 167). Anglophone scholars can seem less wary: see e.g., Jewers, "Fabric" 914ff. For nuanced takes, see Lacy, "Amer" and de Looze, "Gender."

Quant de la foelle espoissent li vergier,
que l'erbe est vert et la rose espanie,
et au matin oi le chant conmencier
dou roissignol qui par le bois s'escrie,
lors ne me sai vers Amors consellier,
car onques n'oi d'autre richece envie,
    fors que d'amors,
ne riens [fors li] ne m'en puet fere aïe.

Ja fine amors ne sera sanz torment,
que losengier en ont corrouz et ire.
Ne ge ne puis servir a son talent,
qu'ele me voelle a son servise eslire.
Je soufferrai les faus diz de la gent
qui n'ont pooir, sanz plus, fors de mesdire
    de bone amor,
ne riens fors li ne me puet geter d'ire. (3180–95)

When the orchards thicken with leaves,
and the grass is green and the roses blooming,
and in the morning I hear the song begin
of the nightingale who cries out through the woods—
then I don't know how to counsel myself in relation to Love;
for I never desired any other riches,
    except from love,
and nothing but her can help me with this.

Never will true love be without torment,
since the slanderers are filled with anger and ire by it.
And I cannot serve in a manner so pleasing to her
that she should choose to allow me to be of her service.
I will tolerate the false words of the people
who cannot do anything more than slander
    true love,
and nothing but her can move me from ire.

This song opens with the traditional *exorde,* as the *je* tunes in to birdsong before submitting to Love. Conrad turns toward Love, therefore, because of what he "overhears" both within the narrative and within the lyric. Indeed, if lyric insertion raises the question of how the lyrics relate to their narrative surroundings, this is in keeping with how lyrics themselves often raise the issue of the harmony of the *je*'s relations with the world around him.

In the second stanza, the dreaded but familiar *losengiers* appear. The love struggles—and here can't quite succeed—at working back to the stability of a refrain; from "ne riens [fors li] ne m'en puet faire aïe" in the first stanza, the song can only get to, "ne riens fors li ne me puet geter d'ire" in the second. At the same time as *losengiers* turn language against the *je*—"I will tolerate the false words of the people / who cannot do anything more than slander"—form is also inciting the poem to turn, to find different words and rhymes so that the lyric, and by extension the love itself, may persevere. The formal movement within the lyric seems, then, potentially correlated to the threat of the *losengiers*; the song may even be producing the threat that it must combat. If this sounds abstract, the romance spells it out for us, since in its narrative context, the song functions performatively. The text insists that it is only once Conrad has sung these verses that the Seneschal goes about stirring up trouble: "Cez .ii. vers li fist pechiez dire, / qu'il en orent puis grant anui" [These two stanzas were ill-spoken by him, as (he and Guillaume) experienced great misfortune on their account] (3196–97). The song about the *losengier* enables this figure's perverse behavior in the narrative. The prospect of deviant use of language within the lyric becomes the deviant use of the language of the lyric.

As we saw in the book's introduction, Derrida speculates that deconstruction may function "by turning the rules in the very sense they were already turning in order to let the other come or emerge in the opening formed by this dehiscence" (*Psyché*, vol. 1, 59). I am, similarly, suggesting that the romance keeps turning the lyrics in the sense that they were already turning: exaggerating their tensions, contradictions, menaces, and slipperiness. "Sameness and difference, from such a perspective, lose their difference without being the same," as Edelman writes of certain figurations of gay sex (*Homographesis* 70).

As importantly, something emanates from this "dehiscence." As recourse to Edelman unsubtly implies, I believe it concerns the interplay between rhetorical "displacements and substitutions" and the deviance of desire. To better grasp how poetics and sexuality intersect in the *Rose*, consider the roundabout manner by which Jouglet introduces Lïenors to Conrad. During this conversation—which, as mentioned, takes place during literal deviations—Jouglet first describes an anonymous "chevalier" (662) about whom he has only heard in a secondhand manner; everything he knows is via "uns bachelers, qui de la vint / ou cë ot esté" [a bachelor who came from where this all happened] (659–60). He then glides from the superlative prowess of this unnamed knight to the beauty of his lady (691–722), and only afterward does he set about introducing Lïenors (744–48) and then her brother (749–52, 763–72).

Once Jouglet has piqued his interest, Conrad just must send for Guillaume. He says,

"Sempres covient savoir qu'ira
querre son frere le matin,   820
a cui ge me doig et destin
por servir de cuer et de cors."
En riant li dit Jouglez lors,
qui ert sages et apensez:
"Del cors, voir, avra il assez,   825
qu'il n'est mie si covoitous;
et Lïenors as blons chevouls
avra le cuer, se m'en creez."
Fet il en riant: "Gars provez,
com ez ore de mal apens!   830
Or cuides tu, voir, que ge pens
mains au frere q'a la seror?
En mon roiaume n'en m'onor
n'afferroit pas q'el fust m'amie.
Mes por ce qu'el n'i porroit mie   835
avenir, i voel ge penser." (819–36)

"Soon we will need to figure out who will go fetch her brother in the morning, to whom I pledge and vow my service in heart and body."

Laughing, Jouglet, who was wise and judicious, then said to him, "Of your body, truly, he'll have plenty, since he isn't too keen for it at all, and the blond-haired Lïenors will have your heart, if you trust me."

Conrad, also laughing, said, "You scoundrel, you have some no-good thoughts in there! Now do you truly believe that I think less about the brother than the sister? In my kingdom, nor for my honor, it would not be fitting that she should be my lover. But because she cannot become this, I'd like to muse about it."

In this remarkable passage, Conrad resists Jouglet's insinuation that he is only interested in the sister—adding that, in any case, it is the distance of this fantasy from reality that makes it permissible. This is not, however, necessarily the only impossible fantasy at play here. For if Conrad's love is predicated on a series of rhetorical reversals, it is in keeping with its modalities to give this passage another twist; this is *a fortiori* the case if the narrative functions by further twisting the already twisty lyrics. This passage provides all the terms we need to make another chiastic reversal, even initiating this movement, as the notion that Guillaume will have the "body" and Lïenors the "heart" is potentially backward, since Conrad eventually comes to "possess" Lïenors, not Guillaume (cf. Zink, *Roman rose* 111). Does Guillaume have his heart? It is tempting to recall Jaufre Rudel's ambiguous, "Que tout can lo faire.m desditz / Aug autrejar a la seror" [Whatever the brother refuses me, I will have granted by the sister] ("Bels m'es l'estius e'l temps floriz" 45–46, p. 11). I am not, however, asserting that Conrad desires Guillaume, whom he has also never seen, as Ben Ramm can seem to be in his queer reading of the romance (esp. 410–15). Yet, *pace* Zink (*Roman rose* 111), I view this not as a violation, but rather as the extension, of how the text construes Conrad's love. The romance "acts out" something akin to what Edelman calls "a calculated sexual ambiguity," which renders "suspect the bond of 'devotion'" between Conrad and Guillaume (*Homographesis,* 201, 165). Same-sex attraction does not, though, cause or capture this ambiguity; rather, it functions as an important—even necessary—corollary to the "substitutions and displacements" that are the mode of the lyrics, of the technique of lyric insertion, and of the romance more generally.

Throughout the romance, rhetorical movement and "sexual ambiguity" continue to intersect, often quite subtly. For instance, Conrad later stumbles upon Guillaume, as he is dreaming about how to make a splash at an upcoming tournament:

> L'emperere, qui mout l'amot,
> le resgarde, s'aperçoit bien
> qu'il entendoit a autre rien,
> ce li est vis, qu'il ne disoit.
> Si fesoit il, car il pensoit
> au tornoi tot vaintre et outrer . . . (1732–37)

> The Emperor, who loved him very much, looks at him, and clearly notices that he was thinking about something else, it seems to him, than what he was saying. And so he was; he was thinking about how to win and conquer all at the tournament.

Guillaume, like tropological language itself, is thinking about something other than what he says. Yet, the romance generally describes Conrad, not Guillaume, as "thinking about something else," since Conrad ostensibly uses Guillaume to get to his sister; this is the insinuation Conrad resisted in the previously cited passage. The act of "thinking about something else" is, therefore, displaced from Conrad onto Guillaume; it is "somewhere other" than where it should be. To add another twist to this language is, it follows, in keeping with the text's movement, or the possibility that the love story is "thinking about something else . . . than what [it] is saying" is one it invites. As the surrounding narrative turns the lyrics in the sense they were already turning, so too can we keep twisting the narrative, and it is in this "dehiscence" that the relation between rhetorical "substitutions and displacements" and "sexual ambiguity" comes out.

Yet, if the indeterminacy of desire comes out in this way, it can't really move forward or go anywhere, since "substitutions and displacements" also constitute the rhythm of this shifty text. Here, for instance, is Guillaume first taking leave of his family:

> Or sachiez que, quant il monterent,
> il i ot ploré maintes lermes.
> .iii. somiers a robes et armes
> orent, et granz chevax de pris.
> Mout a belement congié pris
> a sa seror et a sa mere:
> "A Deu, biau filz! –A Deu, biau frere!
> –A Deu, tuit!," quant il s'en tornerent.
> Or sachiez que tuit en plorerent
> li remegnant por eles deus.
> Or s'en vont, or les consaut Deus! (1274–84)

Now know that, when they got on their horses, there were many tears spilled there. They had three horses to carry robes and arms and also some large, valuable horses. Guillaume very courteously took leave of his sister and mother—"Adieu, handsome son!"; "Adieu, handsome brother!"; "Adieu all"— when they turned to go. Now know that all who remained cried on account of the two women. Now they are leaving, may God watch over them!

The narrator's description of Lïenors's departure almost three thousand lines later is very similar:

> Au matinet, quant ele mut,
> i ot mout besié et ploré:
> "Bele fille, a saint Honoré
> conmant ton cors, quel part qu'il aille.
> —Bele mere, Dex vos i vaille,

> ou ge ai tote ma fiance!"
> Nus ne fust a la dessevrance,
> quant la pucele dut monter,
> s'il deüst lermes emprunter,
> qu'il ne covenist que plorast.
> Ainçois qu'ele s'en par alast,
> par fu trop la dolor conmune. (4074–85)

> In the morning, when she set out, there was much kissing and crying. "Beautiful daughter, may Saint Honoré watch over your body, wherever it may go." "Beautiful mother, may God be with you, in whom I place all my confidence." Nobody was present at this separation, when the maiden got on her horse, who didn't feel the need to cry—even if he had to borrow his tears! Before she had gone away everyone was in distress.

In both moments, the leave-taker looks backward and forward: turning back at family and toward the necessity of appearing at court. At another level, this action of looking both backward and forward (an opposition which, I note in passing, Edelman considers to have "immediate sexual resonance" [*Homographesis* 176]) is performed by the juxtaposition of these instances, which glance reciprocally at each other. The codependence of these moments on each other, which reflects the codependence of brother and sister, gives a nice taste of how the romance is less linear than a series of displacements, as these displacements are also displacements of each other. This text is no *droite voie*, then, where things simply face ahead and move forward.

Yet, by venturing to court, does Lïenors not succeed at setting the record straight or straightening things out? As Krueger underscores, "Lienor's ascension as an active subject in the last third of the romance is remarkable" (*Women Readers* 149). She becomes—to use a term of which Edelman, following de Man, makes much—the "face" of the romance, as well as its brains. And similar to how Edelman understands the reappearance of the stunning Laura in Otto Preminger's 1944 film—after she has ostensibly been murdered—as "cast[ing] out or effac[ing]" (210) other faces, so too does Lïenors's performance lead one man (the Seneschal) to lose face, while others (Jouglet and Guillaume) are displaced, nowhere to be found (de Looze, "Gender" 604). For Edelman, the triumphant return of the female face in *Laura* attempts, more precisely, to overshadow questions about "the male body and the problem of bringing the male body into focus," which the film has been persistently raising (203). Renart's romance evokes similar issues. Lïenors has earlier tricked the Seneschal into accepting "ma ceinture / et m'aumosniere et mon fermal" [my belt, my alms pouch, and my brooch] (4786–87), and before the court she alleges that he has taken these items as tokens of her assault. Then,

> Sanz delai et sanz contredit,
> ou bien li poist ou mal li sache,
> uns chevaliers li tret et sache
> la robe amont et la chemise,
> que chascuns vit qu'il l'avoit mise
> et çainte estroit a sa char nue. (4860–65)

Without delay and without resistance, whether it bothered him or made him displeased, a knight pulled up and removed his robe and his undergarment, so everyone saw that he was wearing it (the belt) and that it girded his bare flesh.

As Helen Solterer has brilliantly observed, "It is the seneschal who is stripped bare for all to see; it is a gendered rose of another order that is made visible" ("At the Bottom" 228). The romance thus "put[s] the male 'goods' . . . on display and into the marketplace," to quote Edelman (*Homographesis* 208). In so doing, it admits the possibility of casting the man as sexual object. Yet, it simultaneously—and aggressively—forecloses it, as Lïenors's behaviors work both to secure a heterosexual union and to contain the disturbing possibility of male sexual passivity by associating it with the deviant seneschal, not Guillaume or Conrad. Lïenors's face and her smarts serve, therefore, to counter the threat of abjection and deviance.

Lïenors's argumentative strategy also exemplifies the conception of deconstruction already rehearsed; for by momentarily admitting to sex with the Seneschal, she exaggerates his allegations past the point which he had intended in order to bring about their crumbling. Yet, because for Derrida (or Edelman) these deconstructive tactics cannot foster stability or resolution, it is fitting to attend to how Lïenors's behaviors in this sequence also go past the point *she* intends, exposing a danger not thwarted by the seneschal's downfall. This seems to manifest itself in two main ways. At one level, Lïenors's performance hinges on rejecting the notion that claims made in language are necessarily true—although her claim to Conrad's heart is, until this scene, a pure linguistic construct. At another level, her performance teaches us to be wary of the visual, because the evidence on the Seneschal's body is planted; what the court thinks they are seeing does not really mean what they think it does. Yet, this is also a dangerous play for Lïenors, whose claims are reliant on the meaningfulness of her beauty. Lïenors's behaviors subject, therefore, both the linguistic and the visual to a "hermeneutics of suspicion," which is as subtly dangerous for her marital prospects as it is extremely problematic for "courtly love" more generally—since it becomes unclear to what one could peg one's beliefs.

In his reading of *Laura,* Edelman proceeds to argue that the film is, finally, "trapped in the destabilizing force field of irony," which "Waldo, as the personification of gay-inflected irony, both embodies and disseminates" (230). In Renart's *Rose,* the Seneschal is "the personification of" sexual deviance, and the romance similarly fails to contain the deviance he "both embodies and disseminates." The text signals this by subtly associating, after this sequence that ostensibly resolves everything, all three major male figures—Guillaume, Conrad, and Renart himself—with the Seneschal's perversity.[6] For instance, when Guillaume returns to court, he approaches his sister, newly crowned as empress, with deference:

> Mout l'a com sa dame honoree;
> et si voel que vos sachiez bien
> c'onqes a li de nule rien,
> fors de parole, n'atoucha. (5270–73)

> He greatly honored her like his lady, and I want you truly to know that he didn't touch her at all, only through his words.

Yet, this is precisely what the Seneschal did (or didn't do); he hasn't touched Lïenors "except through words." By subtly linking Guillaume's and the Seneschal's behavior (through words), the *Rose* makes an unnatural connection between the two, which may reflect the specter of unnatural relations haunting the romance more generally. The text then relates Conrad's consummation of his marriage to the Seneschal's machinations. The barons ask Lïenors to grant the Seneschal clemency:

> Li uns li a sanz delaier
> por aus touz dite la parole,
> que, s'il i muert ou l'en l'affole,
> el i avra mout poi conquis;
> et s'avra a toz jors aquis
> lor cuers, s'ele fet lor proiere.
> Mout estoit en bele meniere

---

6. Cf. Dragonetti, *Mirage* 156–59, 195–99, which compares both narrator and author to these three figures. For him, this comparison figures different qualities of the narrator/author, while the real "author" is Guillaume's mother.

vestue, acesmee et trecie,
que ne l'avoit pas si blecie
la nuit, Deu merci, l'emperere ... (5553–62)

One, without delay, addressed her on behalf of all of them, saying that if he died or was wounded, she will have gained little. She will, however, have forever conquered their hearts if she accepts their request. She was very well dressed and attired, her hair braided, since, thank God, the emperor hadn't overly hurt her the previous night!

Because Lïenors was not mutilated by Conrad—just as she wasn't mutilated by the Seneschal—there is, apparently, no reason for anyone to mutilate the Seneschal. Yet, the romance seems to "gain little" from juxtaposing the softness of the emperor's touch in the bedroom with Lïenors's pardoning of this deviant; this only opens up questions about what has (not) happened between the spouses (Dragonetti, *Mirage* 193). It is equally intriguing how the author then chooses to couch his signature in a description of the Seneschal, writing of his imprisonment and exile: "S'il puet eschaper a cest tor, / dont savra il mout de Renart" [If he can escape from this tower, he will be quite the crafty one] (5420–21; see Dragonetti, *Mirage* 166–67). In a manner, the Seneschal even escapes confinement, by slyly consorting with Guillaume, Conrad, and Renart himself.

These subtle parallels suggest that Lïenors's brilliant performance has not neutralized the threat the Seneschal represents. Rather, he continues to generate literary and sexual ambiguity, as the ensuing description of his departure for the East further suggests:

Toz croisiez i fu amenez,
plorant, devant l'empereriz
rendre les grez et les merciz
de la bonté qu'el li ot fete.
Si vos di que tex s'en deshete
qui pensa poi a son movoir.
Puis voudrent le congié avoir
li baron de l'empereriz ...
Puis departi la cours einsi,
et ralerent en lor païs
ou chascuns ot assez a fere.
Mout est li siecles de mal aire,
que tote joie fine en doel.

Ja ne queïssent mes lor voel
departir, mes il le covint. (5617–24, 5628–34)

Ready for the Crusades he was brought, crying, before the empress, to express his gratitude and thanks for the service she had rendered him. And I tell you that some were distressed who were hardly considering going abroad. The barons then wished to have the empress's blessing. Afterward, the court broke up and everyone went back to their land where all had plenty to do. This world is a terrible place, as all joy ends in pain. They no longer would have wished to depart, but it was necessary.

We get little explanation as to why these barons follow the Seneschal. Yet, their reluctant departure alongside him strongly suggests that the text wishes to cast the Seneschal as a force of profound but enigmatic disturbance. Rather than securing orderly or neat resolution, the romance seems, even, to be pursuing ambiguity and deviance. In fact, not only do the persistent and incessant "substitutions and displacements"—which are the stuff of this romance in its "hybrid form" and "thematic content"—render stability, resolution, or satisfaction unfeasible, but they also invite us to associate pleasure with deviance, as the pleasure of reading this romance is so associated with this seemingly endless twistiness and twistedness.

LE ROMAN DU CHÂTELAIN DE COUCY ET DE LA DAME DE FAYEL

As is well known, we only possess one copy of Renart's *Rose*, as opposed to some 250 of Guillaume de Lorris and Jean de Meun's eponymous text. Yet, suggests Butterfield (*Poetry* 220–21), this statistic does not do justice to Renart's formal legacy, since thirteenth- and fourteenth-century verse narratives continue to stage and "confront" the opposition of lyrics to narratives as Renart does, rather than homogenizing the two in the manner of Guillaume's *Rose*. Later verse narratives would, I shall argue, also follow in Renart's footsteps, by deconstructing this formal opposition in a manner that has important ramifications for *fin'amor*.

Granted, a text like Jakemés's *Roman du Châtelain de Coucy et de la Dame de Fayel* (1285–1300) seems to intercalate lyrics very differently than Renart's romance does.[7] In this fictive literary biography of the Châtelain de Coucy,

---

7. See esp. Huot, *From Song* 107, 122–23, 132–34; also Boulton, *Song* 61–66.

which invents an amorous backstory for six *chansons* it attributes to this twelfth-century trouvère, Jakemés, unlike Renart, focuses on one composer. He also tends to emphasize the composition, rather than the performance, of songs. His engagement with the lyrics is nonetheless similarly intricate. Consider, for instance, the first and fourth stanzas of the second song where the Châtelain sings his love:

> La douce vois dou lossignot sauvage
> Qu'oi nuit et jour quoinciier et tentir,
> Me radoucist le coer et rassouage.
> Or ai talent que canch pour resbaudir.
> Bien doi canter, puis qu'il vient a plaisir
> Celi qui j'ai fait de coer liet hommage.
> Si doi avoir grant joie en mon corage,
> S'elle me voet a son oes retenir.
>
> Je le doi bien siervir a hiretage
> Et sour toutes et amer et cremir
> Qu'adiés m'est vis que je voie s'ymage,
> Si ne m'en puis soëler dou veïr,
> Qu'el mont ne puis si bielle riens coisir.
> Lues que le vi, si laissai en hostage
> Mon coer, qui puis y a fait lonc estage,
> Ne jamais jour ne l'en quier departir. (816–23, 840–47)

> The sweet sound of the wild nightingale,
> Which I hear resound and ring night and day,
> Soothes and appeases my heart.
> Now I desire to sing to brighten my spirits.
> Indeed, I must sing, since it pleases
> She to whom I have sincerely pledged my loyal homage.
> Thus I ought to have great joy in my heart,
> Should she decide to retain me for her use.
>
> I ought to serve her for perpetuity,
> And love and fear her above all;
> For always it seems to me that I see her image,
> And I cannot get my fill of seeing it,
> Because in all the world, I could not find someone so beauteous.
> Since I first saw her, I left my heart captive

And it has been imprisoned for quite long now,
Nor do I ever desire to separate it from her.

According to Dragonetti, "in courtly poetry, the task of invention requires total submission"; the poet submits to "a stylistic tradition" figured by his submission to Love and Lady (*Technique poétique* 539). Yet here, the act of lyric insertion also reflects another profession of loving submission to literary tradition: that of Jakemés's romance to the Châtelain's songs. In the context of Jakemés's romance, this song authored by the Châtelain can, that is, also be read as about the insertion of the song into the romance. The song itself seems to function as the "douce vois dou lossignot sauvage" [sweet sound of the wild nightingale] that Jakemés cannot stop hearing. Jakemés writes this romance as an act of homage to this trouvère: "Bien doi canter, puis qu'il vient a plaisir / Celi qui j'ai fait de coer liet hommage" [Indeed, I must sing, since it pleases she to whom I have pledged my loyal homage]. The song itself is being retained "for the use" of the narrative, "a son oes." Jakemés obsessively reproduces the song's image: "Adiés m'est vis que je voie s'ymage, / Si ne m'en puis soëler dou veïr" [Now it seems to me that I see her image, and I cannot get my fill of seeing it]. He seems to desire not to stray from these songs: "Ne jamais jour ne l'en quier departir" [Never do I desire to separate [my heart] from her]. The final verses of the song proclaim, "Mais j'ai de ce moult cruel avantage / Qu'il m'en estuet sour mon gré obeïr" [But I take from this very cruel "advantage" that I must obey regardless of my will] (854–55). Jakemés's text also has a unique "avantage," which stems from how it remains glued to the Châtelain's *chants*.

If, according to structuralist critics like Dragonetti, courtly lyrics are a "symbolic *mise en forme* of a poetic fiction," whereby the *je* submits to the conventions of poetry, lyric insertion extends this dynamic, therefore, by adding another layer of "poetic fiction": that of Jakemés's narrative's loving submission to the Châtelain's songs (*Technique poétique* 559). This is important to emphasize, because it runs counter to how critics generally understand lyric insertion to function in this romance. "The Châtelain's lyrics are 'fleshed out' by the surrounding narrative, much as a heart is by the body around it," writes, for instance, Solterer ("Dismembering" 105). Yet, as the supplement both invokes and undermines notions of presence, I am suggesting that this romance that provides the Châtelain's songs with a body and face also troubles the ascription of body and face to these lyrics; for as it goes about "fleshing out" the lyric subject, it simultaneously works with the indeterminacy of lyric language, extending its meta-literary and self-referential dimensions.

Another example of how the narrative supplements the lyrics is in order. At one point, the Châtelain is dreaming of his lady,

> Et en ramembrance de li
> Fist il ce cant et dist ensi
> C'on a recordé moult souvent:
>   A vous, amant, ains qu'a nule autre gent,
>   Est bien raisons que ma dolour complaingne,
>   Car il m'estuet partir outreement
>   Et desevrer de ma douce compaingne ... (7343–49)

> And in remembrance of her, he made and declaimed this song, which has
>   since been recalled very often:
>   To you, lovers, more so than to any others,
>   It is fitting that I complain of my pain;
>   For I absolutely must go away
>   And be severed from my sweet companion.

Here, the Châtelain's *ramembrance* of the Dame de Fayel corresponds to Jakemés's act of *recorder* [recalling] the song. The romance therefore substitutes the song for the lady as the thing remembered; and because remembering is also thematized within the song, the song might be said to become something like the object of its own remembering. Within the song, moreover, remembering is predicated on distance, as the *je*'s pending departure occasions this outpouring of emotion: "Car il m'estuet partir outreement" [for I absolutely must go away]. It is, similarly, the displacement of the song into its new narrative context that allows for the act of recalling (*recorder*) it here. As in the *Rose*, lyric insertion does not, then, simply imply tossing the lyrics into a mimetic narrative where the terms are fundamentally different. It is also, and more subtly, engaging with the dialectic of proximity and distance at issue in the song.

Indeed, this dialectic is at stake throughout this romance, as Solterer has shown in an invaluable contribution that notably underscores the importance of the verb *recorder* to the text ("Dismembering," esp. 107–10). Jakemés claims, that is, to write this romance because "On doit tous jours bien recorder / Des boins le bien" [we should always keep in mind the good deeds of good people] (55–56). Throughout the narrative, the protagonists are also persistently recalling each other: for example, "En son coer prent a recorder / Le douc maintien et le parler / De sa dame" [in his heart he begins to recall the lovely countenance and speech of his lady] (309–11; Solterer, "Dismembering" 107). The Châtelain's feats inspire others to recall his prowess, too: "A Faiiel meïsmement / Recordoient son hardement" [Especially in Fayel they recounted his bravery] (339–40). When the lovers come together, they also spend much time recalling together: "La menerent vie d'amant, / Et recorderent leur grietés. . . . Et recordent les grans hascies / Qu'il ont souffiertes" [There they behaved as do lovers, recalling their woes, and they recall the great trials they had suffered] (6078–79, 6081–82; Solterer, "Dismembering" 109–10). Paradoxically, then, *recorder* implies distance (and difference) between the narrative and the lyrics, as the romance recalls far-off songs, and proximity (and similarity), since the narrative, the lyrics, and the act of lyric insertion are each focused on recalling. In a confusing way, the distant is the near and vice versa.

Solterer focuses, more precisely, on the "chronic tension between union and rupture, *recorder* and dismemberment" in the romance's plot ("Dismembering" 110). Yet, I would suggest that lyric insertion troubles this opposition, as the romance simultaneously dis- and re-members the Châtelain's songs. Consider, in this regard, its treatment of the first stanza of the Châtelain's "Au nouviel tans que mais et vïolette," which we also looked at in the *Rose*:

> Le coer ot deduisant et liet,
> Adont fist ce cant envoisiet
> D'amoureuse pensee entaite:
> > Au nouviel tans que mais et vïolette,
> > Et lossignos me semont de canter,
> > Et li dous coers me siert d'une amourette,
> > Si douc present ne doit nus refuser.
> > Or me laist Dieus a tel honnour monter
> > Que celle k'aim entre mes bras nuette
> > Tiengne une fois ains que voise outre mer! (7001–10)

> His heart was joyous and happy. Then and there, he made this lovely song,
> > full of amorous thoughts:
> > In the new season when May and violets
> > And the nightingale encourages me to sing,
> > And my sweet heart provides me a little love,
> > Such a sweet present no one should refuse.
> > Now may God let me rise in such honor
> > That she whom I love I may hold naked in my arms
> > Once, before I go abroad.

This is the only time the romance excerpts one stanza from a song by the Châtelain. Given his integral knowledge of other songs by the Châtelain, Jakemés was no doubt aware that the invective against "fausse amie" and "fausse amours" that follows in the original would be inappropriate here. He therefore voluntarily dismembers this lyric, performing via lyric insertion the very action—dismemberment—that characterizes the romance's gory final sequence, which is about to begin. Yet, to foreground dismemberment is not simply to violate the terms of the lyric. Rather, as we recall from discussion of the *Rose,* this lyric is about loss and dispossession. Jakemés's dismembering may, then, be responding to the lyric's own anxiety about being undone. As the Châtelain will soon order that his heart be removed from his body so as to be forever beside (and then inside) his beloved, so too is the song potentially being both dis- and re-membered by the romance.

Other lyrics in this final sequence develop, in a more ostentatious way, this paradoxical complicity between dis- and re-membering. As the Châtelain lies dying, he declaims three pieces that he could not have written, since they draw on forms—a *virelai,* a *salut d'amour,* and a *congé*—largely posterior to his period of activity; critics thus tend to attribute them to Jakemés himself.[8] The *salut* and the *congé* (which I touch on later) are relayed in octosyllabic couplets; yet the heterometric *virelai* both audibly and visibly contrasts with the surrounding narrative verse. In the refrain and second stanza of this song, the Châtelain sings from his deathbed:

Sans faindre voel obeïr
A ma dame, en qui veïr
   Puis sens et valour.
Sa biauté en sourveïr
Ne me poet asouveÿr,
   Tant ai plus dolour.

Grietés que mes cuers endure
Tout pour amoureuse ardure,
   Ne feroit doloir,
Moi qui ayme outre mesure
La tres bielle a desmesure,
   S'elle euïst voloir

---

8. The *virelai* only appears in one of the two manuscripts of the romance, Manuscript B, BnF nouv. acq. fr. 7514 (Gaullier-Bougassas, "Introduction," in Jakemés 11–12, 83–84, 547 n.81).

> D'aidier son ami; suiwir
> Le voel, se pour moi suiwir
>   Et par ma clamour
> Peusse sans avoir l'aïr
> De li et bien parveïr
>   Pardon de savour.
> Sans faindre, etc. (7563–68, 7582–94)

> Without pretending, I wish to obey
> my lady, in whom I can see
>   wisdom and worth.
> Contemplating her beauty
> cannot satisfy me.
>   It gives me all the more pain.
>
> Suffering that my heart endures,
> all because of love's flame,
>   wouldn't pain me—
> me who loves beyond reason,
> she who is immeasurably beautiful—
>   if she desired
> to help her lover. Accompany her
> I wish to, if by my submission
>   and by my supplication
> I may, without prompting anger
> from her, come truly to enjoy
>   a savory pardon.
> Without pretending, etc.

In the ensuing lines, the narrative describes how the Châtelain, "Ceste cançon fist a grant painne, / Car mout li ert joie lontainne" [made this song with great effort, because he was far from being joyous] (7608–9). If Jakemés here composes rather than recycles this song, he would be exercising more "painne" than usual. The Châtelain's "painne" may, then, reflect Jakemés's. That Jakemés is subtly calling attention to his role in penning this lyric is all the more probable, since the song also invokes terms pertinent to its insertion into the romance. Opening with the question of "faindre" [pretending] resonates, for example, with the attribution of lyrics to the Châtelain that he could not possibly have written. The "biauté en sourveïr" [beauty in contemplating] describes Jakemés's obsession with the Châtelain's lyrics. By writing a *virelai*, Jakemés is loving the Châtelain's lyrics "outre mesure" [beyond measure] and "a desmesure" [immeasurably/outrageously], as the *virelai* represents a new poetic measure. The repetition of the desire to "suiwir" [follow] recalls how this new form is posterior to the Châtelain's *grands chants*.

The Châtelain then tells his secretary what to do with his body after his death:

> ... tantost que mors sera,
> Qu'il l'oevre et em prange le coer,
> Et ce ne laist il a nul fuer
> Qu'il ne l'apareille et atourne. (7619–22)

> Right after he is dead, he should open it and remove the heart. He should not for any reason neglect to arrange and prepare it.

If the Châtelain prepares to die in the narrative, the secretary has already taken over in terms of the lyrics; Jakemés has opened up the body of the lyrics, dressing them up as he sees fit. There is, then, no inviolable border between the lyrics, which belong to the Châtelain, and the narrative, which is Jakemés's domain. Rather, a more confusing interpenetration is at stake, which points to how this romance that so emphatically celebrates the Châtelain's lyrics and fantasizes their embodiment is also, if more subtly, "committed ... to the hope of dismantling the armored identities that keep self and other, inside and outside ... distinct," to quote one of Edelman's descriptions of queerness (*Homographesis* 74).

I will return momentarily to this final sequence. First, though, I want to insist on how, even before things get so gory, deconstructing these different binary oppositions has—as recourse to Edelman suggests—important ethical ramifications: on how, that is, the narrative persistently subjects the lovers' behaviors to a deep "hermeneutics of suspicion." Indeed, it quite literally subjects the Châtelain and the Dame to Fayel to "suspicion," as their relationship, throughout much of the narrative, must negotiate with the jealousy of the Dame de Vermandois (who falls in love with the Châtelain) and then with the watchful eye of the Dame de Fayel's husband. The effect of this jealousy is to compel the lovers to resort to deception, which is hardly unusual in the world of courtly romance. Krueger nonetheless suggests that the "irony," whereby "those whom the narrator exemplifies as 'loiaus amants' are those who lie and betray," is particularly striking in Jakemés's text (*Women Readers* 205). The narrative does both clearly oppose the malevolent antagonists to the righteous protagonists and describe their behaviors in extremely similar terms. The evil

Dame de Vermandois is, for example, initially so dumbstruck by the Châtelain that she cannot eat—"Ensi pensoit et repensoit, / Si que petit but et menga" [Thus she was so preoccupied by her thoughts that she hardly ate or drank] (3801–2)—while the text has earlier said of an amorous Châtelain, "Mais li cevaliers a pensé / Toudis, qu'il ne but ne manga" [But the Knight was so continuously preoccupied by his thoughts that he neither ate nor drank] (236–37). Like the amorous Châtelain, the jealous Dame de Vermandois then enlists an "espie" [spy] (3940) to accomplish her mission. Like the Châtelain and his own proxies, this "spy" is repeatedly disguising himself: "Ses abbis souvent cangoit / Par quoi on ne s'en piercevoit" [He frequently changed his clothing, so he couldn't be recognized] (3971–72). When the Dame de Vermandois tells him about his wife's infidelity, the Sire de Fayel takes to this quasi-amorous behavior. The jealous husband plots to surprise the lovers, so he enlists a servant to seek out "Aucun privé lieu, chi entour, / U nous peussiens iestre le jour, / Si que nuls ne nous puist veïr" [a private place, around here, where we can be during the day so that no one will see us] (4337–39). Yet earlier, the Châtelain has asked the Dame de Fayel to enlist her servant's help in order to find "Aucun privé lieu, biel et gent, / U ne nous sacent nulle gent" [some beautiful and lovely private place where no one will know that we are] (2195–96) in order to consort with him.

The text thematizes this notion of "accord in discord" between the protagonists and the antagonists when husband and wife together learn that the Châtelain is leaving for the Crusades:

> Quant li sires ces mos oÿ,
> De la nouvielle s'esjoÿ.
> La dame aussi en fu joians,
> Qui de çou estoit desirans.
> D'iestre liet a l'oïr s'acordent,
> Mais lors pensees se descordent,
> Car la dame tent a l'aler
> Et li sires al demourer. (6975–82)

> When the Sire heard these words, he was thrilled at the news. The Dame was also joyous about it, who wished for this. Insofar as they were both happy to hear this, they were in agreement, but their thoughts were opposed, as the Lady was ready to leave, the Sire to remain at home.

This "accord" in "discord" directly refers to the Sire's pulling the wool over his wife's eyes. Yet, like homosexuality in Edelman's work, it also functions "to confound the security with which the sameness of [non-deviant sexual] identity can be known" (*Homographesis* 18). For rather than simply casting the righteous lovers as fundamentally different from the awful *jaloux*, the romance also calls attention to their similarities: to how the behaviors of both protagonists and antagonists are in accord despite—or, indeed, because of— their incessant discord.

It is, however, in the infamous final sequence where the confusion of sameness and difference, self and other, right and wrong, and inside and outside reaches an almost fever pitch. At the most basic level, this sequence's status in relation to the preceding narrative brings these issues to the fore. Because there appears to be no record of the eaten heart material being associated with the Châtelain de Coucy before this romance, Jakemés would be ingesting a motif from elsewhere (perhaps the *vida* of Guilhem de Castebanh).[9] Yet, as critics have insisted, this anecdote, far from being an arbitrary appendage to the romance, functions as a sort of *mise en abyme*, since the romance seems to be figuratively embalming and/or ingesting the songs of the Châtelain's heart (more on this in a moment). Paradoxically, then, the trope of the eaten heart, which is a "'foreign' substance," "penetrates and constitutes" the identity of the romance; or, the romance ingests a story of ingestion, which in turn encapsulates its poetics (*Homographesis* 71).

This is similar to how Krueger understands the dynamics at work within this scene. The Dame de Fayel devours the Châtelain's heart; yet, argues Krueger, she is effectively devoured by him, since she "willingly embraces her dissolution into his being" (*Women Readers* 211). Krueger suggests that this is also the case for both Jakemés's lady—whom he mentions only in the prologue and the epilogue—and the "ideal female reader":

> The chatelain and Jakemes live on through their words; the dame of Fayel and "she," the beloved reader, are vehicles of their legend. The ideal female reader who is virtually devoured or consumed by the text in the act of reading the romance embodies the construction of male subjectivity at the expense of female autonomy. (197)

From this feminist perspective, the inversion of the opposition of devourer to devoured is disturbing; yet queer theory seems often to embrace such dynamics of inversion. Edelman argues, in fact, that sexual deviancy—like this sequence—generally raises the issue of who "has been screwed" (*Homo-*

---

9. For the "eaten heart" material, see esp. Gaullier-Bougassas, "Introduction" 63–69 in Jakemés and Vincensini.

graphesis 127). Indeed, for him, gay sex not only abjectly violates boundaries among its participants but also, and more insidiously, threatens the inviolability of the heterosexual male body and by extension the stability of the identity he clings to. Hence, for Edelman, the trope of "shoving . . . homosexuality down the public's throat" (137).

While Krueger (like other critics [e.g., Solterer, "Dismembering" 116]) cautions against overstating the "deviant" nature of this gruesome dénouement, I am turning to Edelman, then, to explore how it mobilizes indeterminacy to trouble the integrity of bodies—both literal and textual—in ways potentially more subversive than it appears. Its use of lyric insertion seems to gesture in this direction. As we have seen, the *virelai* scrambles the distinction between the Châtelain and Jakemés by attributing to the former something no doubt written by the latter. Yet, in the two other pieces pronounced by the dying Châtelain, it is the basic distinction between the lyrics and the narrative that flounders, since these pieces contain ostensibly lyric features—notably evoking a sense of suspended desire—and narrative elements, as they are relayed in octosyllabic couplets and allude to details of the romance's plot.[10] This would appear to suggest that rather than being determinately about how men devour women, this sequence is more generally interested in the indeterminacy of distinctions in relation to both poetics and desire.

The oft-commented tension between the "literal" and the "figurative" at stake here reinforces this idea. At one level, that is, this scene "make[s] literal the poetic topos" of the poet giving his heart to his lady (Solterer, "Dismembering" 104). Yet, as Gaunt emphasizes, "the heart the lady eats, though originally a mere organ from her lover's body," is also "transformed into a fabricated and symbolic object" (*Love* 100). Indeed, from the dutiful servant to the jealous husband to the resolute Dame de Fayel, no one in the text really treats the heart as a "mere organ." In this respect, this sequence serves as a *mise en abyme* for the larger romance, which, if it initially appears to take literally the Châtelain's lyrics, always-already turns this into something "figural" or "poetic" in its own right. Like the romance, this sequence thus both posits and challenges the opposition of the "figurative" or "poetic" to the "literal" or "realistic."

Even more intriguingly, bringing the "literal heart" into play has fostered numerous figurative readings of this sequence, which seems "pregnant with symbolism" (*Homographesis* 138–39). Solterer, for instance, observes how the romance "assimilates the body of the Châtelain in the form of his poems. The

---

10. For *saluts* and their relation to the opposition of lyrics to narratives, see Butterfield, *Poetry* 237–39.

text contains and sustains him, much as the Dame de Fayel does physically" ("Dismembering" 117). This implies a suggestive parallel between Jakemés and the Dame de Fayel that crosses gender lines and casts Jakemés as the Châtelain's lover. Yet, as we have seen, Krueger finds the Dame de Fayel to be most similar to Jakemés's anonymous lady and "the ideal female reader." We might also compare Jakemés to Gobiert—the Châtelain's servant, who removes, prepares, and transports the heart—since Jakemés adopts a similar posture of subservience in relation to the Châtelain's lyrics (cf. Allen 34–35). There is also a parallel to be drawn between Jakemés and the Sire de Fayel, as like the jealous husband, Jakemés's final act is to orchestrate this gruesome dénouement. He oversees this horror.

Paradoxically, then, implicating the literal excision of the heart appears to confer a pressing sense of figural meaning onto this scene. Yet, if this scene appears to hold a mirror up to this text, it also fails to provide the illusion of coherence that the Lacanian mirror stage provides for the subject. Like queerness in Edelman's work, it even reads as a sort of reverse mirror stage, the "fall *back* . . . from the fantasized achievement of coherence and autonomous agency" embodied by discrete individuals in determinate positions to a messier interpenetration, "a state of mirror-like receptivity that appears . . . inherently 'self'-negating" (*Homographesis* 104–5; original emphasis).

Recourse to the mirror stage is all the more pertinent here, because this scene is concerned with how body parts convey meaning, especially in relation to the gaze of the other. Edelman focuses on these questions throughout *Homographesis*—perhaps most startlingly in his subtle reading of (of all things) media accounts of George H. W. Bush's vomiting in the Japanese Prime Minister's lap on January 8, 1992. He suggests that the act of regurgitating belies the President's inability to serve as "signifier" or "face" of the Republic. Vomiting reveals, that is, an "impurity" in Bush's body, which is uncontainable in his mouth and "threatens to interrupt the production of [symbolic] meaning" (141). Edelman then concentrates on how Barbara Bush grabs the mic in an effort to control the damage inflicted by her husband's indisposition. Yet,

> in the process of substituting her face for his she gives his face away, calls attention to the fact that he has no face, that he is, instead . . . only a mouth in desperate pursuit of a face to call its own. (144)

Jakemés's romance, and its final act in particular, are chewing on similar (and similarly complex) issues, albeit in somewhat different ways. Until the Châtelain's lyrics are incorporated into Jakemés's romance, they are as a mouth "in desperate pursuit of a face," or language without an anchoring in corporeal identity. Jakemés provides this mouth with a face (which, for Edelman—and following de Man—figures a "totalized, coherent" identity [*Homographesis* 193]) and anchors this heart (metaphor for true feeling in courtly tradition) in a body. Yet, both mouth and heart constantly risk being exposed as "only a mouth [and/or heart] in desperate pursuit of a face to call [their] own." More precisely, in this final sequence, the Châtelain's heart is in "pursuit of a face" and a body; it needs to be made meaningful by the Dame de Fayel. Yet, similar to Barbara Bush's taking up the mic, the fact that the Dame de Fayel must *become* the mouth, face, and body of their love exposes something potentially grave: how this heart does not necessarily go with the Châtelain's mouth, face, or body. What's more, the gruesome manner by which all this *goes down* illustrates how the relationship between mouth, heart, face, and body can be horribly disfigured. The mouth can defile rather than express the heart; in a reversal of what happens with President Bush, it serves here to introduce into the body something that doesn't belong and shouldn't be incorporated in this fashion. And this is, I think, also how this scene functions in relation to the romance, as it stuffs into Jakemés's text the notion that containing the "heart" is a potential violation and represents the passage through the mouth—whether the Dame de Fayel's, the Châtelain de Couci's, Jakemés's, or even ours—as delicious but deeply problematic.

Jakemés's epilogue pursues similar questions in a less horrifying way. In it, the author first denounces, at length, men who indiscriminately seduce women:

> Mais tels dist qu'il est vrais amis
> Qui son coer moult lonc en a mis,
> Car li coer sont diviers souvent.
> Une maniere y a de gent,
> S'il voient dame u damoisielle,
> Tantost lor lance une estinciele
> Telle qu'il sont en une esrour . . . .
> Cheaus tient Amours a anemis
> Qui en çou faire se sont mis,
> Et s'il goent, c'est sans savour
> Savourer des dous biens d'amour. (8196–202, 8214–17)

> But such a man says he is a true lover, whose true feelings are quite far from this; for hearts are often deceptive. There is a certain type of person, who if he sees a lady or a maiden, receives a spark which leads them astray. . . . These men are considered enemies of Love, when they behave in such a way.

And if they play around, it is without knowing how to savor Love's sweet rewards.

It would initially seem that Jakemés is "moult lonc" [very far] from proposing a reasonable moral for his romance, since no man disingenuously seduces women within it (with the exception of the Châtelain's seducing the Dame de Vermandois). Yet this passage is coherent, even incisive, insofar as it is calling attention to the problematic discrepancy between the mouth, the face, and the heart. What's to say that the mouth or the face expresses any sort of heartfelt truth? Unfortunately for medieval *fin'amor* or modern heteronormativity, the mouth and the face—which may well not correspond to each other—also might not correspond to a true heart. The line between normativity and deviancy will, therefore, always be invisible or illegible. Perhaps more importantly, this rhetoric also reveals how "courtly love" is predicated on a fantasy, whereby mouth, face, heart, and body do *genuinely* go together. Both the everlasting love between the Châtelain and the Dame de Fayel and this romance depend on this illusion—as the text puts a "genuine" face, body, and heart (in)to the Châtelain's mouth. Yet, in invoking the presence of the Châtelain's lyrics, person, and love, this romance—like the Derridean supplement—is also relentlessly undermining them, exposing their troublesome but seductive indeterminacy, vulnerability, and contingency.

LE DIT DE LA PANTHÈRE

Like Renart's *Rose,* Jakemés's *Châtelain* thus deconstructs charged binary oppositions. And if within both romances, "sameness and difference . . . lose their difference without being the same," this may, in turn, also describe the relationship between these texts. Indeed, while critics have (as mentioned) often contrasted Renart's means of inserting lyrics with Jakemés's, it is worth emphasizing how these romances caution us to be wary of the oppositions they seem to affirm.

It has also been suggested that romances and *dits,* the genre that inherits the mantle of lyric insertion, relate to lyrics in opposing ways. Cerquiglini-Toulet's dichotomy, in particular, seems to imply that lyrics tend to be "ornamental" in verse romances, whereas they drive the narrative in later *dits*; she refers to the former technique as *collage,* the latter as *montage* (see "Pour une typologie"; *Engin* 23–32). I turn now to Nicole de Margival's *Dit de la Panthère,* though, in order to explore how it, too, troubles the oppositions of lyrics and narrative, inside and outside, and self and other. Juxtaposing Nicole's *dit* with

Renart's and Jakemés's romances also suggests that any opposition between how romances and *dits* intercalate lyrics is as unsteady as the binaries that are deconstructed within these texts.

Granted, Nicole's *dit* appears quite different from, say, Jakemés's romance, with which it is probably roughly contemporaneous. The vast majority of the *Panthère* is comprised of a dream-vision, where Nicole catches a glimpse of a stunning panther. The God of Love informs him that the panther represents various facets of the marvelousness of his lady. Heated debate then erupts between Nicole, Amours, and Venus, over whether he should reveal his sentiments to his beloved. Nicole feels that he just can't muster the courage. Finally, he wakes up and proceeds to author a series of lyrics that further describe his passion.

Gone, then, is Jakemés's precise geography of northern France, which gives way to an allegoric dreamscape. And rather than a love affair with a beginning, middle, and end, we get a story where nothing seems to happen, as the lover can't overcome his trepidations. Nicole's *dit* nonetheless shares something crucial with Jakemés's romance, since it, too, focuses on one trouvère: in Nicole's case, Adam de la Halle. Nicole does not invent a backstory for Adam's songs. Instead, as he and Venus debate whether lovers should confess their love, they toss around citations from Adam's *grands chants,* seemingly positioning him as the ultimate authority in the art of love. Inventing a backstory for songs seems quite different from citing lyrics over the course of debate; yet the effect on the lyrics can be similar. In Nicole's *dit* as in Jakemés's romance, the inserted *chants* may be understood as describing not only the protagonist's feelings for his lady but also those of the author for the trouvère's lyrics. Consider, for example, the first two stanzas of Adam's "Grant deduit a et savoureuse vie," one of two songs that Nicole cites in its entirety:

Grant deduit a et savoureuse vie
En bone Amor honorer et servir;
Qui la maintient si qu'il doit, sans boisdie,
Qu'Amours rent plus c'on ne puist deservir.
Pour ce le serf, miex faire ne porroie;
Et se ja merci n'avoie
Quant tant avrai deservi,
Si me plaist il ma vie user ainsi.

Car je la fais pour la miex ensaignie
C'on puist du cuer penser ne d'ieux veïr;
De tant appert a tous sa seignorie

Qu'il est tous liez qui la puet conjoïr.
Hé! las! je ne m'os mettre en la voie,
Car poy parans y seroie,
Si n'ai qui la soit por mi,
S'Amors n'y est, et Pitié que je pri. (1589–1604)

There is great delight and a rich life
In honoring and serving good Love,
For he who treats her as he should, without trickery,
As Love gives back more than one could ever deserve.
For this I serve her: I could do no better,
And even if I were never to be rewarded,
Despite serving her such,
Still I prefer to spend my life in this way.

For I do it for the best learned
That one can conceive of in one's heart or see with one's eyes.
So much is her superiority obvious to all
That he who can please her is overjoyed.
Alas! I dare not put myself in her path,
For I would hardly be noteworthy;
And I have nobody pulling for me,
Should Love not be there, and Pity to whom I pray.

Nicole ostensibly turns to Adam's song in order to describe how he will behave toward his lady. Yet, in the context of this *dit,* the song more suggestively resonates with his relationship to Adam's lyrics. By relentlessly appealing to Adam's songs, Nicole appears to experience "grant deduit" [great enjoyment] in honoring and serving Adam's poetry, which he views as second-to-none: "Pour ce le serf, miex faire ne porroie" [For this I serve him: I could do no better]. In the *dit,* Adam more emphatically than the lady emerges as "la miex ensaignie / C'on puist du cuer ne d'ieux veïr" [the best learned person [fem.] that one can conceive of in one's heart or see with one's eyes]. Nicole's excessive reliance on Adam presumes that his "superiority [is] obvious to all": "de tant appert a tous sa seignorie." He evidently considers that "he who can take pleasure" in these songs will be "overjoyed": "il est tous liez qui la puet conjoïr."

The other song cited in its entirety, "Merci, Amour, de la doulce doulour," can also be read in terms of the *dit*'s relationship to Adam's lyrics. The *je* insists, for example, that he has found "la plus belle et toute la meillour / Qu'en puist ou mond ne amer ne servir" [the most beautiful and entirely the best lady that in this world one could love or serve] (2558–59). He then adds, "Car n'est pas pareil de nous" [for we are not equals] (2588). By obsessively citing Adam's and only Adam's lyrics, the *Panthère* implies that Adam is both the best trouvère in the world and seemingly far above him. Adam's song concludes, "Ne je ne vueil point guerir, / Car mon espoir vault d'autrui le joïr" [nor do I wish to be healed, as my hope is worth as much as another's joy/success] (2599–600). The *Panthère* takes these verses almost literally, as the helpless Nicole's hopes correspond to the (poetic) feats of another: Adam.

As in Jakemés's romance, lyric insertion adds, therefore, another level of "poetic fiction" to the lyrics. Not only does the trouvère submit to poetic convention in the song, but the *dit* also submits to the trouvère's act of submission. The *Panthère* even renders this more explicit than Jakemés's romance does, by calling attention to how lyric sentiment and "poetic fiction" interpenetrate in three smaller inserted *dits*, which are included in the larger *Panthère*. In the second and third inserted *dits*, Venus and Amours literally deliver to the feeble narrator the expression of his own effusive sentiments; the narrator says of Venus's *dit*, "Dedens ce dit moult bien escript / Avoit la deesse descript / De mon cuer toute la matiere" [Within this very well-written *dit*, the goddess had described all the substance of my heart] (1147–49). As in the *Rose*, the protagonist's subjectivity, therefore, "vibrates with an energy not its own" (*Homographesis* 17). And as if to insist on this, the particular relation of this *dit* to the protagonist then pierces through the *je*'s expression of "his" amorous sentiments. The *dit*, for instance, begins,

> Dame, cilz qui amors fine
> Destraint por vous, vous estrinne
> De son cuer sans ja mouvoir. (1151–53)

> My lady, he who true love torments on account of you, presents you his heart without ever wavering.

Otherwise banal sentiment here comes alive through play on the verb "mouvoir" [to move]. Not only does the faithful Nicole place his heart in his lady "sans ja mouvoir" [without ever wavering] but he also becomes the lyric *je* literally without moving at all, since Venus hands the *dit* to the bedridden narrator. As it continues, the *dit* alludes even less subtly to how Venus provides Nicole with these verses. In the third stanza, the *je* declares,

> Sans faire plus longue atente,
> Vous doins mon cuer, bele et gente;

Ne veilliez por mal tenir
Se par escript le presente. (1175–78)

Without any more delay, I give you my heart, beautiful and noble lady. Please do not consider it wrong if I present it in writing.

Rather than describing what Nicole will do with this *dit,* these lines recall how Venus already has given the narrator "by writing" his own heart, which we might consider "wrong" or at least unconventional. And if the inserted *dits* intertwine lyric sentiment with meta-poetic concerns, this would authorize readings of Adam's songs in the context of the *dit* that similarly attend to the interplay of amorous feeling and "poetic fiction."

This is important to emphasize, because it invites us to conceive of Nicole's relations with Adam in a new way. For while Nicole seems (not) to approach Adam's lyrics as he does the panther—casting both beast and songs as terrifyingly superior to him—the interplay between lyric sentiment and lyric insertion points to messier, subtler relations (cf. Solterer, *Master* 61–78; Berthelot, esp. 6). Consider, for example, the narrator's third citation, which is the second stanza of Adam's "Li jolis maus que je senc ne doit mie":

Folz est qui trop en son cuidier se fie.
On voit aucun seur le point d'enrichir
Emprendre tant dont il aprez mendie;
Tout ce me fait de li proier cremir,
Car miex me vault user toute ma vie
En mon joli souvenir
Que par trop taillant desir
Perdre tout a une fie. (1099–106)

He is reckless who has too much confidence in his own convictions.
We often see one who is on the point of becoming rich,
who undertakes so much that afterward he is forced to beg.
All this makes me afraid to make any request of her,
as it suits me better to spend my whole life
happily contemplating her,
than, because of my overly sharp desire,
to lose everything at once.

The narrator understands this stanza as Adam's instruction to lovers not to reveal their love. This is not, however, quite the message of Adam's song, as the *je* comes to implore his beloved to "moi metre en volenté de jehir / Mon cuer" [Give me the will to reveal my feelings] (*Oeuvres complètes* II.26–27, p. 42). Nicole's protagonist seems not to grasp how the lyric *je*, rather than simply being paralyzed by fear, is torn between concealing and revealing; the song is even self-consciously addressing the lady about the very impossibility of addressing her. Yet, if the protagonist is not attuned to this tension, the *dit* may be engaging with it, since lyric insertion deflects the issue of revealing and concealing onto the *Panthère*'s relationship with the song. It exacerbates the irony whereby the song is saying what it apparently cannot say or revealing what it purports to conceal, by excerpting it in such a manner as to make it say, or reveal, what it doesn't necessarily mean to.

Nicole's second citation engages with the fourth stanza of Adam's "D'amourous cuer voel canter" in a similarly intricate way:

Ançois voit on refuser
Celui qui trop prie
Que celui desamonter
Qui trop s'umilie.
Pour ce sueffre sans renier
En espoir d'avoir merci,
Et bien veil qu'il soit ainsi;
Car a seignorie
A on mainte foys failli
Par trop haster. (1085–94)

We are more likely to see refused
someone who asks for too much
than someone stumble
for being overly humble.
For this reason, I suffer without renouncing,
in the hope of benefiting from her mercy,
and I do desire that it be so,
since, to attain a superior position,
one has many times failed
by acting too hastily.

As in the previous citation, Nicole is "dismantl[ing] the carefully developed argument of Adam's" piece (Armstrong and Kay 152–53), since this song does not simply advocate restraint and timidity. Rather, it seems more concerned with persistence, especially in the face of slanderers. Nicole's recourse to this stanza rings, moreover, ironically; for while it denounces "celui qui trop prie" [he who begs/implores too much], it is hard not to see Nicole as doing a version of the same, since he is "celui qui trop prie" Adam. Yet, Nicole also "trop s'umilie" [overly abases himself] before Adam's poetic authority. He appears, then, to be behaving both as he should and shouldn't, and the *Panthère* might also be understood as treating this stanza both as it should and as it shouldn't. At one level, that is, the effect of lyric insertion is to twist Adam's language, giving the impression that it means what it doesn't quite mean; yet this ties back, at another level, to the question that dominates Adam's song: that of the *je*'s (in)capacity sincerely to express himself. Nicole's act of citation restitutes the tension between sincere expression and its impediments (internal and external), by raising the question of whether he is revealing or perverting the song's true sentiment.

Not unlike sodomy in Edelman's *Homographesis,* lyric insertion in the *Panthère* has, therefore, the effect of "confounding and dismantling . . . the active/passive distinction" (58). If Nicole initially appears so passive before Adam's poetic authority, he is, on closer inspection, exercising something akin to what Edelman calls a "passive agency" (112), as the ostensible submission to Adam's songs reflects a more fervent engagement with their terms.

The issue with "passive agency," however, is that it is almost necessarily difficult to locate. Indeed, as with the *Rose* and the *Châtelain,* we might ask whether Nicole is necessarily engaging with Adam's songs so subtly? One response to this query would be to point to how certain allegations suggestively resonate with non-cited elements of songs, which implies a more complex engagement with the lyrics than meets the eye. Venus's first citation, for example, doesn't do much to explain why *gehir* (revealing) should give the lover courage to endure his pain, although this is ostensibly why she includes it (1517–27). Yet what Venus does not cite from Adam's "Pour coi se plaint d'Amours nus" is perhaps more relevant to Nicole's *dit*. Adam's song begins,

> Pour coi se plaint d'Amours nus?
> Mais Amours se deüst plaindre,
> Car ele rent assés plus
> C'on ne puist par sens ataindre
> Ne par bel servir.
> Or veut on sans deservir
> Recouvrer joie et amie . . . (XI.1–7, p. 62)

> Why should anyone complain about Love?
> Love should be the one complaining,

> as she provides considerably more
> than one can attain through wisdom
> or through devoted service.
> Thus one wishes, without deserving it,
> to obtain joy and his beloved.

The lofty sentiment Adam expresses here is almost literally true in this *dit*, where Venus and Love provide this extremely feeble lover—who doesn't think he should do anything—with much more than he appears to deserve. Later, the *je* complains that before his lady, "le langue m'est loïe / Aussi que se faerie / Me venist entour" [my tongue is tied, as if a fairy had appeared around me] (XI.51–53). This is, again, similar to what occurs in the *dit*, where a *féerique* Venus appears before a hopelessly tongue-tied lover. Adam's song concludes,

> Canchon, fai toi de maisnie
> A me dame tant c'oïe
> Soies par douchour!
> S'on t'en cache, fai un tour,
> Si rentre a l'autre partie. (XI.56–60)

> Song, infiltrate the household
> of my lady until you are
> heard with approval!
> If you are chased away, think up some ruse,
> and find another way in.

It is tempting to read the *dit* as inviting us to *faire un tour*, to *rentre a l'autre partie* of the song, which is what the song advocates for itself. As sodomy, for Edelman, "is interpreted as the practice of giving precedence to the posterior and thus as confounding the stability or determinacy of linguistic or erotic positioning," so too can the *Panthère* be "interpreted as . . . giving precedence" to backdoor ways of entering into Adam's songs, in a manner which troubles the "stability" of Nicole's "positioning" vis-à-vis the trouvère's lyrics (*Homographesis* 183–84).

In fact, the *Panthère* engages in a backdoor manner with Adam's lyrics on a considerably larger scale. In the context of the debate, the citations justify opposing positions, like in a *jeu-parti*. Adam's own *jeux-partis* often treat similar subjects. Such *jeux-partis* as "Adan, s'il estoit einsi," "Adan, amis, je vous dis une fois," and "Adan, liquels doit miex trouver merchi," are all, for instance, about whether or not the tormented lover should go for it. The *jeux-partis* also persistently, and playfully, discuss Adam's authority in love in terms of *clergie*, as Nicole and Venus do. Considering Nicole's obsessive citation of Adam's *grands chants* alongside Adam's own *jeux-partis* brings to the fore, however, a series of ironies. Although he seemingly confines Adam to one lyric genre, Nicole in fact pushes him into another; and although he seems to over-cite Adam in a servile manner, Nicole potentially dramatically under-cites him by not alluding to the *jeux-partis*. Even more suggestive is how the move from Adam's *chants* to his *jeux-partis* echoes that of the famous trouvère Chansonnier W (BnF fr. 25566), which is generally acknowledged as the first attempt to unite the *oeuvre* of a single author and which proceeds from Adam's *chants* to his *jeux-partis*.[11] While on its surface, the *Panthère* is effecting "a fortification of boundaries"—both between lyric genres and between Nicole and Adam—it thus also demonstrates "a willingness to allow the boundaries of their identities to be penetrated," as the *dit* is more elusively engaging with Adam's corpus (*Homographesis* 69).

The final segment of the *dit*, sometimes referred to as the "epilogue" (Hoepffner, "Poésies lyriques" 214; Huot, *From Song* 203), supports this hypothesis. After waking up, Nicole inserts, alongside two more citations from Adam's songs, six works he claims as his own. As Ernest Hoepffner first noted, the principal feature distinguishing Nicole's six *chançons* from Adam's *chants* (to employ the terms Nicole does) is the presence of refrains ("Poésies lyriques" 216). This is somewhat paradoxical, however, since refrains are "anonymous, inclusive forms of speech and melody [that] do not easily admit a notion of original, authorial creation" (Butterfield, *Poetry* 244). Nicole thus finds his own voice by drawing on the very type of language that, as Butterfield argues, "both set[s] up and break[s] down barriers . . . between mine and yours, ours and theirs, hers and his" (*Poetry* 243). Even more curious is the notion that *chansons à refrain* mark a progression away from Adam's lyrics, since Adam authored many *rondeaux* with *refrains*. Nicole was, moreover, no doubt aware of Adam's *rondeaux*, as, according to Butterfield, his first *rondeau* "has the same distinctive formal structure as Adam's rondeau, 'Je muir, je muir d'amourete'" (*Poetry* 284). What's more, the move from *grands chants* to *jeux-partis* to *rondeaux* is also precisely that of Chansonnier W. Rather than having graduated from obsessive citation of Adam's *chants* to Nicole's proto-*forme fixe* lyrics, the *Panthère* seems, then, to be elusively shad-

---

11. For this Chansonnier, see e.g., Huot, *From Song* 64–74.

owing the movement of Adam's *oeuvre*.[12] Nicole is persistently engaging with it through a sort of backdoor, which reflects a more twisted interpenetration between the poets' corpuses.

As I have been suggesting, this relationship resonates with Edelman's argument in *Homographesis*, according to which queer sexuality effects an uncomfortable "disorientation of positionality" in relation to seemingly stable meaning. Edelman writes, for instance, of "the reversal of front and back, proper and improper, socially productive and narcissistically wasteful, that renders sodomy a practice essentially inimical to essence" (131). Similarly, Nicole's *dit* engages with the "front and back" of Adam's lyrics, in "proper and improper" ways: in manners that simultaneously exult, violate, and probe the terms of the lyrics. The effect of Nicole's engagement with Adam's lyrics is also to underscore what we might call their "narcissistically wasteful" quality: to emphasize their indeterminacy and self-reflexivity, or how the language more emphatically refers to layers of "poetic fiction" than to any actual lady. This "narcissistic wastefulness" then infects Nicole's *Panthère*, as sexuality in this navel-gazing *dit* is certainly not "productive" in the sense of inducing any sort of activity vis-à-vis the lady.

Yet, similar to how "passive agency" resists being located, so too does emphasis on the "narcissistically wasteful" raise problems for the analogy between lyric insertion in the *Panthère* and Edelman's work on queerness. If the *Panthère* seems to be a "narcissistic" text, where almost nothing happens, could we not simply argue that its interest lies in literary questions rather than sexual ones? My response is twofold. At one level, the fact that the love story between Nicole and his lady is underdeveloped does not mean that the erotic sentiment expressed in either Adam's lyrics or Nicole's *dit* is void. Rather, as we have seen, desire and erotic feeling are at play, although they often seem to pertain more to the funny relationship between Nicole and Adam's textual corpus. At another level, the *Panthère* also has a (somewhat) more precise relationship to sexual deviance, as its opening lines suggest:

> A dame bele et bone et sage,
> Noble de cuer et de lignage,
> Cilz qui son dous non n'ose escrire,
> Que par ce ne puist de mesdire
> Aus mesdisans ouvrir la voie,
> En lieu de salu li envoie

---

12. See Hoepffner, "Poésies lyriques" for Nicole's lyrics in relation to fourteenth-century *formes fixes*.

Son cuer et toute sa pensee,
Avec ceste oevre que rimee
A pour li especïaument.
Mais comment que principaument
L'ait por li faite et acomplie,
Toutevoies ne l'ose mie
Droitement a lui envoier,
Car il ne veult pas anoier
Les envïeus de mal penser,
Ains les en veult, s'il puet, tenser. (1–16)

To the beautiful, good and wise lady, noble in heart and lineage, he who does not dare write her sweet name—so that by this he does not open the door for slanderers to slander—sends her instead of salutations his heart and all his thoughts, along with this work that he has rhymed especially for her. But even though he principally wrote and accomplished it for her, he nonetheless does not dare send it right to her, as he does not wish to burden the envious with bad thoughts; rather, if he can, he wishes to keep them from this.

Throughout the *dit*, the threat posed by *mesdisants* remains pressing; at one point, Nicole even finds himself stuck in thorns that represent these nasty slanderers (581–94). Similarly, the *Panthère* might be described as profoundly entangled with the threat they represent. For as this prologue claims, the *mesdisants* are crucial to how this text presents itself; it is (ostensibly) because of them that the *dit* cannot be sent right to the lady or directly invoke her. As Edelman writes that "the historical positing of the category of the 'homosexual' textualizes male identity as such, subjecting it to the alienating requirement that it be 'read'" (*Homographesis* 12), so too does the "positing of the category of the" *mesdisants* "textualize" the protagonist's amorous identity, since it is because of them that this love must be "read" and "interpreted" (by his lady and us).

And as in *Homographesis,* the textualization of desire both reflects and fosters a troublesome "hermeneutics of suspicion" that spreads in dangerous ways. Indeed, in a curious turn, suspicion in the *Panthère* is perhaps best embodied by Nicole's lady. This lady but fleetingly appears in a dream sequence within the larger dream-vision, where Nicole tries to give her the *dit* that Venus had written about his feelings. She tells Nicole that she does not wish to read a sealed letter, "Car chose qui est sëelee / A prendre pas ne li agree, / Car il y avoit souspeçon" [for something that is sealed she does not wish to take, as there (would be) suspicion] (1423–25). We might say something analogous about the *Panthère,* where the "hiddenness" of meaning invites suspicion in regards to Nicole's true intentions. The lady will, however, agree to look it over; yet she complains that Nicole should not have included a ring inside his letter:

> Que mal de chief et mal de dens
> Puist avoir corps si po loiaus
> Com cil qui aimme por joiaus! (1450–52)

> That a headache and a toothache should befall the body of one so uncommitted that he loves for jewelry's sake!

Again, a similar critique might be leveraged against this *dit,* where Nicole risks coming off as "po loiaus" [uncommitted] because he "aimme por joiaus" [loves for jewelry]: with the jewels being Adam's lyrics that glimmer throughout this *dit.* And in any case, the lady adds, she is just not interested in loving him (1456–62). This is an interesting objection here, too, since it is the mirror image of the question of whether Nicole is interested in loving her in the *Panthère.*

I would suggest, then, that the *Panthère* resonates with Edelman's work in *Homographesis,* because it has the effect of subjecting to a contagious and corrosive "hermeneutics of suspicion" the narrator's desires—as well as the desire expressed in Adam's lyrics or even courtly letters more generally. The *Panthère* may also go further than Edelman seems to in *Homographesis* (though not further than in *No Future,* as we shall see in the next chapter), by explicitly embracing the very qualities most threatening to the stability of *fin'amor.* Witness, in particular, the *dit*'s mascot of sorts: the magnificent panther. In an account indebted to bestiary tradition, the *Panthère* stresses two of the beast's features. One, the panther assimilates the colors of all other animals into itself, except the dragon:

> Qu'il n'i avoit beste nis une,
> Tant fust estrange ne commune,
> Qu'ele n'eüst de lor coulour,
> Tant recevoit elle du lour
> Sans faire a elles nul domage. (99–103)

> For there was no animal but one, however unusual or common, whose color it didn't incorporate into itself. This much did it receive from others without damaging them at all.

Two, the panther exhales a most "douce alaine" [sweet breath] (111) that can cure other animals: "s'alaine qui en issoit / De trestous mauls les guarissoit" [the breath that came from it can cure all ills in them] (113–14). When it comes time to explain the "signifiance" (151) of these marvels, Love argues that the colors represent the "graces bonnes, / Qui en toutes autres persones / Sont communement espandues" [good graces, which are commonly distributed among all other people] (475–77); yet, in the panther, they are "en son corps seul retenues" [retained in its unique body] (478). As regards the sweet, healing breath, "Ce senefient les paroles" [this signifies the words] (499) of the lady. Her words are so sweet that "Chascuns volentiers les eschange" [everyone happily exchanges them] (504), and they also teach all to "entendre a bien faire" [strive to do well] (517). As Love puts it, "La fault il bien prendre examplaire" [in them you can find a model] (518).

This marvel and its interpretation curiously overlap with the threat posed by sexual deviancy, as Edelman understands it. For him, male homosexuality confronts masculinity with an indeterminacy it cannot bear. Normative masculinity then attempts different maneuvers to defuse this threat. It strives, for instance, to counter the invisibility of homosexual difference by pretending to be able to read it on gay bodies, which implies "effecting a denaturalization of the gay male body, translating every move into a spectacle, every gesture into a representation or a performance of that gesture" (*Homographesis* 207). Not dissimilarly, the panther's every gesture is quite literally a spectacle to be interpreted. Masculinity, according to Edelman, also attempts to contain the threat of indeterminacy, by casting gay men as the embodiment of it.

> The gay male body ... must be *marked and indeterminate at once*; consequently, it is imagined to be marked *as* indeterminate with the result that indeterminacy effectively ceases to *be* indeterminate and becomes, instead, the gay male body's determinate mark (*Homographesis* 237; original emphases).

One of the panther's "determinate marks" is similarly—and similarly paradoxically—its indeterminacy. Indeed, the panther is marvelous because it is able to "naturalize, or present as proper, that which is improper or alien or imported from without," to borrow Edelman's definition of metaphor (*Homographesis* 90). The *Panthère* is therefore celebrating the indeterminacy of borders and meaning, which, recourse to Edelman would suggest, is all the more intriguing since this is what makes normative masculinity so anxious.

We can also go further. Not only is the *Panthère* celebrating potentially risky things, but it is also not clear how determinately the indeterminate panther is related to the lady in Nicole's *dit*. Eliza Zingesser has, for instance, suggested that while it ostensibly symbolizes the lady, the panther also resembles Nicole's text, since both incorporate into their fabric a wide variety of different sources (307). The *Panthère* does explicitly gesture to such diverse texts as the *Roman de la Rose,* a French translation of Andreas Capellanus's infamous treatise, and a vernacular lapidary. Yet, the panther may also represent not Nicole's text but Adam's function in it. Surely, in the world of this *dit,* Adam's words are the loveliest and the most renowned, exemplary, and instructive. As we have seen, his lyrics also seem curiously able to incorporate elements of their evolving surroundings into themselves. It seems, therefore, that the panther is both symbol of indeterminacy and itself an indeterminate figure in this text. Or, as in the *Châtelain,* the panther-figure functions both as a mirror being held up to this text and effects a sort of reverse mirror stage, since it disrupts the stability of contours, positions, and identities. I have, moreover, argued that this is also how Nicole's *dit* relates to Adam's lyrics, as it both celebrates them and deconstructs their contours. We might also describe its relations with queer work like Edelman's in a similar way. The interest of the connection between the *Panthère* and *Homographesis* lies in how both engage—and embrace—the relation of poetics and desire to indeterminacy, so this connection is fittingly only determinate in its seductive indeterminacy. And because this paradox also applies to the other texts studied in this chapter, it brings me to the conclusion.

In my mind, the "signifiance" of this chapter is twofold. One, that romances and *dits* both posit and deconstruct the difference between lyrics and narratives. Two, that lyric insertion is not immune from the "inescapable politics" (*Homographesis* 21) of form. Indeed, there is not much less reason to study the gender and sexual politics of verse narratives that insert lyrics than there is to consider gender and sexual politics in relation to, for example, genre. Obviously, not every verse narrative with inset lyrics will resonate as suggestively with queer work like Edelman's. Yet, others will, because inserting lyrics into narratives effects a "disorientation of positionality" in relation to the lyrics and to the love they champion, and this has the potential—which is mined by the texts I have explored here—of putting pressure on the indeterminacy of literary language and of the desire that, in courtly letters, is always at its heart.

As in the last two sections, the subject of this chapter also provides ways of reconceptualizing the relations both between verse romances and *dits* and between the courtly and the queer. If lyric insertion often serves to deconstruct charged binaries, then we might be similarly wary of using binary oppositions—such as those of orality and literacy, song and book, *collage* and *montage,* code and message—to oppose how verse romances and *dits* intercalate lyrics. We might also be wary of using binaries to oppose these genres *tout court.* My point is not, of course, that we can do without such oppositions as orality to literacy—or that verse romances and *dits* are identical. Yet, as with the confrontation of lyrics and narratives within texts, things get most interesting when "sameness and difference . . . lose their difference without being the same": when criteria of sameness and difference, rather than being asserted or assumed, are challenged and destabilized.

This chapter has particularly attended, furthermore, to how the terms of the lyrics bleed into the surrounding narratives; I have read romances and *dits* as "long poems" rather than verse narratives. Similarly, we might attempt to conceive of the story of lyric insertion—and of the relations between verse romances and *dits* more broadly—as a "long poem" rather than a verse narrative. There is an important irony underlying much work on lyric insertion; for while scholars tend to be determined not to let the lyrics be drowned out by the surrounding narratives, lyric insertion is often cast as a largely chronological narrative, moving from Renart to Machaut (and beyond). This gives narrativity the last word. It seems to me more fitting to conceive of the story of lyric insertion—and even of the evolution from verse romance to *dits*—as taking the form "of a spiral staircase, constantly turning round, though moving to new locations," to borrow Judith Peraino's description of the trajectory of her majestic book on song, which wiggles its way from the troubadours through to Machaut (32). Such an approach takes to heart the resistance to determinacy and linear progression—or narrativity—characteristic both of lyric pieces and of the verse narratives that incorporate them.

I glance to Peraino, too, as a gesture toward the *grand absent* from this chapter: music. Various factors explain my lack of insistence on music when discussing lyric insertion in these verse narratives. None of the texts studied here contains music, for instance, and I have concentrated on the lyric genre of the *chanson courtoise,* for which "no music exists in romances" (Butterfield, *Poetry* 29). This chapter may nonetheless have a theoretical contribution to make to more musically oriented readings than my own. Peraino notably decries how "proponents of [a] literal, word-oriented view" of lyrics "see melodies as supplemental rather than integral to the expression of the song" (27). With Derrida, this chapter has troubled the opposition between the "supplemental" and the "integral" by countering that "supplementarity" is paradoxically "integral" both to these lyrics and to the texts that contain them. And if supplemental logic is so pertinent to how these texts function, it may be that musicologists like Peraino could work with it: no doubt to supplement literary readings like my own.

Finally, this chapter's *matière* also has ramifications for conceiving of the relationship between courtly literature and modern queerness. It is interesting (and in the spirit both of work on queer temporalities and of "post-historicist" approaches to medieval literature) to think of nonnarrative ways in which the two may interact—and which, in turn, challenge both our narratives about the Middle Ages and a (sometimes unexamined) reliance on narrativity lurking within queer histories. In an issue that I touch on in the next chapter, a queer narrative may, in important respects, even be an oxymoronic formulation.

I bracket this larger issue for now, however, to observe how the practice of lyric insertion can more precisely help us theorize new ways for the courtly to relate to the queer. If, throughout this chapter, I have emphasized how, in these verse narratives, "sameness and difference . . . lose their difference without being the same," an analogous dynamic may characterize an important facet of the interactions between courtly literature and queer theory. No doubt this sounds abstract (and it is). Yet, this chapter has also performed this tension, as Edelman's queer theory has functioned in this chapter in a manner not entirely different from lyric insertion in these verse narratives. I have *inserted*—used and no doubt abused—queer theory (to employ terms that require more rigorous definitions than I can provide here, as the propriety of interactions is never a given in queer studies). In the prologue to his *Rose*, Renart writes,

> s'est avis a chascun et samble
> que cil qui a fet le romans
> qu'il trovast toz les moz des chans,
> si afierent a ceuls del conte. (26–29)

> It is the impression of all and seems that he who made the romance composed all the words of the songs, so well fitted are they to those of the tale.

My goal in this chapter has not been to imply that Edelman might as well have been writing about courtly letters—or that I have incorporated Edelman's queer theory so wonderfully that I could have up with it. Rather, it has been to *insert* Edelman's work in such a way as to destabilize, even deconstruct, notions of sameness and difference between the courtly and the queer: to employ this insertion to signal both the recognition and the fervent—even abject—flaunting of contours that lyric insertion represents.

The irony of this chapter's methodology, then, is that the least medieval element I have treated—Edelman's poststructuralist theory—has functioned *like* the most distinctly medieval element: the insertion of lyrics into verse narratives in the thirteenth and fourteenth centuries. And speaking of irony, it will be the subject of the next chapter.

CHAPTER 4

Queer Irony in Chrétien de Troyes and Guillaume de Machaut

The two previous chapters have studied the knotty interactions between narrative levels and segments and between lyric pieces and their surrounding narratives. This chapter focuses on the rhetorical figure most closely associated with incongruity: irony. It does so, moreover, by effecting a seemingly incongruous juxtaposition of its own, considering in tandem romances by Chrétien de Troyes and *dits* by Guillaume de Machaut. Despite being two of the most towering figures in medieval French letters, these giants have never before been brought together.[1]

The association of these authors with irony should surprise no one. Scholars such as Haidu, D. H. Green, and Gaunt have so successfully debunked the "assumption" that "the Christian and scholastic Middle Ages" are "*de facto* non-ironic" that courtly literature now seems about as intimately tied to irony as Lukács famously argues the novel to be.[2] In their studies, each of these critics first situates the trope in relation to ancient and medieval rhetoric, before claiming that courtly letters use irony in more modern ways, too, for which rhetoric cannot account. Each must, then, advance a working definition of the trope. Green's is most concise:

---

1. See, nonetheless, Hoepffner, "Crestien."
2. Quoted in Reiss 211, another important take on medieval irony.

> Irony is a statement, or presentation of an action or situation, in which the real or intended meaning conveyed to the initiated intentionally diverges from, and is incongruous with, the apparent or pretended meaning presented to the uninitiated. (9)

It is not hard to see why irony, defined in this way, would be a good fit with courtly literature. Medieval courts and irony both exclude many in order to create solidarity among a happy few, "the initiated." It makes sense that authors wield irony, since irony requires sophistication, which serves as cultural capital for medieval aristocrats.

Such a conception of irony conceives of the trope as largely constructive. Sure, it can have bite, but irony seems to have "a positive function" in—and for—courtly society, "unlike the admittedly often nihilistic corrosiveness of modern irony" (Green 393). Irony is even more patently constructive in terms of literary texts, where it emerges as a key player in what Foucault refers to as "the author function." Even if we know nothing about the author's biography, as with Chrétien, irony points to the skill of the implicit author; recognizing irony implies sliding a center of gravity beneath a shifty surface. Indeed, it often seems that the more ironic elements of a text are, the surer we can be of the masterful author, lurking behind the teasing façade.

De Man, however, vehemently disputes any notion that irony is constructive. Like others, he understands irony as standing out, insofar as it implies "a more radical negation" of explicit meaning than "an ordinary trope such as synecdoche or metaphor or metonymy" (*Aesthetic Ideology* 165). De Man's original gesture is, though, to harness irony's particular stress on deviation and negation to argue that it figures the ineradicable threat of linguistic deviancy and the negation of any positive affirmation. If irony raises the possibility of not grasping what is meant, argues de Man, then rather than quashing the doubt raised by irony by claiming to get it, we might read with the ever-gnawing specter of uncertainty. "But what," he asks, "if irony is always ... the irony of understanding, if what is at stake in irony is always the question of whether it is possible to understand or to not understand?" (*Aesthetic Ideology* 166).

De Man develops his conception of irony by looking, in particular, to Schlegel's *Lucinde* (1799). He focuses on "a short chapter, called 'Eine Reflexion' ... which reads like a philosophical treatise," although "what is actually being described is ... sexual intercourse" (*Aesthetic Ideology* 168). For de Man, this chapter is so compelling because

> it's not just that there is a philosophical code and then another code describing sexual activities. These two codes are radically incompatible with each

other. They interrupt, they disrupt, each other in such a fundamental way that this very possibility of disruption represents a threat to all assumptions one has about what a text should be. (169)

For de Man, Schlegel's piece is emblematic of irony, because there is no synthesis to be had between the competing codes. The persistent interruptions will not add up to anything positive; rather, they color the reader's experience with unrelenting uncertainty. And because, for de Man, "irony is unrelieved *vertige,* dizziness to the point of madness," it follows that it impedes, rather than fosters, the coherence of narratives (*Blindness* 215). "Irony is precisely what makes it impossible ever to achieve a theory of narrative that would be consistent" (*Aesthetic Ideology* 179).

I am dwelling on this example for two reasons. One, to provide a taste of deconstructive irony, which I shall argue to be more prevalent in Chrétien's romances and Machaut's *dits* than criticism has hitherto allowed. And two, because it points to an undertheorized element in de Man's work on irony. For despite stressing this particular chapter of Schlegel's, de Man never treats the trope's relationship to desire. He is more interested in how "philosophical" and/or "narrative" systems teeter than in the "sexual" per se.

Edelman's *No Future* contends, however, that sexual politics are not incidental to de Manian irony. In this polemic, Edelman argues that "politics, however radical," necessarily "works to *affirm* a structure, to *authenticate* social order, which it then intends to transmit to the future" (2–3; original emphases). If, according to de Man, irony disrupts positive affirmations and the illusion of authenticity, it would, therefore, be not apolitical but antipolitical. Indeed, for Edelman, queers embody "the radical threat posed by irony" (24), since like de Manian irony, they "figure . . . the resistance, internal to the social, to every social structure and form" (4). Somewhat more precisely, queers represent "the social order's death drive" by flaunting a sexuality divorced from "reproductive futurism" and thus at odds with the logic of heteronormativity's narrative, according to which desire has "*con*sequence" (3, 35; original emphasis). "*Embodying* the remainder of the Real internal to the Symbolic order" or "the drive" (to invoke the Lacanian concepts on which Edelman draws), queerness therefore means puncturing desire's promise of eventual meaningfulness with the disruptive allure of meaningless pleasure: with a bliss (*jouissance*) that "exposes sexuality's inevitable coloration by the drive: its insistence on repetition, its stubborn denial of teleology, its resistance to determinations of meaning . . . and, above all, its rejection of spiritualization through marriage to reproductive futurism" (25, 27; original emphasis).

While *No Future* is best known for this last element, the motif of the child will not be my emphasis here. Rather, I am interested in how deconstructive irony and the deviance of desire intersect. Accordingly, this chapter has two aims: one, to explore how two romances attributed to Chrétien (*Erec et Enide* and *Cligés*) and several *dits* by Machaut (the *Jugement* cycle and the *Voir Dit*) are haunted by a radically negative, deconstructive irony, which neither fosters the coherence of narratives nor plays into the "author function." And two, to resist a tendency to associate irony with aesthetics by stressing the trope's queerness: its relentless antagonism toward the coherence or meaningfulness of desire, its imbrication with "the drive."

CHRÉTIEN

Erec et Enide

Chrétien's first romance, usually dated to 1170, is perhaps a counterintuitive place to begin, because it has been described as his least ironic text (Maddox and Maddox 118–19). It also appears loudly to proclaim the "author function" at the end of its famous prologue:

> Des or comencerai l'estoire
> Que toz jors mais iert en memoire
> Tant con durra crestïentez.
> De ce s'est Crestïens ventez. (23–26)

As of now I will begin the story that will remain in memory as long as Christianity lasts. Of this Chrétien has boasted.

These lines nonetheless match up nicely with Edelman's contention that "politics" always works "to *affirm* a structure, to *authenticate* social order, which it then intends to transmit to the future." The futurism of these verses is hardly subtle. *Erec et Enide*'s prologue serves, moreover, not only to "affirm" and "authenticate" Chrétien's achievement but also to anchor it in notions of "structure" and "order," as the author here famously coins the principle of "conjunture": "Crestïens de Troies ... trait [d']un conte d'aventure / Une mout bele conjunture" [Chrétien de Troyes extracts from an adventure story a most beautiful composition] (9, 13–14). Kelly has, in particular, traced this notion of "conjunture" back to the Horatian *iunctura,* where it means something like the art of elegant transitions ("Source" and *Art* 15–31). He then argues that "conjointure" defines the art of medieval romance, as the romancer is tasked with weaving together disparate *matières* in an elegant and meaningful way. Structure and ordering play no small part, then, in "affirming" and "authenticating" the achievement Chrétien bestows to posterity; and if Chrétien's literary feat has proven so successful, this is no doubt to some extent because it resonates with what Edelman views as the deep structure of politics.

Yet, something else is also happening here, as this "miniature treatise on literary theory" (Maddox 18) curiously rubs up against the ensuing storyline. For example, it begins,

> Li vilains dit en son respit
> Que tel chose a l'en en despit,
> Qui mout vaut mieuz que l'en ne cuide.
> Por ce fait bien qui son estuide
> Atorne a sens, quel que il l'ait;
> Car qui son estude entrelait,
> Tost i puet tel chose taisir
> Qui mout venroit puis a plesir. (1–8)

> According to the peasant's proverb, one may hold in disdain something that is worth far more than one might think. For this reason, he does well who turns his learning into something clever, whatever this may be; for he who neglects his wisdom may easily keep silent something that could later produce much pleasure.

"It is not an exaggeration," declares Tony Hunt, "to say that the dialectic of the work (*teisir/dire, celer/aprandre*) can be derived from the prologue" ("Chrétien's Prologues" 156). As Hunt observes (156), this "dialectic" is most noteworthy for the "series of *jeux-partis*" where Enide "ne set le quel saisir, / Ou le parler ou le taisir" [doesn't know which to choose: to speak or to be silent] (3723–24). The prologue seems, then, to be saying something about the ensuing storyline, which it doesn't quite come out and say; it is itself hovering between *dire* and *teisir* and the related opposition between *celer* [to hide] and *aprandre* [to reveal/teach] that Chrétien is about to invoke. Other turns of phrase resonate, too, with the ensuing drama. In the fateful conversation where Enide explains to Erec that he is perceived as having become "recreanz" [cowardly] (2462), Enide emphasizes, for instance, the verb *entrelaissier*, saying, "granz damages est de vos / Que vos armes entrelessiez" [it is a great pity for you that you abandon your arms] (2542–43). The peasant's proverb may also be understood as a subtle yet poignant indictment of Erec's behavior throughout the romance. If one "thing" is worth more than "someone believes" in this text, it is surely Enide, whom Erec "holds in disdain" until she proves that she "is worth far more" than he realized.[3]

The ostensibly literary terms in this prologue trip, too, over those of the ensuing tale. According to the historian John Baldwin (188), *coniunctio* is one of the common terms used in high medieval medical treatises to describe coitus. It is also, as the theologian Philip Reynolds has shown (483–85), a key term in twelfth- and thirteenth-century definitions of marriage, where it refers to the initiation of marriage and/or to the "resulting bond" between spouses. As this is a marriage with too much physical affection, and then seemingly too little emotional affection, it is no given that *Erec et Enide* is describing a *bele conjunture* from one end to the other (cf. Burns 162). It is also unclear whether Chrétien has transformed a *conte d'aventure* into a *bele conjunture*. When a triumphant Erec finally narrates his story to the court, he ticks off a series of battles against foes, and his speech is prefaced with, "Ses aventures lor reconte" [He recounted his adventures to them] (6468) and followed by, "Ses aventures lor conta" (6485). Perhaps, then, Chrétien's boasts about his achievement don't quite hold up? This is a text that repeatedly warns of the dangers of bragging—Erec quips, "Tex vaut petit, qui mout se loe" [He is worth little, who extensively praises himself] (4432)—and of counting one's chickens before they have hatched: "Tex cuide avoir / Le jeu joé, qui puis le pert" [He may think he's finished the game, who then loses it] (5916–17).

"With irony," writes Gaunt, "as soon as the ironic meaning has been deduced, the literal meaning is undermined and, in part at least, discarded" (*Troubadours* 23). While I am not claiming that the literal, and literary, meaning of this prologue should be discarded, it is undermined by a "surplus" of "sen" (Marie de France, "Prologue," v. 16, p. 22), which lurks in its elusive engagement with the ensuing *matière*. Or, more precisely, these lines appear infested by what Edelman calls "the constitutive *surplus*" that characterizes "the drive" (*No Future* 10). Following Lacan, Edelman conceives of "the drive" as the ineradicable lure of antisocial pleasure, which haunts normativity's pretensions as an "irrepressible remainder" (10). To get only slightly ahead of ourselves, "the drive" is akin to the *surplus* of pleasure that Erec experiences in *dosnoier* [taking pleasure] (2434) with Enide; for the licit institution of marriage is tainted by an involuted overindulgence, which is in excess to Erec's marital responsibilities and in opposition to his "social viability" (*No Future* 9). Similarly, *Erec et Enide*'s prologue contains a *surplus* that appears not to partake of Chrétien's public responsibilities but instead to reflect a more private, involuted, and disruptive pleasure in engaging the upcoming *matière*.

---

3. For Enide and the formulation "tel chose," see Burns 161–62.

Indeed, if the prologue is tinged with irony, it is surely because the narrative is so concerned with the perverse *surplus*, which casts irony on any attempt to render desire productive, notably via the institution of marriage. Such issues were, moreover, generating much anxiety around Chrétien's time. Twelfth-century thinkers generally held that marriage "first began in Paradise, where it was instituted for the procreation of children"; yet, "after the Fall, marriage was reinstituted outside of Paradise . . . this time for protection against fornication" (Brundage 271). Theologians and canonists realized, however, that rather than protecting against fornication, marriage could abet it. In fretting over the issue of "immoderate marital affection," Peter Lombard, Gratian, and many others look to the same passage from Saint Jerome's *Adversus Jovinianum*, where he writes,

> Hence Sextus says in his *Sentences*, "The man who loves his wife too ardently is an adulterer. Of course, any love for someone else's wife is sinful, but so is too much love for one's own." A wise man ought to love his wife with discretion, not with passion; he will control the force of his desire, lest he be carried away headlong into sexual intercourse. There is nothing more foul than to love one's own wife as if she were a mistress. (182–84)[4]

Erec et Enide is engaging with this issue of much concern to contemporary canon law. It may well even be gesturing toward this passage of Jerome's, since the romance pairs terms for wife (*fame* or *dame*) with those for lover (*amie* or *drue*) four times (2434–35, 3322–23, 3478, 4682–83). These terms most forcefully collide when Count Oringle asks Enide whether she is Erec's "fame" or "amie," to which she responds, "l'un et l'autre" [the one and the other] (4682–83).

Like canon law, *Erec et Enide* is therefore concerned with the irony, whereby marriage, which serves as "affirmation" and "authentication" of "social order," is also haunted by a perverse *surplus* that risks unraveling its pretensions to order. The text's representation of sex corroborates this hypothesis. As if to insist that the romance is interested not in the illicit per se but rather in how perverse irony haunts and infests the licit, the text only includes two sex scenes, neither of which appears "immoderate." In the first, Erec and Enide consummate their marriage, and in the second, they seal their reconciliation: "Or ont lor amor refermee" [Now, they reaffirmed their love] (5249). The irony of the latter scene is striking, as indulging their desire, formerly the

---

4. See Samuelson, "Affirming Absence" 83, for sources that cite this passage. This paragraph draws on this piece, pp. 83–84.

problem in this marriage, now figures its resolution. Yet, irony perhaps more perversely rears its head when Erec and Enide first consummate their nuptials.

> Quant vuidie lor fu la chambre,
> Lor droit rendent a chascun mambre;
> Li huil d'esgarder se refont,
> Cil qui d'amors la voie font
> Et lor message au cuer envoient,
> Car mout lor plait quanque il voient.
> Aprés le message des iauz
> Vint la douceurs, qui mout vaut miauz,
> Des baisiers qui amors atraient . . .
> De baisier fu li premiers jeus;
> Et l'amors qui iert entr'aux deus,
> Fist la pucele plus hardie:
> De rien ne s'est acohardie,
> Tot soffri, que que li grevast.
> Ainçois que ele se levast,
> Ot perdu le non de pucele;
> Au matin fu dame novele. (2085–93; 2097–104)

When the chambers were cleared for them, they rendered the debt due to each member. Their eyes are invigorated by contemplation—these eyes which open the path to love, and send their message to the heart—as they are so pleased by all they see. After the message from the eyes, comes the sweetness, worth far more, of the kisses that bring love forth. Kisses were the foreplay, and the love that united them made the maiden all the bolder: she did not recoil in fear from anything; she endured all, however much it hurt her. Before she had risen from bed, she had lost the title "maiden." In the morning, she was a new lady.

This passage initially seems orderly. Things neatly progress from the eyes, to the heart, to kissing, to coitus; consummation caps the larger sequence of the rites of initiation of marriage; and this, in turn, reflects marriage's role in fostering order in society. A perverse *surplus* nonetheless haunts these verses. For example, the line "Lor droit rendent a chascun mambre" [They rendered the debt due to each member] appears to be an allusion to the conjugal debt; yet, for Gratian and others, the debt only comes into effect after the consummation of marriage (Brundage 241). It is also not rendered unto "members," which are, instead, associated with perversion; twelfth-century thinkers spoke of the "law" and "tyranny" of "members," *lex membrorum* and *tyrannus membrorum*, both associated with carnal sin.⁵ Even stranger is the description of Enide's experience of coitus, which announces her upcoming peripeties. "Because of love," Enide will become "emboldened" and "suffer greatly, whatever it costs her." As the romance concludes, she ostensibly emerges as a "new lady." These lines contain a worrisome *surplus*, then, because the drama in store for the couple seems to be curiously embedded in (or in bed with) the couple's seemingly licit consummation of their marriage (cf. Samuelson, "Affirming Absence" 100).

The reader is even faced with a temptation not dissimilar to Erec's—that of overindulging the *surplus* that haunts this scene—or to Enide's—that of calling out a menacing danger. This temptation will not go away, even after "Erec sets out with his wife: he knows not where, but in search of adventures" (2762–63). Indeed, while *Erec et Enide* has been read as a romance "of simple linear structure," where "each encounter . . . marks a definite step toward the reconciliation of the lovers" (Zaddy 611, 610), this "movement toward realization cannot be divorced . . . from a will to undo what is thereby instituted," to borrow from Edelman's description of "the drive" (*No Future* 9). For each adventure, "far from partaking of this narrative movement toward a viable political future," also "comes to figure" a "resistance, internal to the social" and textual, "to every social structure or form" (4). Consider, for example, four of the first five adventures the spouses encounter, which are structured similarly. In each instance, Enide worries that her husband is in an unfair situation, either because multiple knights threaten him or because he is too injured to fight: "N'est pas igaux partiz cist jeus / D'un chevalier encontre trois" [This is not a fair fight, with one knight against three] (2832–33), she reflects, for instance, in the first case. These episodes have been read in terms of numerical progression, as Erec gradually encounters more opponents (Haidu, "Episode" 666–67). Yet, something else is also at stake, since they persistently return to the problem of inequality. So doing, they pick at a dangerous scab. For while the text has presented Erec and Enide as "igal et per" [equals and peers] (1500), Enide hardly seems to stand on equal footing in relation to her husband (Burns 168–69). When, then, Enide offers such observations as, "ne fu pas igaus la joste, / Que cist fu foibles et cil forz" [the joust was not equal, since the one was weak and the other strong] (5010–11), her comments also, and ironically, resonate with her unjust marital situation. The movement toward marital reconciliation and Erec's political "realization" is therefore compet-

---

5. Lottin 82, 84, 91; Baldwin 117, 318.

ing with—and haunted by—an irony that evokes the woeful, even intolerable inequality of Erec and Enide's union.

"The drive" is perhaps more vicious in the adventure packed between these unequal *partiz*. Erec and Enide encounter Count Galoain, who is overwhelmed by Enide's beauty. He offers to make her "m'amie chiere / Et dame de tote ma terre" [my dear lover and lady of all my lands] (3322–23). Certainly, he tells her, she can do better than her current arrangement:

> Haÿ! fait li cuens, mout me poise
> Quant vos alez a tel vitance,
> Grant duel en ai et grant pesance....
> Bien sai et voi que vostre sire
> Ne vos aimme ne ne vos prise. (3312–14, 3326–27)

"Oh!" says the Count, "it quite pains me when you are in such a shameful way; I feel great pain, great sorrow.... I can clearly see and understand that your husband doesn't love or value you."

Enide has no interest in Galoain's proposition. Yet, when Galoain threatens to slay Erec, she pretends to acquiesce to him: "Trop ai menee ceste vie, / Je n'ain mie la compaignie / Mon seignor" [I've lived this life too long, and I do not appreciate my husband's company] (3391–93). Lying through her teeth—"El pense cuer que ne dit boche" [Her words don't reflect her heartfelt feelings] (3380)—she tells Galoain that she has not spoken "par orguil" [out of pride] (3364) but so as to "esprover" [test] (3365) his love for her. She then has time to warn her husband.

After she warns him, Erec will reflect that "bien se prueve / Vers lui sa fame lealment" [his wife is faithfully proving herself to him] (3482–83). Galoain, too, finally admires Enide's loyalty and cunning (3638–39), and the narrator notes that "Ses cuers ne fu dobles ne faux" [her heart was neither duplicitous nor false] (3462). Yet, I have quoted at length from this scene, because it foments an ironic *surplus* that undoes this notion that Enide is simply proving her loyalty. As the count "ne repose / De regarder de l'autre part" [is incessantly looking somewhere else] (3280–81), so too is this scene "look[ing] over its own shoulder" (Simpson 48), since Enide's words to Galoain trip over the terms of her predicament with her husband, as scholars have remarked. When, for example, she invokes such motifs as speaking out of pride or testing another, a *surplus* in her language seems to be whispering something about her marital situation, to which these terms equally pertain (McCracken, "Silence" 117, 119–20). Or not whispering, as this scene explicitly brings up the question of the acceptability of Erec's treatment of his wife. Sure, we aren't meant to sympathize with Galoain, whose motives are dubious, and Enide is being ironic when she claims that she has had enough of Erec's mistreatment. This scene nonetheless introduces, *qua surplus,* the prospect that Erec's treatment of his wife should be questioned and perhaps not tolerated. It also functions by embracing irony. Yet, while Enide puts irony to a constructive purpose, her actions and words open the door to a more insidious irony that, rather than working to save Erec, indicts his behaviors.

This sequence even allows us to observe similarities between Enide and the notion of constructive irony, which we can contrast with the mobilization of another, more deconstructive irony in the romance. As we saw, constructive irony is the fantasy that irony, however much it misbehaves, contributes to the "author function" and to "politics." Similarly, when Enide speaks out of turn, as is her wont, she always does so in the name of what we might call the "husband function": that is, to aid her husband, not to subvert patriarchy. Erec finally realizes that "the transgression of his command" is "proof" of her love for him (Dulac 41). This seems, too, to be the fantasy of constructive irony, which, however mischievous or unruly it might appear, is finally "redemptive," a "reaffirmation" of courtly values.[6]

Likening Enide to constructive irony is useful, because it allows us to navigate between the two poles that have defined critical conceptions of her. According to the one, Enide is a proto-feminist hero.[7] This reading can downplay how problematic this commitment to the "husband function" is. According to the second pole, the romance is about silencing women.[8] This interpretation seems to encourage us not to put too much weight on the striking prominence of Enide's thoughts, feelings, and words throughout the adventure sequence. It also risks erasing her from the text, by casting Enide as merely the male fantasy of a woman who comes to relish her own submission. Yet, the dangers of likening Enide's relation with her husband to the notion of constructive irony should be equally apparent, as this comparison risks mimicking the outmoded gesture of morphing a female character into an element of language—and thus also erasing her. I would, however, maintain that wielded carefully, the comparison usefully allows us both to distinguish modes of disobedience—constructive or deconstructive—and to situate them in relation to Enide. Put more simply, if Enide is committed to the "husband function," there is another irony operating in the text and enabled by her behaviors, which figures an immoderate and antisocial *jouissance.*

---

6. Nightingale 140; Buckbee 68. Both terms are used to describe the romance.
7. Armstrong, "Women" 32–37 and "Enide"; P. Sullivan. See Haas 134.
8. See e.g., Ramey; McCracken, "Silence"; Kinoshita, "Feudal Agency" in Stahuljak et al.

As this is a complex argument, it makes sense to look to another adventure that dramatizes this tension between constructive and deconstructive irony. Not long after escaping Galoain, Erec appears to succumb to battle injuries. Enide worries that, "Par ma parole l'ai ocis" [I killed him with my words] (4619), and she begs Death to come fetch her (4614). Yet, instead of Death, another predatory count stumbles on Enide. Overwhelmed by her beauty, Oringle of Limors offers to marry Enide; yet, when she refuses, Enide is "a force donee" [given by force] (4764) to him. Oringle reminds her that she should be grateful—"Povre estïez, or estes riche" [You were poor, and now you're rich] (4795)—but Enide refuses to be. The infuriated Oringle slaps her. Enide screams out, awakening Erec who then slays the count. Those who can escape run off, convinced that Erec is "deables ou enemis" [the Devil or a demon] (4887).

Erec understands this scene as Enide's definitively proving her love for him (4914–25), and there is a certain (constructive) irony in how "la voiz sa fame" [his wife's voice] (4853), rather than offending Erec, saves him. Yet, Enide's shrieking, which "shatter[s] . . . with irony's always explosive force" (*No Future* 31), also jolts the reader. Her shrieks alert us to ironic similarities between Oringle's and Erec's behaviors, since both demand gratitude from a woman who does not have much choice in the matter (Burns 175–76; McCracken, "Silence" 120–21). This sequence even showcases "the repetitive compulsion" and "the violence intrinsic to the drive" (*No Future* 142), since it repeats the initial terms of Erec and Enide's marriage but does violence unto them, by inviting an unflattering comparison between Erec and Oringle. In this sense, Oringle's violence toward Enide is also a violence toward her marital situation. What's more, the horror that is Erec is fleetingly exposed to us, when he is resuscitated as the Devil—even Death itself (4872). While there is the blatant irony, whereby Erec isn't really dead, there is also a deeper irony, as this scene lets us glimpse an Erec without "any redemptive humanism," to borrow from Edelman's description of "the drive": an "impossible and inhuman" Erec, who entirely unintentionally embodies the negativity of "the drive" (*No Future* 100, 109).

Early in the romance, Erec says to Guinevere, "se je puis, je vengerai / Ma honte ou je l'eng[r]ignerai" [if I can, I will avenge my shame—or I will increase it] (245–46). This binary, I have been arguing, does not hold up. While each adventure seems to carry Erec's story forward, each also reflects "the drive" to undo any progress being made. But what, then, to make of the romance's concluding sequence, where Erec twice triumphs, emerging victorious over Maboagrain in the "Joy of the Court" episode before being coronated by Arthur at Nantes? While critical accounts of the romance's conclusion (e.g., Maddox and Maddox 114–16; Haas) generally hold that it trumpets a redeemed Erec—as loudly as the horn into which Erec triumphantly blows—the final sequences may more precisely speak to Edelman's notion that

> the structuring optimism of politics . . . is always . . . a negation of [a] primal, constitutive, and negative act. And the various positives produced in its wake by the logic of political hope depend on the mathematical illusion that negated negations might somehow escape, and not redouble, such negativity. (*No Future* 5)

This sense whereby "political optimism" depends on "negated negations" is particularly striking in the "Joy of the Court" episode. As Erec arrives at a castle, he is greeted by exclamations of, "Ahi! Ahi! / Chevaliers, Joie t'a trahi" [Oh my, Knight, you have been betrayed by Joy] (5697–98). Afterward, he must not only negate this threat to his own honor but also conquer joy by assuring the defeat of the negation of joy, as the peculiarly named custom is called the "Joie de la Cort" because the court will be joyful once it is overturned. To conquer this joy, Erec combats Maboagrain, a knight whose possessive Lady has forced him to "abidcat[e] his sovereignty," trapping him in this orchard until he is conquered by another knight (P. Sullivan 329). Maboagrain's relationship with his Lady is "an inverted and sinister reflection" (Dulac 46) of Erec and Enide's; it is an antisocial union, as Erec and Enide's once was, yet one where the woman calls the shots, as Enide never has. When he combats against Maboagrain, Erec is therefore negating a negation of his own predicament. And this sense of negating negations continues even after Erec's victory. Maboagrain's lady is heartbroken, since she can no longer exercise tyrannical control over him; yet, she is suddenly overcome with joy, when she recognizes Enide as her long-lost cousin.

But if the "Joie de la Cort" episode functions as a series of "negated negations," is it necessarily a "mathematical illusion" that the romance can "escape" and not "redouble" such "negativity"? Upon hearing the name "Joie de la Cort," Erec wrongly claims that "en joie n'a se bien non" [in joy there is nothing but good] (5458). Similarly, I submit, the ensuing coronation sequence is not "joy, which contains nothing but good," as it too is haunted by perverse irony. Or, put differently, this sequence where Erec is paraded around in wondrous garments that showcase the glory of the Quadrivium does not necessarily succeed at "mend[ing] each tear, however mean, in reality's dress with threads of meaning," to quote Edelman (*No Future* 35). At one level, it is evident that the sequence contains "tears" in its fabric, since the narrator interrupts Erec's version of his story to tell us that we already know why he set out with his wife on *aventures*: "Bien savez le voir / Et de ce et de l'autre chose" [You know the truth about this and the other thing] (6472–73). Yet, as critics have long observed (e.g., Lacy, "Narrative" 355), we don't. For Hunt, this is "an egregious example of narratorial *teisir* in place of the process of revelation so lauded in the prologue" ("Chrétien's Prologues" 160). I will say no more about this moment, however, because "you already know the truth about it." Yet, there are many other loose threads dangling about in this sequence. For example, the narrator prefaces his description of Erec's coronation as follows:

> Dont vuil je grant folie enprendre
> Qui a[u] descrire vuil entendre;
> Mais, puis qu'a faire le m'estuet,
> Or aviegne qu'avenir puet,
> Ne laisserai que je ne die
> Selonc mon sens une partie. (6699–704)

> Now I am undertaking great folly, who will attempt to describe it; but since I must do it, come what shall, I will not refrain from saying my bit as well as I can.

If Enide is sidelined in this sequence, the terms of her struggles are not. Rather, they haunt these lines as a sort of *surplus,* since the narrator is gratuitously recalling the notion of hesitating to speak and deciding to say his part, come what will. But why recall Enide's dilemma, when things have ostensibly been resolved—unless to suggest that they aren't quite or that there is more to say? A similar irony haunts the narrator's final intervention, where he discusses the banquet that follows the coronation. He first says about its arrangement,

> Mais je ne vuil pas faire croire
> Chose qui ne semble estre voire.
> Mençonge sembleroit trop granz,
> Se je disoie que .v^c.
> Tables fussent mises a tire
> En un palais; je nou quier dire. (6915–20)

> But I don't want to make you believe something that won't seem true. It would appear to be too big a lie if I said that five hundred tables were lined up in a palace—I don't wish to claim that.

And then about the meals at this banquet:

> Neporquant, se je ne les vi,
> Bien en seüsse raison rendre,
> Mais il m'estuet a el entendre
> [Que a raconter le mangier. (6932–35)
>
> Nevertheless, if I didn't see them, I am able to give a good account of them, but I have other things to do besides recounting the feast.

A few lines later, the romance is done. Arthur rewards all handsomely, everyone goes home, and there is nothing left to say. Yet, the narrator is most strangely bowing out of this romance, which is Chrétien's only completed text not to contain an epilogue. When he frets about not making us "believe something which wouldn't seem true," he necessarily introduces doubt in the reader. The gratuitous detail that the narrator did not see the banquet may also hint at what we aren't seeing—Enide—as well as her association with the visual throughout the romance. It is curious, too, that the narrator's final words are, "il m'estuet a el entendre" [I must focus on something else], which recall Enide's fateful words to her husband: "Tot en perdez vostre pris," she says, "Ne ne querez a el entendre" [You're losing all your esteem and you don't wish to do anything else] (2560–61). In this passage, Erec's *pris* is being celebrated, but like everything else in this romance, the final sequence allows the possibility that it "a el entendre" to remain. "The drive" has not, and cannot, be put to sleep.

Cligés

The romance of Chrétien's considered the least ironic is, then, infested with deconstructive irony, which I have been calling queer because it reflects the force of immoderate, antisocial desire. I turn now to Chrétien's second romance, *Cligés* (c. 1176), in order to explore how queer(ing) irony can also shake up our understanding of a text renowned for its reliance on the trope.

Haidu's 1968 *Aesthetic Distance in Chrétien de Troyes* first advanced the argument that "irony is the reigning tone of" *Cligés*, "the play between reality and illusion its stuff" (89). As Haidu contends that *Cligés* is flooded by irony, so too has his thesis pervaded critical work on the romance, with most studies substantially engaging with it.[9] Yet, despite so much interest in *Cligés*'s irony,

---

9. E.g., Grimbert 124; Kelly, "Honor" 45; Bruckner, "Cannibalism" 31n.9.

de Man would no doubt caution that scholarship has routinely employed common tactics for "defusing" the trope, such as "reduc[ing] irony to an aesthetic practice or an artistic device" (*Aesthetic Ideology* 169). De Man in particular mocks the notion that "irony allows one to say dreadful things because it says them by means of aesthetic devices, achieving a distance, a playful aesthetic distance, in relation to what is being said" (*Aesthetic Ideology* 169). This is, in a nutshell, Haidu's argument about *Cligés*. It is, however, hardly the only way in which the romance has been cast as a "playful aesthetic" exercise. The notion that *Cligés*'s relation to the Tristan material represents "by far the thorniest problem to sort out when dealing with" it suggests, too, that it is primarily concerned with literature (Freeman 98). Critics have also played up the romance's meta-literariness, by conceiving of different episodes in terms of different literary genres. The initial sequence, for example, opposes *chansons de geste* and Ovidian rhetoric, while "the story of Cligés and Fénice begins in the register of the chanson courtoise" but "resorts precipitously to the comic style of the chanson de malmariée" (Grimbert 131). Sustained interest in secondary characters, namely the narrator's "*louche* doubles," Thessala and Jean, has equally fed into the notion that this is a romance self-consciously about romance aesthetics.[10]

Considering *Cligés* in terms of aesthetics nonetheless runs the considerable risk of negating the romance's engagement with anything beyond the literary; it occludes the irony whereby *Cligés* is "the most self-consciously literary and 'intertextual' of Chrétien's romances" and that which is "closest to 'real' life" (Polak 94). It also neglects how irony rears its head in characters' interactions with each other, where it assumes ethical rather than aesthetic proportions, as we shall see. This notion of aesthetic distance generally presumes, too, that the reader is "the privileged observer for whom [the text's] world is spread out without secrets," whereas this is not necessarily the case (Haidu, *Aesthetic Distance* 89). What reader, for instance, knew to be on her guard for the epilogue, where we suddenly learn that the heroes' adventures have caused all subsequent Byzantine emperors to imprison their wives? At stake is whether there is a neat opposition between the illusory and uncertain world of the characters and that of author and reader, who, protected by aesthetic distance, escape infection by radical doubt.

Granted, to observe that criticism of *Cligés* has persistently understood irony in one potentially limiting manner—in relation to aesthetics—does not mean it functions differently in the romance; it merely introduces the possibility. So too, I think, does the first section of the text, which evokes the menace of deconstructive irony without allowing things to get too out

---

10. Quote from Kay, *Courtly Contradictions* 242. See e.g., Freeman 109–19.

of hand. The first third of *Cligés* tells the story of Cligés's father, Alixandre. As in Schlegel's chapter, there are two competing "codes": a love story, which recounts the amorous trepidations of Alixandre and Soredamors; and a war story, where Count Engrés rebels against Arthur, whose victory is assured by Alixandre's might and cunning. If, in "eine Reflexion," the two codes persistently "interrupt" each other, so too in *Cligés* do "episodes of war interrupt the static time of love and . . . interludes of love interrupt the action of war," as McCracken has shown ("Love" 11). But how disruptive are these interruptions? As in de Man's reading of Schlegel's piece, there is a tension between more literal and more figurative registers, although in *Cligés* it seems reversed, since the erotic is associated with lofty reflections, war with physicality or violence against bodies. For instance, Love initially exacts vengeance on Soredamors "Dou grant orgueil et dou dangier / Qu'ele li a touz jorz mené" [for the incessant pride and the resistance that have always characterized her attitude toward him] (458–59), and once Love "a prise bataille" [has begun battle] (574) against her, she realizes she can no longer control her eyes: "Mes euz ne puis joustisier / Et faire autre part esgarder" [I can't govern my eyes and make them look elsewhere] (484–85). Yet, this amorous rhetoric is clearly "looking elsewhere," since it alludes to Arthur's circumstances, where he must assert his control over a prideful and rebellious baron. One effect of the "shared vocabulary" (McCracken, "Love" 11) between the love and war plots is to chide the naïve loftiness of the amorous monologues, consistent with Gaunt's notion that irony "brings down to earth" (*Troubadours* 35). Soredamors's extensive reflections on whether she could possibly call Alixandre her "ami" (1374–410) are, for instance, sandwiched between fierce debate over the fate of captured traitors, whom Arthur wishes to execute, although Alixandre has delivered them to Guinevere. The young maiden's naïveté contrasts with these consequential political deliberations over men's lives. Yet, while de Man argues that crisscrossing codes fundamentally undermine narrative logic in Schlegel, this doesn't seem to be the case in *Cligés*'s first section. The narrator says of the two lovers, "Ambedui par contençon / Sont d'une chose en cusençon" [Both are striving for the thing they each desire] (2209–10). Similarly, love and war seem to want the same thing in this sequence where "passion and political expediency . . . exactly coincide" (Kinoshita, "Poetics" 346). Yet, while Kinoshita contends that the "dialogism between love and war is resolved in favor of the *public* discourse of the epic" ("Poetics" 353; original emphasis), the two registers seem to me finally to interact in the mode of love not war, as they come together "honorably," similar to what Guinevere pushes the lovers to do: "Par mariage et par ennor / Vos entr'acompeigniez ensemble" [Come together by marriage and with honor] (2264–65). Guinevere brings together Alixandre and Soredamors, that is, because, as she says to them, "de .ii. cuers avez fet un" [you have made two hearts into one] (2258). And while, as we shall see momentarily, the narrator contends that this is not really possible, this impossibility initially takes a backseat to the compatibility of the love and war intrigues.

Things don't, however, end here, as this romance where Fénice will fret about being torn between two men is divided between the stories of the father and the son. In this next generation, irony flares up even more, particularly viciously casting its sights on Alixandre's younger brother, Alis. When Alixandre was presumed dead, Alis was crowned emperor of Greece. Upon returning to Constantinople, Alixandre allows him to retain the title of emperor, so long as he swears never to marry in order not to impede Cligés's claims to succession. Yet, after Alixandre's death, Alis reneges on his word, marrying Fénice, the daughter of the German emperor. Alis is, however, betrayed by Fénice's governess Thessala, who concocts a potion that leads Alis to believe that he consummates his marriage, although nothing happens:

> Tenir la cuide, n'en tient mie,
> Mais de neent est a grant ese,
> Neent enbrace et neent baise,
> Neent tient et neent acole,
> Neent voit, a neent parole,
> A neent tence, a neent luite.
> Molt fu bien la poisons confite
> Qui si le travaille et demaine.
> De neent est en si grant poine,
> Car por voir cuide et si s'en prise
> Qu'il ait la forteresce prise. (3312–22)

He believes he holds her, but he doesn't at all; yet with this nothing, he is most pleased. He embraces and kisses nothing; he holds nothing and hugs nothing, sees nothing and speaks to nothing. He struggles with nothing and wrestles with nothing. The poison was very well prepared which overcomes and controls him. He works himself up over nothing, as he truly believes and considers himself to have "conquered her fortress."

If "an ironic statement depends upon the possibility that someone will misunderstand and take it literally," this is basically what's happening here (Gaunt, *Troubadours* 22). This sequence even exemplifies constructive irony, as this amusing deception both serves a political function—that of furthering Cligés's claims by preventing Alis from reproducing—and implies a nice neat separation between those who realize what is happening and those who don't, "Com s'entr'eus .II. eüst .I. mur" [as if there were a wall between the two of them] (3160).

Yet, the "wall" separating Alis from the protagonists is not perfectly solid, because persistent echoes link his deluded predicament to those of other characters. Haidu first observed, for example, how Alis's lovemaking with *neent* recalls an earlier sequence where Alixandre "Se delite en vain et soulace" [delights and enjoys himself in vain] (1629) with a hair of Soredamors's (*Aesthetic Distance* 85). This is, though, hardly the only instance where the protagonists' behavior is entangled with the terms of Alis's humiliation. In introducing Fénice, for instance, the narrator claims that he cannot describe her beauty, "Que ce seroit poine gastee" [because it would be wasted effort] (2699). Similarly, Alis is up to "poine gastee" here. When the narrator shortly thereafter explains how Cligés and Fénice, though overcome by love for each other, do not share one heart, he also alludes to Alis's upcoming betrayal. According to him,

> Il n'est voirs ne estre ne semble
> Que .I. cors ait .II. cuers ensemble;
> Et s'il pooient assembler,
> Ne porroit il voir resembler.
> Mais s'il vos i plest a entendre,
> Bien vos savrai le voir aprendre,
> Coment dui cuer a .I. se tienent
> Sanz ce qu'ansemble ne parviennent. (2779–86)

> It is not true or seemingly the case that one body contains two hearts together, and if they could come together, this wouldn't seem credible. But if it pleases you to listen, I can tell you the truth about how two hearts come together like one without becoming one.

This lengthy digression comports a *surplus* of *sen*, by announcing how Fénice and Alis, rather than Fénice and Cligés, come together "without really coming together." The romance is even bringing together two moments that won't fully come together, as the lofty courtly rhetoric is elusively caught up in the terms of Alis's unhappy predicament.

Speaking of Cligés and Fénice's passion for each other, the narrator will later digress on how love without fear is impossible:

> Amors sanz crieme et sanz poor
> Est feus sanz chaut et sanz chalor,
> Jorz sanz soleil, ree sanz miel,
> Estez sanz fleurs, ivers sanz giel,
> Ciel sanz lune, livre sanz letre. (3841–45)

> Love without doubt and without fear is like a fire without warmth and without heat; daytime without sun, honeycomb without honey, summer without flowers, winter without frost, the sky without the moon, or a book without letters.

Or perhaps, like a "marriage without consummation"? Not only, moreover, should Alis fear his wife more than he does, but this persistent imbrication of Alis's predicament with the "courtly loves" of father and son also suggests that Alis's situation is tapping into larger fears, too. Indeed, at one level, this sequence speaks to a practical fear: that of impotence caused by sorcery, *maleficium operatione diaboli* (see esp. Shirt 82; Polak 89–90). Contemporary canon law was actively debating whether this form of impotence constituted legitimate grounds for the dissolution of marriage (Brundage 290–92). Yet, similar to *Erec et Enide*, *Cligés* is perhaps less interested in the clerical debate than the underlying issue: here, the problem of the "absence of the sexual relation," to wax Lacanian. For while this scene euphemizes the "absence of the sexual relation" into a good thing—Fénice is right to betray Alis—the echoes linking Alis's predicament with the protagonists' point to how Alis risks casting irony back on them. Alis's behaviors seem, that is, dangerously to reduce desire "to the meaningless circulation and repetitions of the drive" (*No Future* 39). Like queer sexuality as Edelman describes it, they "den[y] the spiritualization that would bathe" desire or love "in the warmth of Symbolic meaning" (*No Future* 44). And so doing, Alis's behaviors raise dangerous possibilities about the potential meaninglessness of all sexual behaviors in—and even beyond—the romance.

This is not, moreover, the only danger Alis represents. His predicament also relates to another equally pressing concern: that of Cligés and Fénice's excess desire. Indeed, the romance fosters a tension between lack and excess; while *neent* happens between Alis and Fénice, Fénice and Cligés take things too far. Like Erec, Cligés even falls into the trap of confusing wife and lover. When they finally get married, Cligés,

> De s'amie a faite sa femme,
> Mes il l'apele amie et dame,

>   Car por ce ne pert ele mie
>   Que il ne l'aint come s'amie,
>   Et ele lui tot autresi
>   Com amie doit son ami ... (6671–76)

> Took his lover as his wife, but he calls her lover and wife, because it is still the case for her that he loves her as a lover, and she also loves him every bit as much as a lover should love her beloved.

Medieval canonists would be appalled by this. It is also, as Sally Burch has insisted, not clear that adulterers could later marry each other (187–89). Fénice's claim that Saint Paul advises lovers unable to contain themselves to try to be discreet (5258–63) further demonstrates how Fénice and Cligés are pushing the envelope, since "Paul of course said nothing of the sort" (Haidu, *Aesthetic Distance* 91).

In *Cligés* as in *Erec et Enide*, there is therefore a sense that "tex cuide ... Venchier sa honte qui l'acroist" [he believes he is avenging his shame who increases it] (2885–86). Fénice and Cligés's vengeance against Alis is, in part, motivated by Cligés's legitimate political interests; yet it goes too far, with the licit morphing into the illicit. What's more, both Alis and Fénice's *neent* and Cligés and Fénice's excess passion demystify Love rather similarly, since both "reduc[e]" it "to the status of the letter," insisting on the gap between the signified and the signifier (*No Future* 37). As regards Fénice and Cligés's relationship, we see this in the romance's tendency to cast their behavior as the literalization of more abstract courtly rhetoric. For example, if Soredamors must "suffer" abstract "assaults of Love" [sofrir son asaut] (932), Fénice will suffer literal assaults because of Love; she will subject her body to a dangerous potion—and then nearly have not the life but the death beaten out of her by doctors who realize she is alive. If Soredamors feels she couldn't possibly be so forward as to declare her love to Alixandre—"Ce n'avint onques / Que fame tel forsen feïst / Que d'amer home requeïst" [It has never happened that a woman was so outrageous as to request a man's love] (994–96)—Fénice takes female affrontery to a whole new level, in concocting the romance's elaborate dénouement. While the narrator reflects, as we saw, on how the amorous Cligés initially fears the stunning Fénice—"Dex! ceste crieme dont li vient, / C'une pucele sole crient"? [God, where does this fear come from, whereby he fears a lone maiden] (3795–96)—Fénice will give one every reason to be afraid of a "simple" woman. And if Fénice claims that her heart accompanied Cligés to Britain and left her as an empty shell—"En moi n'a rien fors que l'escorce, / Car sainz cuer vif" [In me there is nothing but the bark, as I live without my heart] (5140-41)—she will, because of her love, become a sort of lifeless shell after having ingested the potion.

I am not merely echoing Haidu's observation that "brief notations in one part of the romance . . . recall a more extensive narrative development in the other part" (*Aesthetic Distance* 107). Rather, I am suggesting that Fénice and Cligés's antics in the final sequence often read as a collapse, into the level of the signifier, of loftier amorous rhetoric. Similar to the doctors, who should be welcome authorities but instead come off as perverse thugs who beat a helpless woman, the thing—Love—which is supposed to "affirm" and "authenticate" courtly politics is reduced to a troublesome literalness or physicality. This suggests that this final sequence is not merely "low" comedy (Grimbert 134); or if it is comic, it risks taking the joke too far, similar to how Fénice claims, "Je [me] cuidai gaber et feindre, / Mes or m'estuet a certes plaindre" [I thought I was joking and pretending but now I have genuine complaints] (6191-92).

The final sequence of *Cligés* even exposes how desire threatens not to further politics but "to destroy" the political (cf. *No Future* 137). The romance exposes the fiercely ironic proximity between Cligés and Fénice's desire and "the drive" in a series of lengthy monologues that purport to denounce Death. In the first, the townspeople, desolate at the prospect of losing their queen, exclaim,

> Dex! quel annui et quel contraire
> Nos a fait la mort deputaire!
> Morz covoiteuse, Morz englove,
> Morz, assez es pire que love,
> Qui ne puez estre saoulee.
> Onques mais si male golee
> Ne poïs tu doner au monde.
> Morz, qu'as tu fet? Dex te confonde,
> Qui as toute biauté esteinte!
> La meillor chose et la plus sainte
> As ocise, s'ele durast,
> C'onques Dex a faire endurast. (5711-22)

God! What distress and misfortune did bastardly Death inflict on us! Greedy Death, voracious death: Death, you are considerably worse than the she-wolf who can never be satiated. Never before have you so wretchedly swallowed something from our world. Death, what have you done? God curse you, who has extinguished all beauty! You have killed the best and most saintly thing in this world—were she to remain—that God ever permitted to be made.

Lying just beneath the surface (like Fénice) is the irony whereby Fénice isn't dead. Yet there is a deeper irony, as we could substitute Love for Death in this passage, and it would be true. The voracious she-wolf of Desire has taken the empress from the people. And by showcasing the reversibility of Love and Death, this passage risks "removing all beauty" from the world, by taking "the best and the holiest thing that God has devised," Love, and "killing" it, or exposing its "coloration by the drive" (*No Future* 27).

This sequence hints at the imbrication of love and "the drive" in other ways, too. For example, the cemetery in which Fénice is temporarily buried ironically resembles the tower where she is stowed away with Cligés (Haidu, *Aesthetic Distance* 102–3). The epilogue then turns the heat of queer irony up a notch. While Cligés gets his throne and Fénice becomes his "fame" and his "amie," her behaviors, we learn, have disastrous consequences for future Byzantine empresses. Fénice

> Unques ne fu tenue anclose
> Si com ont puis esté tenues
> Celes qu'aprés li sont venues,
> Qu'ainc puis n'i ot empereor
> N'eüst de sa fame peor
> Qu'ele nel deüst decevoir,
> Se il oï ramantevoir
> Comant Fenice Alis deçut
> Primes par la poison qu'il but
> Et puis par l'autre traïson.
> Por ce einsi com an prison
> Est gardee an Costantinoble,
> Ja n'iert tant riche ne tant noble
> L'empererriz, quex qu'ele soit,
> Que l'empereres ne la croit
> Tant com de cesti li remanbre. (6680–95)

was never imprisoned, as have been held all those who have come after her. For never again was there an emperor who didn't fear that his wife would be unfaithful to him—whenever he heard told how Fénice betrayed Alis: first with the poison he drank and then the other betrayal. For this reason the empress is guarded in Constantinople like a prisoner. Never will the empress be so rich or noble, whoever she is, that the emperor trusts her—as long as he remembers that one.

Critics have described this passage as "burlesque, anticlimactic" (Polak 72), "amusing" and "ironic" (Grimbert 134). It is "ironic" that Fénice was "closed up in a tower" to consort with her lover, while later empresses are imprisoned so as to keep them away from Love (Grimbert 134). It is even more ironic that Fénice's "arrogant search for total blamelessness" throughout the text "leads to . . . a posthumous reputation far worse than Iseut's, since she is remembered for deceit by all the emperors of Constantinople" (Polak 91). Fénice seems "caught in the very narrative tradition she sought to escape" (McCracken, *Queenship* 44).

There are also more deconstructive ironies at play here. As we have seen, de Man argues that irony "makes it impossible ever to achieve a theory of narrative that would be consistent" (*Aesthetic Ideology* 179). This epilogue radically impedes the coherence of the narrative, since it is inconsistent with anything that has come before. In this sense, the epilogue itself functions as a sort of "traïson," since it fails to redeem the actions of Fénice, which the preceding text has always treated with compassion. It resonates, therefore, with Edelman's notion that queerness resists compassion's logic (67–109), embracing the unintelligible and the unredeemable. It is, moreover, particularly ironic that the epilogue refuses a happy future to Fénice's descendants. De Man and Edelman both insist on how irony "interrupts" narrative temporality (*Aesthetic Ideology* 178–79; *No Future* 87); it is opposed to the promise of future meaning, which de Man and later Edelman associate with allegory (see *Blindness* 187–228). Yet, in *Cligés*'s final lines, it is futurity that has been infected with the temporality of irony, as it "shatter[s] . . . with irony's always explosive force" (*No Future* 31). Futurity functions, that is, as the perverse *surplus*. It has become the excessive "remainder" that is the stomping ground of queer irony, in this romance where nothing seems able to escape the uncontrollable appetite of "the drive."

MACHAUT

The *Jugements*

Chrétien's romances and Machaut's *dits* may not appear to have much in common. While Chrétien's romances are action-packed, far less happens in Machaldian *dits* such as the *Jugement dou roy de Behaingne* (before 1342) and the *Jugement dou roy de Navarre* (1349). The *Behaingne* recounts how Guillaume stumbles upon a Knight and a Lady, both of whom are suffering. As Guillaume hides in the bushes, the two debate whose situation is worse: that of the Lady, whose lover is dead, or the Knight, whose lover has been unfaithful. When the Lady's dog sniffs out Guillaume, he offers to bring the matter before King John of Bohemia, who eventually rules in favor of the Knight. The *Navarre* opens with a harrowing account of the 1347–49 Plague, during which Guillaume stays at home. Once the air is clear, he goes hare hunting; yet he is soon interpellated by Dame Bonneürté [Lady Happiness] who accuses him of having defamed women in the *Behaingne*. A trial ensues, where Bonneürté and her maidens (all allegorical personifications) trade *exempla* with Guillaume as they debate how men and women suffer for love. Charles of Navarre finally finds for Bonneürté; Guillaume has defamed women, and death is worse than infidelity. As punishment, Guillaume is condemned to write three lyrics, of which the "Lay de Plour" may be the first.

I turn to the *Jugements* because, like *Cligés,* they are flooded with irony. The "problem of quantifying heartache" is "absurd" (Moreau 106), and it is ironic that to win this debate one must prove that one has lost the most. It is equally ironic that John finally instructs the Knight and Lady to "tout oublier" [forget everything] (1981), when the purpose of the debate is to crown the most insurmountable suffering. Irony also colors the *Navarre*. The initial Plague sequence, with its gory "realism," "contrasts ironically" with the ensuing allegorical trial (Boutet 35). In this trial, it is ironic that "both parties compete in the court of Happiness in order . . . to have their exclusion from her realm recognized" (Kay, *Place* 115). The *exempla*, which often seem "totally inconclusive" and "irrelevant," also brim with irony (Moreau 133, 103). There is, too, "the irony of a court poet being 'punished' by having to write more poetry" (Moreau 136 n.76).

As importantly, critics have interpreted Chrétien's and Machaut's irony in similar ways. Like in *Cligés,* irony in the *Jugements* seems to foster aesthetic distance and to feed into the "author function." Indeed, the *Jugements* are, by all accounts, important stages in Machaut's literary development, and the "evolution from one *Jugement* to the other can . . . be seen as indexical of the promotion of the poet figure to a more central status in fourteenth-century literature" (de Looze, *Pseudo-Autobiography* 71). The *Jugements* appear, that is, to foster an increasing distance from the amorous plights of the characters, which is "aesthetic," as it reflects the increasing prominence of the metaliterary (e.g., Palmer, "Metafictional" 33–39).

The *Behaingne*—which even comes to function similarly to the first segment of romances like *Erec* or *Cligés,* as a situation appears resolved over roughly two thousand lines that is then taken apart over the course of the next four thousand—does seem to exemplify constructive irony; for it sets about translating the most insurmountable negativity into a courtly *jeu-parti*. While the Knight says to the Lady, "Mais vraiement / On trouveroit plus tost aligement / En vostre mal qu'en mien" [But truly, one could sooner find relief from your troubles than mine] (248–50), the irony of the *Behaingne* is that the text stands to foster "aligement." Or, put differently, if John will rule that the Knight "plus long / Est de confort" [is further from comfort] (1952–53), the debate itself creates this "distance" from the negativity of the lovers' predicaments. At one level, as William Calin observes, Guillaume's stance as "a spectator, not an actor . . . creates distance and a greater sense of objectivity" (48). Almost cheeky self-referential moments that dot the *dit*—such as Machaut's allusion to a romance-reading clerk, whose name he just can't recall (1474–75)—equally remove us from the pangs of suffering. The *dit* also has a clever tendency to reinscribe terms pertinent to the lovers' plights in the context of the debate. The Lady, for instance, claims "que j'ay plus de tourment, / Et moult visible / Est la raison" [that I am suffering more, and the reason is quite visible] (923–25), and the "visibility" of her logic counteracts the impossibility of her ever again *seeing* her deceased lover. Similarly, the Knight says of his Lady, "en .i. lieu son cuer n'arresteroit / Nés que feroit .i. estuef seur .i. toit" [her heart cannot remain in one place any more than a ball on a roof] (962–63), since God and Nature "loyauté a mettre y oublierent" [forgot to put loyalty in her] (699). This Lady's inconstancy appears, however, to give way to the very definitive judgment of the King, who "loyauté aimme" [loves loyalty] (1305).

The *Behaingne* seems, therefore, to illustrate what Edelman calls normativity's "imperative" to "translate the insistence, the pulsive *force*, of negativity into . . . some stable and positive *form*," which it does by literally putting amorous suffering into poetic form (*No Future* 4; original emphases). As Huot writes, "poetic discourse . . . allow[s] the pain of desire, loss, bereavement, or betrayal to be sublimated into art" ("Guillaume de Machaut" 184). The *Behaingne*'s poetics may nonetheless be more entangled in issues of unresolved suffering than it would seem. For Palmer, that is, the *dit* is "about the anomalous position of its maker" ("Metafictional" 30). Because the poet must "assume the burden of supporting the emotional life of the class above," "the identification of love and poetic services is effectively deconstructed" (39, 30). Yet, like those of the Lady and the Knight, the poet's love—fleetingly mentioned in the prologue (11–12) and then forgotten by the *dit*—might be described as impossible, even hopeless. Important elements of the Knight's description of his luckless love even pertain to Guillaume's predicament. The Knight's greatest complaint is that his beloved, "Mon guerredon ailleurs donne et depart, / Ne je n'en puis avoir ne part ne hart" [gives away and divides my just reward among others, and I get no part or piece of it] (1577–78). Similarly, in the *dit,* Guillaume is not able to have "any part" of the amorous intrigues, which are allocated to others. The Knight describes it as, "ma mort et mon destruisement / Quant je li voy / Autrui amer, et n'a cure de moy" [my death and destruction when I see her loving another, and she doesn't care about me] (979–81); and there is, too, a sense whereby the *dit* "doesn't care" about Guillaume's love life, which is a "destruction" of his amorous pretensions. According to Edelman, "No subject, try as it may, can ever 'get over' itself—'get over,' that is, the fixation of the drive that determines its jouissance" (36). Similarly, I am suggesting that in the *Behaingne,* Machaut might not "get over" the force that desire exerts on him as neatly as it seems.

The *Navarre* more explicitly raises the problem of "getting over oneself." As it was written years after the *Behaingne,* it shows that there is something in the earlier *dit* that has proven difficult to digest. It is not, however, clear what this is. The range of terms critics have used to describe the *Navarre*'s relationship to the *Behaingne*—a "parallel text" and "inverted response," "gloss," "interrogation," "interpretation," "exploration" and "rewriting," "supplemental narrative," and so forth—speak to the difficulty of pinning down how it relates to the earlier *dit*.[11] There is nonetheless some consensus. In the *Navarre,* the opposition of death to unfaithfulness seems to take a backseat to the "significance of gender difference" in the "responses to the sorrow" love "causes" (Leach 168; also Huot, "Guillaume de Machaut"). Perhaps the *Behaingne*'s interest in the "doctrine and form of love debate poetry" even becomes, in the *Navarre,* "merely the source of this poem's engagement with the dilemmas and discontents of authorship" (Palmer, "Introduction" 31 in Machaut, *Complete Poetry*). The *Navarre* may, that is, "get over" amorous issues almost entirely, replacing them with interrogation of the "author function." If so, it would epitomize constructive irony even more than the *Behaingne,* by inverting the negativity of erotic pain into the positivity of Machaut's literary achievement.

Yet, as critics have recognized, the *dit*'s challenging opening sequence suggests that it is engaging with suffering. As mentioned, it opens with an Apocalyptic account of the recent Plague, which "reads like a veritable anthology of plague histories" (Moreau 113–14). Disgusted by the sorry state of humanity, Guillaume shuts himself up in his home. From there, he witnesses "signes et demoustrances" [signs and demonstrations] (156) of "Les meschiés qu'a venir estoient" [the ills that were to come] (168). Dissention rules the world, the

---

11. Boutet 37; de Looze, "Masquage" 205; Palmer, "Transtextuality" 297; de Looze, *Pseudo-Autobiography* 79.

Jews poison Europe's wells, and heretics descend on her cities. Nature is horrified, so "Elle vuet . . . l'air corrumpre" [she wishes to contaminate the air] (282). God then "Fist la mort issir de sa cage" [released Death from its cage] (355), unleashing havoc on His creation.

Because the "realism" (Calin 124) of the Plague account jars with the allegorical trial that follows, the *Navarre* (like the opening section of *Cligés*) appears to be staging a clash of registers. But how "disruptive" is this clash of "codes," to return to de Man? It has been argued that the *Navarre*'s opening sequence serves both to ground the text in historical circumstances and to "distance it" from them, as the ensuing trial "suppresses the political in favor of mystifying it" (Butterfield, "Pastoral" 26; see also Boutet). Yet, the "realistic" and "allegorical" codes are also more curiously intertwined; for like the fateful weather that announces the Plague, the Plague narrative announces important themes in the upcoming text, namely its "pervasive . . . preoccupation with death" (Lanoue 2). Beyond putting death in the air, the Plague narrative also functions disruptively, as the disruption caused by the Plague seems reflected, albeit in a quite different key, in the disruptive relation between the Plague narrative and the ensuing trial. According to the text, for example, once the Jews have poisoned the waters, God "Ceste traïson plus celer / Ne volt, eins la fist reveler" [no longer wanted to hide this act of treason, so He revealed it] (231–32). In the ensuing trial, Guillaume's "traïson" is also "revealed" to all. Both the Jews in this account of the Plague and Guillaume in the trial function, moreover, as "scapegoats," as different critics have suggested.[12] But can there really be a parallel between this antisemitic trope and Machaut's writing of the *Jugements*? Immediately thereafter, the text turns to the Flagellants, who rose to prominence during the Black Death, whipping themselves in order to appease God's wrath. After initially tolerating their behavior, the Church

> Et tous les escommenia . . .
> Pour itant que leur baterie
> Et leurs chans estoit herisie. (253, 255–56)

excommunicated them all, because their drumming and singing was heretical.

The *Behaingne*, it seems, was first tolerated—until the *Navarre* declares it defamatory, even heretical. In a sense, Machaut also flagellates himself in the

---

12. For the Jews as scapegoats, see Girard 7–21; for the narrator as scapegoat, Calin 118.

dit, by relentlessly calling attention to his own shortcomings. But is his behavior comparable to that of these heretics, or does a comparison between the author and the Flagellants itself smack of heresy?

These are genuine, not rhetorical, questions. I am suggesting that the juxtaposition of the account of the Plague with the allegorical trial fosters, for the reader, an "unrelieved *vertige*," which—to some extent—reflects and maintains the radical negativity epitomized by the Plague. The ensuing trial is also flooded by deconstructive irony. More precisely, the numerous *exempla* that comprise the bulk of the *Navarre* are subject to "the drive," as they counter what de Man and Edelman call allegory's promise of meaningfulness—here embodied by actual allegories—with a "stubborn denial of teleology" and a "refusal of determinations of meaning" (*No Future* 27). For rather than proving their points, *exempla* are often remarkable for how their "energies of vitalization ceaselessly turn against themselves" (*No Future* 7). In the first *exemplum*, for instance, Bonneürté draws on natural history to compare the behaviors of the dove and the stork. Upon losing her mate, the female dove is so devastated that she forever shuns society. Yet, upon discovering that his mate has been unfaithful, the male stork,

> Par les nis des oisiaus reverche
> A ceuls qui sont de sa samblance
> Tant qu'il en ha grant habondance;
> Puis entour son nif les assamble,
> Et quant il sont la tuit ensamble,
> Il y tiennent .i. grant concire,
> Puis mettent celui a martire
> De mort qui l'a, ce dit, forfaite. (1678–85)

> seeks out in different birds' nests those of his kind, until he has found a great number; then, he assembles them around his nest and when they are all together they have great deliberations. Then they condemn to death that (bird) which, it's said, wronged him.

Apart from the dubious message—Guillaume seems to wonder if Bonneürté is suggesting that men should murder unfaithful lovers (1815–19)—is the irony whereby the male stork's behavior resembles that of Bonneürté in the *Navarre*. In order to seek vengeance on someone disloyal, Bonneürté brings together many "of her kind," and they have an "assembly" to come up with a suitable punishment. This irony sits uncomfortably with Bonneürté's point, according to which men have recourses unavailable to women. In a similar vein, in the next *exemplum*, Attemprance [Moderation] describes how doctors attend to a lovesick maiden. After feeling her "feet, pulse, and then temples" (1907), the physicians

> Et puis si moustroient exemples
> Des cures qu'il avoient faites
> En pluseurs lieus et bien parfaites;
> Et que plus d'exemples moustroient,
> De tant plus esbahi estoient. (1908-12)

> Then discussed examples of successful treatments they'd used and perfected in different places. But the more cases they discussed, the more they were stumped.

The *exempla* within this *exemplum* only serve to stump the doctors, who can do nothing for this dying girl. This *exemplum* thus (needlessly) alludes to the uselessness of *exempla*, which points to how a "pulsive *force* of negativity" can haunt tales in the *Navarre* (*No Future* 4; original emphasis, punctuation modified).

The *exempla* can also seem to take on a life of their own. Tellers get caught up in "superfluous details" (Picherit 114, referring to Souffissance); or the *exempla* speak to a pleasure in storytelling divorced from meaning and utility, "jouissance in place of access to sense" (*No Future* 37). Their content appears, that is, not only trivial or counterproductive but also seductive, and I have glanced to Edelman in discussing how irony functions in *exempla* in order to plant the idea that the *exempla* are indeed concerned with sexual politics.[13] The qualities associated with the use of *exempla* in the debate do also apply to their content. For example, as the debate goes nowhere productive, the *exempla* almost invariably go nowhere good, culminating in death and/or madness (Kay, *Place* 118). As the debaters' arguments can be self-defeating, so too are the behaviors described within *exempla*: particularly the numerous suicides and infanticides (Dido, Medea, Hero). *Exempla* equally foreground the gratuitousness of passion. For instance, Guillaume tells the tale of a man who has promised his beloved never to remove a ring she has given him. The lady asks for her ring back, so he amputates his ringed finger, which he sends to her. For Guillaume, this speaks to the man's exemplary devotion; yet the lover's gesture is, in Prudence's view, utterly gratuitous: "Car il y avoit .iij. ou iiij. / Voies qui deüssent souffire, / Et il prist de toutes la pire" [for there were three or four

---

13. For their gender politics, see Huot, "Guillaume de Machaut" esp. 179-85.

other options that would have been acceptable, and he chose the worst of all] (2996–98). The same could be said about this *exemplum*—and most *exempla*—in this *dit* where the debaters choose about the worst ways of expressing their ostensible points. In this sense, the almost flamboyant futility of the *exempla* in the debate corresponds to the gratuitousness and self-destructiveness of passion as expressed within *exempla*.

I am suggesting, then, that the *exempla* "fly *through* and not *from*" issues of gender and sexuality, to use Edelman's terminology (*No Future* 135; original emphases). The *Navarre* also reflects on the nature of "the drive" by interrogating the relationship between temporality and suffering. The *dit* is particularly concerned with whether "li maus qui termine / Est mendres que cils qui ne fine / Einsois dure jusqu'a la mort" [suffering that ends is lesser than that which does not end but persists until death] (3067–69). These issues come to a head in Honnesté's response to Guillaume's tale of a clerk who, upon learning that his lady has married, goes permanently mad. She argues that he suffers but momentarily:

> Mais tantost, celle heure passee,
> Sa grant grieté fu trespassee.
> Car combien que lonc temps dura,
> Onques puis grieté n'endura
> Qui point fëist a son cuer touche.
> Et s'aucuns griés au cuer li touche,
> Il n'i a point de sentement,
> Dés qu'il n'i a consentement. (2581–88)

> But once that moment had passed, his great grief was overcome. For even if it lasted a long time, he no longer endured any suffering that touched his heart. And if there is any pain touching his heart, he doesn't feel it, because he is no longer able to consent to it.

At stake is the tension between the negativity of persistence and that of death. If death figures the most radical negativity but is a one-time deal, and persistent pain is worse than suffering that passes or is no longer felt, can something be worse than death? This question is at the core of Edelman's Lacanian-inspired thinking on "the drive," too. He discusses "the death drive's 'immortality,'" which "refers to a persistent negation that offers assurance of nothing at all: neither identity, nor survival, nor any promise of a future" (*No Future* 48). While it embodies the radical antifuturistic negativity of death, "the drive" paradoxically cannot itself die, because its horror results from its unrelenting persistence. The *Navarre,* I submit, fixates on something similar. Sure, Charles does rule that

> de tous les crueus meschiés
> La mort en est li propres chiés;
> A dire est que tous meschiés passe,
> Et pour ce que nuls n'en respasse. (3621–24)

of all the horrible ills, death is the true apogee, which is to say that it surpasses all other ills because no one recovers from it.

Yet, because it spawns tale after tale of suffering—death after death—the debate seems, in a manner, to "recover" from each instance of this gravest of "ills." Each dark *exemplum* keeps both alive and dead the paradoxically persistent "life" of "the drive."[14]

Thus, in the *Navarre,* the purposelessness of the *exempla* in the context of the debate performs the meaninglessness of "the drive." The *dit* also both thematizes "the drive" within *exempla* and interrogates it by reflecting on its paradoxical temporality. This idea that the *dit* fervently engages with "the drive" forces, in turn, a radical reexamination of its relation to the "author function." As we have seen, de Man argues that irony is "an endless process that leads to no synthesis" (*Blindness* 220). Yet, faced with both two *dits* and a trial that take the form of thesis and antithesis but go nowhere, critics have regularly posited a synthesis in the form of the "author function," as it is assumed that behind the ironic text lurks the masterful Machaut (cf. esp. de Looze, *Pseudo-Autobiography* 71). While the jury is deliberating, Mesure says to Guillaume, "Se tu ne mes Mesure en toy, / Elle s'i mettra maugré tien" [If you don't bring (some) Measure into yourself, she'll make her way in against your will] (3562–63). But must the cool light of moderation, figured by the implicit author, insert itself into the *Navarre?*

Kay has observed how the manuscript BnF fr. 1587 contains an intriguing miniature, where in a representation of the trial, Guillaume's head appears scratched out (*Place* 104–5; also McGrady, "Textual Bodies" 15–17). Similarly, we might attend to how Machaut scratches himself out in the *Navarre*. This is less abstract than it might seem, as the *dit* hardly shies away from the shortcomings of Guillaume, Machaut's "comic fall guy and alter ego" (Kay, *Place* 113). According to Pais, "Tels cuide vangier sa honte / Qui l'accroist et qui plus s'ahonte" [He believes he is avenging his shame who increases it and

---

14. For "living death," see Gilbert.

shames himself all the more] (1213–14); and Guillaume gets himself in more and more trouble as the debate progresses, in particular because he "evinces the very anti-feminism he has been accused of" (Palmer, "Transtextuality" 292). Guillaume will, more precisely, accuse women of inconstancy—"en cuer de femme n'a riens ferme, / Rien seür, rien d'estableté, / Fors toute variableté" [in a woman's heart nothing is firm or constant, no stability except total instability] (3020–22)—whereas, as Doubtance observes (3109–14), he is plagued by these very qualities. Interestingly, if we substitute "dit" for "cuer de femme," Guillaume's misogynistic outburst also serves as a reasonable summary of the *Navarre*. This points to a connection between stereotypically feminine inconstancy, the narrator, and the *Navarre*'s poetics, which doesn't fall back on the notion that a "ferme et seürs, / Sages, esprouvez, et meürs" [firm and constant, wise, tested, and mature] (3047–48) author necessarily calls the shots, to borrow from Guillaume's description of the male heart. Earlier, the *dit* has also invoked the possibility of a chaotic disunity characterizing texts written by Machaut. When Bonneürté first accuses Guillaume of having defamed women, he responds,

> J'ay bien de besongnes escriptes
> Devers moy, de pluseurs manieres,
> De moult de diverses matieres,
> Dont l'une l'autre ne ressamble. (884–87)

> I've many texts by me, of various sorts and with all kinds of different subjects—and which hardly resemble each other.

While critics have tended to interpret these lines as "loosely disguised bravado," they may, as McGrady suggests, also "contain an equal measure of anxiety over a corpus" that the author "does not control and, perhaps, does not want to control" ("Textual Bodies" 11). Indeed, these lines, which ostensibly refer to Machaut's burgeoning authorial corpus, also nicely—and ironically—summarize this *dit*, which is composed of many different "matieres" that barely cohere. And if they accurately summarize the *dit*, the *dit* is admitting the possibility of text(s) that function via the centrifugal energy of "the drive."

Responding to Guillaume's story about the clerk who, after discovering that his lover has remarried, goes mad, Charité tells a short anecdote about a man in love with a grafting ("ente," feminine in Middle French). The grafting grows up and becomes a tree ("arbre," masculine). The man's gardener then says to him,

Ne demandez plus que fait elle,
Mais demandez me bien qu'il fait,
Car vostre ente .i. arbre parfait,
Et en tel guise se deporte
Que flours, fueilles, et bon fruit porte,
Dont perdu a d'ente le nom,
Et d'aubre a recouvré le nom . . . (2462–68)

Don't ask me anymore how *she* is, but ask me how *he* is, because the grafting has become a grown tree, and has achieved such a state that he has flowers and leaves and bears good fruit. So it is no longer properly a she-graft but has become a he-tree.

Machaut criticism often effects an analogous operation, morphing the immature protagonist-narrator Guillaume into the mature author: even repudiating the stereotypically feminine inconstancy of Guillaume in favor of the implicitly masculine constancy of the "author function." This amounts to straightening out the author-figure; yet this gesture should not be self-evident. The protagonist and the implicit author, the grafting and the tree, are not one-and-the-same; yet there is no neatly divorcing the author-figure from the qualities he curiously chooses to emphasize in his "alter ego." According to de Man,

> Ironic language splits the subject into an empirical self that exists in a state of inauthenticity and a self that exists only in the form of a language that asserts the knowledge of this inauthenticity. This does not, however, make it into an authentic language, for to know inauthenticity is not the same as to be authentic. (*Blindness* 214)

For de Man, the fallibility of the comic narrator-protagonist (here, Baudelaire), though not identical to that of the author-figure, is similar, since both are trapped inside "inauthenticity." Irony, in turn, is the admission of and submission to the impossibility of authentic meaningfulness—which, as Edelman emphasizes, procures both pain and pleasure. This does not mean that Machaut is not a great author or that the *Jugements* aren't poetic feats. It does, however, mean that these are misleading statements. If Guillaume de Machaut is a great author, it is because these *dits* take up something akin to Edelman's call not to "disown" but to "assume" the pain and pleasure of pointless perversion (*No Future* 24). The importance of the *Jugements* as poetic texts cannot be divorced from the paradox whereby their cohesion is their lack thereof, their utility or meaningfulness their utter inutility and persistent meaninglessness. After all, in these *dits,* triumph and suffering are two sides of the same (damn) coin.

LE VOIR DIT

Reading the *Jugements* as embracing queer irony goes against the grain of Machaut studies, which generally considers them in relation to the "author function." An analogous reading of the *Voir Dit* plays, however, for higher stakes, because it is unanimously considered Machaut's, and fourteenth-century French literature's, most profound exploration of authorship.

It certainly places literature front and center. The *Voir Dit* recounts a love affair inspired by and focused on poetry. The adolescent Toute Belle sends a *rondeau* to the aging poet Guillaume de Machaut in which she declares her love for him. The two then enter into an elaborate correspondence, trading some 58 lyric pieces and 45 prose letters (Hanf 24) over the course of about nine thousand lines of verse narrative. These exchanges chart the yoyoing dynamic of their emotional states, and they far overshadow the one sequence, occurring in the first half of the *dit,* where Guillaume and Toute Belle come into closer proximity.

Like "eine Reflexion," the *Voir Dit* stages, therefore, a sort of interpenetration of two codes: here, the amorous and the literary. Yet, unlike in de Man's reading of Schlegel, critics have not found this to be radically disruptive. Rather, the relationship of these two codes is generally understood in two (overlapping) ways. Because "scholars agree that the *Voir dit* deals less with its purported principal concern, the love affair, and more with the poet's efforts to produce a compelling written record of that affair," love appears to take a backseat to literature (McGrady, *Controlling Readers* 46). Love nonetheless remains complementary to letters. A recent monograph, for instance, opens by reflecting on how Machaut's "art of love is an integral part of his poetry" (Kelly, *Machaut* 1).

Yet, as in *Erec et Enide, Cligés,* and the *Jugements,* love in the *Voir Dit* also communes with "the drive." It has been suggested that the larger *dit* unfolds from Toute Belle's first *rondeau* (Williams 212; Cerquiglini-Toulet, *Engin* 53). In a similar vein, my reading will unfold from the *Voir Dit*'s opening lines. After quickly praising Love and Hope, the narrator claims that for his "gracieuse dame" [gracious lady] (5), whom he loves "Sanz comparison plus que mi" [incomparably more than (himself)] (8),

> Vueil commencier chose nouvelle,
> Que je feray pour Toute Belle.

Et certes je le doy bien faire,
Qu'elle est de si tresnoble affaire,
Tant scet, tant vault, qu'en tout le monde
N'a de villenie si monde
Ne de bonté si bien paree
Ne de biauté si aournee;
Quar Nature qui la fourma
Mis en li si douce fourme ha
Qu'onques mais œuvre si subtive
Ne fist, si plaisant ne si vive:
Assez y puet estudier,
Penser, muser et colier,
Quar jamais ne fera pareille.
Brief, tous li mondes se merveille
De sa bonté, de sa biauté
Et de sa tresgrant loyauté. (11–28)

I wish to begin something new, which I'll do for Toute Belle. Certainly I ought to do this, since she is of such a noble sort; she knows and is worth so much that in the whole world no one is so free of villainy, so attired in goodness or adorned with beauty. For Nature, who formed her, put such a lovely form in her that never before had she made a work so sophisticated, pleasant, or alive. She can study, reflect, muse, and ponder plenty, but never again will Nature make her equal. In short, everyone marvels at her goodness, her beauty, and her very great loyalty.

Irony is simmering here. According to Isidore of Seville, "It is irony when . . . it is desired that something different from what is said be understood. This is the case when we praise what we want to vituperate."[15] Because the text casts considerable doubt on Toute Belle's "loyauté" to Guillaume—no less than five *médisants* accuse her of infidelity—the excessive praise in these lines sounds rather like "false praise." The rhyme "nouvelle / Toute Belle" (11–12) hints in this direction, as "nouvelleté" (5195) will be the term used to describe her potential infidelity (Attwood, "Image" 143). Rather than proclaiming that Toute Belle "douce fourme ha" [has a lovely form], this sequence may, then, "double fourme ha" [have a double form] (7842), to borrow from a later mythological description of Vulcan's monstrous son Erichthonius.

---

15. *Etymologiae* 11.21.41, vol. 1, p. 102. Translated and discussed in Gaunt, *Troubadours* 9–10.

This passage nonetheless serves another function, since much of it applies to the *Voir Dit*, which Machaut may love "without comparison more than" Toute Belle. By all accounts, he "never before made so sophisticated, pleasant, or lively a work," and never again would he achieve its "equal." As critics have shown, one "can study, reflect and muse on, and ponder plenty" the *Voir Dit*. Many a reader "marvels at its quality and beauty."

If the *Voir Dit* comes to "elid[e] the woman and leav[e] only Machaut and his artistic creations" (de Looze, *Pseudo-Autobiography* 100), this may, then, already be the case in its opening lines. This introduces, however, another irony, by calling the text's "loyauté" into question. Guillaume later denounces any *losengier*, "Que un feroit et l'autre diroit / Et sa dame ainsi traÿroit" [that would do one thing and say another, and thus betray his lady] (3195–96). Yet, this may be what the *dit* is doing, as it voices praise of Toute Belle while its principal interests seem to lie in its own craft. As we shall see, Desir is closely associated with doubt in the *dit*, and I am suggesting that rather than overcoming the doubt figured by Desir through poetry, the *dit* twists but retains this doubt, by rendering persistently uncertain the text's commitment to this love affair.

In what follows, I explore how irony functions in the *Voir Dit* by elaborating on the issues raised by this sequence. First, I suggest that the text may be "false praise" not of Toute Belle in particular but of *fin'amor* more generally. I then argue that rather than merely shifting its focus from love to letters in the mode of constructive irony, the *dit* invites a critical analysis of this turn. I back up this assertion by showing how "the drive," far from being quashed by the text's meta-literariness, ironically comes to overwhelm the *Voir Dit*.

Granted, if critics have long understood the *Voir Dit*'s praise of love as perhaps sincere, perhaps half-hearted, the *dit* has never been read as a critique of *fin'amor*. It nonetheless resonates with poststructuralist thinking which has interrogated sexuality's reliance on discourse. Machaut does not, of course, invent the notion of discourse inspiring desire; yet the *Voir Dit* distinguishes itself from other medieval texts about *amor de lonh* in how adamantly it sets about deconstructing this love, by showing how what constitutes it— discursivity—also constitutes its undoing. "Mais en li est de moi faire ou deffaire" [But in her is the power to make or unmake me] (1306), Guillaume says of his beloved, but this notion better describes language's role in the affair. Because Toute Belle falls for Guillaume, "pour les biens que de vous dit / Tous li mondes communement" [because of all the good things that everyone is constantly saying about (him)] (210–11), and because the affair is conducted via literary exchanges, it seems inevitable that any claim to ground sentiment in extra-linguistic truth will prove tenuous here. For example, "Je ne ressemble pas le jai / Qui n'a que plumes et paroles, / N'en moi n'a nulles paraboles" [I don't resemble the jay who's only got nice feathers and words; there are no untruths in me at all] (1945–47), protests Toute Belle. This assertion cannot hold up, however, and Toute Belle is so vulnerable to slander, because this is a love built entirely on ever-shifty *paroles*. No less than Foucault, the *Voir Dit* calls out, then, the illusion whereby love exists before or beyond discourse. By the same token, it debunks love's claim to being personal or private. For instance, "Se tous li mondes me looit ou consilloit une chose et le contraire vous plaisoit, vostre douce volenté seroit assevie et laisseroie la volenté de tous les autres" [If everyone encouraged or advised me to do one thing and you preferred the opposite, your lovely wish would be granted and I would ignore those of all others] (XVIII.318), proclaims Guillaume. Yet, the text unravels this opposition, since this affair is blatantly constituted by and dependent on deeds and words of—and for—others.

The *Voir Dit* can, therefore, be understood as critically interrogating sexuality's reliance on discourse. It also seems to have the courtly lover in its crosshairs. That the feeble and self-pitying Guillaume isn't a stellar lover is a staple of criticism. Cerquiglini-Toulet has, moreover, argued that Guillaume fails as a lover because he is a clerk, and loving ladies is for knights only (*Engin* 125–38). Yet, rather than being an insufficient lover in his own right or *qua* clerk, Guillaume might also be understood as exaggerating basic traits of the courtly lover. Indeed, the *Voir Dit* brings to the surface what critics have had to unearth about the mechanisms of *fin'amor* in earlier texts. In his Lacanian reading of troubadour *fin'amor*, for instance, Jean-Charles Huchet observes how troubadours choose "as objects of desire the most inaccessible Lady: she who everything (geographic distance, difference in social class) renders impossible" (111). Hard to fit this bill better than Toute Belle, who is removed from Guillaume by both of these factors. Huchet reasons, furthermore, that troubadours fall for unattainable ladies, because they can only grapple with their wonder and horror of women in the space of the *canso*, which serves both to generate the illusion of the lady's magic and to keep her at a safe distance. Certainly, Toute Belle is both the product of lyrics and kept at a distance from Guillaume through literary exchanges, which frequently dis- or replace the lovers' coming together. In fact, Guillaume's response to his secretary's digression late in the text—"Vous m'avés fait un long sarmon / Adfin que ma dame ne voie" [You have made this long speech to me so that I don't go see my lady] (7191–92)—appears to apply to the larger *dit*, written so that Guillaume does not have to spend much time in Toute Belle's presence. Or, as Huchet would have it, poetry serves to keep female sexuality at bay, since singing the wonder of Love obfuscates troubadours' horror of sex. This is not subtle in the

Voir Dit, either. During the sole bedroom scene, Venus descends, enveloping the lovers in a murky cloud (3988–4011). Instead of seeing the lovers' (perhaps) having sex, we hear songs about love (4032–74, 4172–79). This sequence shows how poetry disavows "the impasse of sex by idealizing" love (Huchet 133). It also illustrates, in retrospect, why sex is so threatening: it fails to satisfy the subject's sense of lack. Indeed, if it occurs, sex appears to change little for our insecure Guillaume.

Rather than simply lacking as a courtly lover, Guillaume may, then, excessively embody many of his traits. The *dit* would therefore be deconstructing *fin'amor* by exaggerating its gestures. There is, nonetheless, a good reason why this negativity toward love has been downplayed: the *dit* appears to exemplify the move, equally inherited from troubadours, of "displacing sexual activity toward poetry" (Huchet 17). Indeed, it presents as a textbook case of sublimation. As in Freud's elaboration of the concept, the subject redirects his frustrated libido in order to produce something socially useful (see e.g., Valls 308–10). Or, to stick with irony and Edelman's Lacanian-inspired work, the *Voir Dit,* like the *Behaingne,* speaks to

> the demand to translate the insistence, the pulsive *force,* of negativity into some determinate stance or "position" whose determination would thus negate it: always the imperative to immure it in some stable and positive *form.* (*No Future* 4; original emphases)

The text takes everything menacing about love—anxiety about women, sex, Fortune—and immures it into the (relatively) more "stable and positive form" of the literary artifact we read.

Certainly, criticism routinely understands the *Voir Dit* in terms of sublimation—or constructive irony.[16] It even participates in this turn from unstable love to great poetry, which it locates in the text; for many literary questions debated by critics seem to reflect amorous issues raised within the *dit*. For instance, while scholars have wondered which literary form inspires the *Voir Dit*—"the narrative unfolds, like a Japanese flower, from the lyric pieces," argues Cerquiglini-Toulet (*Engin* 24)—the narrative raises a similar issue in relation to the love affair; reflecting on its genesis, Guillaume insists, "Que ce fu de son mouvement" [that it was all her initiative] (877). Similarly, while critics have studied which form dominates in this hybrid text, the *dit* repeatedly raises the issue of "Signourie," but always in relation to Love, not poetry (e.g., II.80, 5994). Critics have also studied the tension between "accord" and

---

16. For "sublimation," see e.g., Calin 200; Poirion 176; Lechat 220; Leupin 182–87.

"discord" among literary forms, but the text treats it in relation to the love affair. "Ainsi fumes nous racordé" [thus we were reconciled] (8966), Guillaume proclaims at the end of the *dit*,

> Et grant bien est du recorder
> Quant on voit gens bien acorder,
> Et plus grant bien de mettre accort
> Entre gens ou il ha descort. (8970–73)

> And it's a great thing to recall when people harmoniously come together—
> and even greater to bring people together when there is conflict among them.

For many (e.g., Boulton, "Idéologie") the *Voir Dit*'s real triumph lies, however, in how it brings together different *forms*.

It is important to emphasize how critics have translated amorous questions into aesthetic ones, because it suggests the possibility of proceeding differently. More precisely, we can ask whether the unresolved turbulence of the love affair is satisfactorily overcome in the refuge of the meta-literary (in the mode of constructive irony)—or whether a more vicious, deconstructive irony is at stake. Consider, for instance, Guillaume's repeated insistence that Toute Belle has "saved" him. At one point, he claims,

> Car unques mais je ne vi certes
> Faire miracles si apertes
> Com elle fist a ma personne;
> Et ce si bon renon li donne
> Qu'on dit, quant elle finera,
> Qu'en paradis sainte sera,
> Car bien puis dire en verité
> Que .II. fois m'a ressuscité.
> Car j'estoie tous arrudis
> Et d'oÿr leesce assourdis;
> Et, perdu mon entendement
> Et mon amoureus sentement . . . (818–829)

> For certainly never before have I seen anyone perform such a manifest miracle as she did unto me. This gives her such great renown that, it is said, when she dies, she will be a saint up in Heaven. For I can say in total truth that she resurrected me twice. I had become completely brutish and unable to take in happiness—and had lost my head and any loving feeling.

Today, no critic worth his salt buys this "miracle." Toute Belle hardly comes off as saintly in the text, and she doesn't redeem the limited Guillaume. Yet, an analogous miracle, whereby the *Voir Dit qua* literary text "resuscitates" the insipid love affair, seems to be largely accepted. Poetry, rather than Toute Belle, miraculously morphs a mess into a masterpiece. If, however, we understand the text as inviting us to be wary of Toute Belle's purported miracle, perhaps we should be similarly wary of the miraculous transformation of silly love affair into poetic achievement. Indeed, the text cautions against idolizing both women and art. Guillaume's obsession with Toute Belle's Ymage (statue or painting)—to which he is constantly offering, "loial hommage / De mains, de bouche et de courage, / A genous et a jointes mains" [loyal homage, with my hands, mouth, and heart, on my knees and with my hands clasped together] (1494–96)—is, in particular, unquestionably excessive. Rather than simply being part of the text's artistic self-consciousness, it may be a warning not to fall into the trap of fetishizing art.

Granted, to raise the possibility that the love-code infects the literary-code with the ever-negative kiss of irony does not mean that it does. Rather, it pushes us to think more about whether the literary text functions like the child in Edelman's thought, where the child figures the redemption of the meaninglessness of the parents' (non)relation. This metaphor is, moreover, apt, since the *Voir Dit* lends itself to this equation of writing and procreation (esp. Huot, "Reliving" 63–65). Critics have emphasized how, late in the text, the *Voir Dit* describes two motherless births, which have been understood as "images of the emergence of the poet's craft."[17] The accounts of these two births are nonetheless quite different. The first, relayed by the cornaille [crow] in a dream-sequence, tells the story of Erichtonious.[18] Failing to consummate his desire for Athena, Vulcan "son germe en terre espandi" [let his seed spill on the earth] (7831). Afterward, the earth conceives a monstrous child, which Pallas stashes away in a chest that ought forever to remain closed. The other motherless child fares better. After the corbiaus [raven] has informed Apollo about Coronis's "avoutire" [adultery] (7961), he mortally wounds her. Dying, she tells him that she is carrying his child. Apollo removes this child from inside her, who "fu puis de moult grant renon" [went on to be very distinguished] (8027):

---

17. Cerquiglini-Toulet, *Engin* 154; also Leupin 181–82; Lechat 236–37; de Looze, *Pseudo-Autobiography* 98–99.

18. Anglophone critics have very often mistranslated the names of these birds, rendering "corbeau" as "crow" and "corneille" as "raven."

> Esculapius ot a non,
> Et si sceut plus de surgerie
> Que nul homme qui fust en vie,
> Car il faisoit les mors revivre ... (8028–31)

> His name was Asclepius and he knew more about surgery than any man alive; for he brought the dead back to life.

The *Voir Dit* is generally understood as Asclepius. Born from the sacrifice of the unfaithful woman, the poetic text, *qua* child, operates magically, healing the insufficiencies in the love-narrative, bringing it back to life as something more meaningful. But this neglects how, more like Erichtonious, the text risks *not* redeeming the parents, instead reflecting the horror of its birth "contre nature" (7856).

At issue is whether the *Voir Dit* overcomes or reflects the parents' desire, which accounts for its emergence. To respond necessitates closer analysis of how Desir functions in the text. Often overlooked, this allegorical persona is the most frequent instigator of trouble for the lovers.[19] He frequently presents as a sort of renegade warrior. The text describes, for example,

> Comment il vient, lance sur fautre,
> Assembler a l'un et a l'autre
> Comment il les assaut et detaille
> De sa lance dont li fers taille ... (3525–28)

> how he comes, lance readied on the felt, to attack both [lovers]; how he assaults and stabs them with the sharp iron of his lance.

Desir the anarchic knight resembles "the drive," insofar as he attacks without warning, "shattering" the subject's stability.[20] Indeed, like "the drive," Desir is destructive. For example,

> Adonc Anemis-qui-ne-dort
> —C'est Desirs, qui m'a fait maint tort—
> Tenoit en sa main un tison,
> Et si s'en vint en traÿson

---

19. E.g., 1766–69, 2386–96, XI.270, 3241–46, 4626–32, 5162–79, 6070–78, 6289–302.

20. See *Engin* 65–67, where Cerquiglini-Toulet considers Desir in relation to two verbs: "courir seure" [attack/assault] and "bestourner" [destabilize/upend]. See the conclusion for Bersani and "shattering."

Et dedens mon cuer se bouta,
Si que prés le manoir tout ha
A force ars, malgré mien, par m'ame,
Et mis tout a feu et a flame. (5162-69)

Then the Devil-who-never-sleeps—namely Desire, who had done me many wrongs—held in his hand a firebrand, and came treacherously and made his way into my heart, so that, I swear, he almost violently burned down the entire manor, despite my best efforts, reducing everything to fire and flames.

The "manoir" that Desir nearly burns down is, though, less the love affair per se than Hope, with whom Desir is depicted as grappling no less than eleven times in the *Voir Dit*.[21] As "the drive" is, for Edelman, opposed to futurity, "refus[ing] the insistence of hope itself as affirmation," Desir is threatening because "because it declines to affirm as certain any future at all" for Guillaume and Toute Belle's love (*No Future* 4, 118). It refuses Hope's promises.

I am insisting on similarities between "the drive" and Desir, because it introduces a new possibility for Machaut criticism: that of embracing "the drive," as Edelman calls on queers to do. For while Desir is "essentially an evil force for Machaut," it is not clear that this text functions to "abaissier le haussage / De Desir" [counter the rise of Desire] (1754–55) with the "*auctoritas* of Hope" (Attwood, "Temps" 246, 249). Instead, the irony is that the *Voir Dit*, rather than surmounting Desir, resembles him in key ways. Edelman, for example, insists on how "the drive" troubles linear or narrative temporality; it "severs the continuity essential to the very logic of making sense" (*No Future* 24). The *Voir Dit* seems up to something similar, as for over a century, critics have fretted over "internal contradictions" and "gross chronological errors" that make this narrative not add up (Calin 169). The rhythm of the text recalls the temporality of "the drive," too, insofar as it is comprised of "surprises and interruptions" (Hughes 195). Similar to the "messengers, valets, and friends" who "burst onto the scene with letters, poems, and portraits," Desir always shows up unannounced—and uninvited (Hughes 195). It is particularly ironic that even Hope appears in this way. Midway through the text, Guillaume encounters her, as he makes his way through lands ravaged by the free companies. He is interpellated by a lady. "Toutes fois que Desirs t'assaut, / Je me met ou premier assaut" [Every time Desire assaults you, I put myself on the front lines] (4238–39), she says; yet,

---

21. 1380-83, XI.270, XVI.308, 3521-36, 4238-43, 4358-65, 4491-92, 4546-61, 4626-39, XXV.424, 4893-904.

tu ne me prises un double,
Ne tu n'as encor de moi dit
Rien d'especial en ton dit... (4247-49)

I'm not worth two slivers of silver to you, and you haven't yet said anything about me in particular in your *dit*.

Ironically, Hope is behaving like Desir. Like her nemesis, she surprises and assaults; like him, she threatens violence. And like him, she demands quick and tangible satisfaction of her will.

The *Voir Dit* resembles Desir in other ways, too. "The drive," as we have seen, is related to excess. The *dit* certainly advertises its excessive length, which, as Guillaume says at one point, "is already three times longer" than the *Fonteinne amoureuse* (XXXI.522). The text's length is related, moreover, to its fondness for seemingly superfluous details. To cite but one, Guillaume mentions to Toute Belle how, "Je vous fais faire aucune chose a Paris, laquele je ne puis avoir si tost come je cuidoie pour la mortalité" [I'm having something made for you in Paris, but I can't get it as quickly as I thought because of the Plague] (XXXV.572), later adding, "On m'a dit que li orfevres est mors, si croi que j'arai perdu ma besongne et mon or" [I was told that the goldsmith has died, so I'll probably have lost my work and my gold] (XLI.680). Critics once interpreted such details as evidence that the story was autobiographical. More recently, they have been understood as Barthesian *effets de réel*, fostering the illusion of realism.[22] Yet they might also be *effets de Réel*, to risk a neologism that combines the Barthesian notion with Lacan's Real. For rather than simply being contingent, such details—as the preceding examples concisely express— give the impression of something particular, chaotic, futile, and/or unnecessary, which does not have its place in the symbolic order of the narrative. Such superfluous (*surplus*) details account, furthermore, for much of the text's repetitiveness, which it seems to embrace. As Guillaume says early in the text,

Et s'aucunes choses sont dittes
Deulz fois en ce livre ou escriptes,
Mi signeur, n'en haiez merveille... (508-10)

And if some things are said or written twice in this book, you shouldn't, my lords, be astonished.

---

22. E.g., Calin 172; Cerquiglini-Toulet, *Engin* 42; de Looze, *Pseudo-Autobiography* 98.

According to Edelman, the "repetition compulsion" is the mode of "the drive" (*No Future* 142). By embracing irregular repetition, the text is not necessarily merely submitting to Toute Belle's wish that everything be included in it, then, but also signifying its openness to inappropriate *redites*, to use the medieval term (cf. Kelly, *Machaut* 4, 7–8). Or more generally, it is submitting to the disorder of "the drive." Guillaume says at one point,

> Car cilz qui aimme par amours
> Ha des joies et des clamours
> Et des diverses aventures
> Et des joieuses et des dures,
> Des grans desirs et des pensees
> Diversement entremellees. (1568–73)

For he who loves as a lover has joys and tumults and many sorts of experiences—some joyous, some painful—variously mixed together with many great desires and worries.

A description of the lover subject to Love, this is also one of the *Voir Dit*. Literary forms, allusions, contingent details, sentimental reflections, and so forth are "diversement entremellees."

Despite singing the praises of Hope, the *Voir Dit* therefore ironically resembles, in many ways, Desir. This argument nonetheless necessitates a precision, because the text's relationship to Fortune has been of particular interest to scholars. Cerquiglini-Toulet has notably advanced that the *dit* is modeled on Fortune's wheel (*Engin* 56–89). Since both Fortune and Desir are similarly "harmful forces" (Cerquiglini-Toulet, *Engin* 68), why emphasize Desir, when Fortune dominates the final segment of the *dit*? Both because the elements just rehearsed seem, on the whole, more closely related to Desir than Fortune (Fortune is not, for example, associated with excess per se) and because there is a tendency to conceive of Fortune in the mode of constructive irony. Cerquiglini-Toulet, for instance, understands the wheel of Fortune as "a rhythmic model" that becomes a source of "harmony" for Machaut (*Engin* 76, also 57). Representing the form of the wheel of Fortune can paradoxically become a means of rising above Fortune's instability, by finding geometric order. There is, however, no harmonizing Desir's antics, which are (therefore) a graver threat to these lovers and to the text's pretensions to order.

Another objection, though: could the *Voir Dit* really be about Desir, when it seems so phobic of sexual activity? The text may be less prudish than many of its critics, as Calin has suggested (176). More thoroughly, Huot has shown how studying the *Voir Dit* in relation to the *Rose* brings out an eroticism, often verging on the obscene, in Machaut's text. As she suggests, this sits uncomfortably with a certain image of him as prudish ("Reliving" 52–53).

It would nonetheless be a stretch to argue that the *Voir Dit* is focused on sexual behaviors. This does not, however, detract from its queerness, which lies in the irony whereby the ostensible turn away from sexual behavior augments rather than quashes its engagement with "the drive." This is what has been at stake in pointing out similarities between Desir and the *dit*. It is also a movement that the text fosters within itself, as what would appear to be a turn away from the love affair within the narrative does not "escape" but "redoubles" the negativity of "the drive," to return to Edelman's terminology. More precisely, the slew of *exempla* that dominate the final third of the text have often been seen as leaving the love affair behind: "The lover-narrator gives way to the clerk," writes Lechat (215). Yet, like in the *Navarre*, the *exempla* retain key characteristics of "the drive," such as the unflagging refusal to be productive or meaningful. At instances, we see this within *exempla*. The crow's plea to the raven not to be a bearer of bad news fails, for example, to alter the bird's behavior in any way. More generally, the text signals these *exempla*'s engagement with uselessness by refusing explicitly to connect them to Guillaume's predicament. Guillaume's secretary believes, for example, that it would be unadvisable for Guillaume to go to Toute Belle, because he is weak, the weather treacherous, and the countryside unsafe. He (therefore?) launches into an account of Circe's unrequited love for Picus, who rebuffs her for Canens. The secretary concludes,

> Mais de Circé l'enchantement
> Ne de Piquus le hardement
> Ne de Caneüs le chanter
> Ne porroient si enchanter
> Le vent, le froit et les Compagnes
> Qui sont au bois et aus champagnes,
> Qu'il vous menassent la seür
> Sens avoir aucun maleür. (6734–41)

> But neither Circe's spells, Picus's boldness, nor Canens's singing would be able to so enchant the wind, the cold, and the free companies—who are in the woods and the countryside—that you would be able to make it there safely, without having some mishap.

As, for the secretary, there should be no coming together of Guillaume and Toute Belle, so too is there no meaningful coming together of the *fiction* and Guillaume's predicament. If the *Voir Dit* is about the absence of the sexual relation (to return to Lacan), this *exemplum*—like others—extends this problematic, by having no satisfactory relation with Guillaume's situation.

Or, I should say, no explicit relation to it. For the *exempla* also resemble "the drive," by "excee[ding]" their "use-value in the service of signification" (*No Future* 65), fostering an ironic *surplus* that, as critics have observed, does pertain to Guillaume's predicament. This is particularly pronounced in the crow's and raven's tales, the ostensible moral of which is that bad news will never be well received. Yet, there is a "flagrant discrepancy between the lesson taken from the story and the fable itself," as Lechat, for example, remarks of the raven's tale (231). "The narrative highlights Coronis's infidelity at least as much—more, even—than the dangers of slander" (231).

Not unlike the raven and the crow, the *exemplum* says what it shouldn't say about Guillaume and Toute Belle's (non)relationship. *Exempla* can also say what they shouldn't say about the *Voir Dit*. This is notably the case in the tale of Polyphemus, which, "in a manner similar to the character, assumes a gigantic place and importance" in the text (Cerquiglini-Toulet, "Polyphème" 221). The secretary's version of this myth, indebted to books XIII and XIV of the *Ovide moralisé* (Lechat 243), begins with an account of the one-eyed giant's cannibalism. The secretary then explains how Polyphemus was blinded by Ulysses. Finally, the myth loops back to the giant's beloved, Galatea, who relays "la chanson au dÿable" [the devil's song] (7149). In this roughly 250-line lyric, copied almost verbatim from the *Ovide moralisé* (Thomas 384–94), Polyphemus notably praises his own beauty, while insisting on the ugliness of men less hairy than he.

Critics have pointed out the irony, whereby Guillaume resembles Polyphemus. Both are *borgnes* and less than handsome; both are clerks.[23] Yet, the larger irony is that this *exemplum* resembles the *Voir Dit*: that as "nothing can escape" the giant's fangs of death ["rien ne li puet eschaper"] (6758), the *Voir Dit* risks being devoured by this myth, which challenges the critic to swallow the truth, whereby the greatest masterpiece of fourteenth-century poetry is, like Polyphemus's mouth, also "Puant comme charongne de mors" [stinking of dead corpses] (6774) or spewing the ugly song of "the drive." More precisely, this fable raises the possibility of resisting what Edelman calls "the lure of redemptive humanization," instead embracing the "impossibility" and "inhumanity" of "the drive" (109). Certainly, there is no redeeming the monstrous Polyphemus. Try as he might, he cannot convince Galatea—or the secretary, or us—that he or his love is beautiful. Perhaps more importantly, the

---

23. Cerquiglini-Toulet, *Engin* 167, 245; "Polyphème"; Leupin 186; Singer 180–83; Calin 180–81.

giant's *song* is not redeemed, either. Indeed, according to Cerquiglini-Toulet's wonderful reading of it ("Polyphème," esp. 224–25, 227), the myth shows how poetry can commune with death rather than life, presence rather than hope, and the material rather than the transcendent. Yet, Cerquiglini-Toulet—giant on whose shoulders I am standing here—seems to stop short of forcefully applying this analysis to the larger *Voir Dit*. But why would the *Voir Dit* foreground this myth, if it didn't say something about it? Naturally, one wants to find beauty and meaning in fourteenth-century French literature's greatest masterpiece. But the irony is that the *Voir Dit*, like Polyphemus's song, is wonderful not in spite of but because of its ugliness: because it submits to and embraces "the drive."

Over the course of this chapter, three texts have invoked variations of the proverb, "Tex cuide ... Venchier sa honte qui l'acroist" [He thinks he is avenging his shame who increases it] (*Cligés* 2885–86; *Erec* 245–46, 919–20; *Navarre* 1213–14). Analogous formulas exist in the *Voir Dit,* where they are applied to Toute Belle: "En vous est tout de moi faire et desfaire" [In you is the power to make or unmake me] (6122) and "Qui tout me donne, tout me tost" [Who gives me all, takes all from me] (2742). Edelman makes a similar argument about desire. For him, there is a "general misrecognition of sexuality ... as ... securing the collective reality it ... threatens to destroy" (*No Future* 137). This is, too, my thesis about irony. Contrary to a critical tendency to view irony as always to the credit—glory, even—of the implicit author, I have argued that the (aesthetic) distance between the butt of irony and the implicit author should not be taken for granted. In Chrétien's romances and Machaut's *dits,* irony is also what unravels pretensions to structure and order, in both literary and—insofar as it communes with "the drive"—more politicized terms.

This conception of irony can, in turn, be brought to bear on the relationship between Chrétien and Machaut, verse romances and *dits*. If a deliciously perverse irony infests texts by Chrétien and Machaut, it would be logical that something analogous characterizes the relationship between their works (and the genres they represent). As mentioned, Chrétien and Machaut have, that is, not before been studied together, which is surprising. Yet, they have implicitly—and almost constantly—been folded into a similar story; these are two great authors, who speak to the progress of aesthetic self-consciousness in the genres they represent and in courtly letters more generally. In place of this narrative, which is a sort of monumental history, I have not attempted to slide another one. Rather, consistent with de Man's and Edelman's notion that irony functions to undo, not to recreate, narratives, I have been interested in what exceeds and threatens this narrative: in the radical negativity that this narrative fails to stomp out—and the chilling pleasure we might experience from engaging with it.

At a quite different level, the relationship between the courtly and the queer might be productively—or, as it were, pleasingly but perversely unproductively—conceived of in the mode of deconstructive irony. If the medieval courts for which these texts were produced hardly seem (on the whole) to be synonymous with queer politics, it is ironic how these works, which are hardly marginal to the tradition of courtly letters, are so receptive to queer work like Edelman's. Yet, the goal of this chapter—or, for that matter, this book—is not simply to recognize this irony. My argument is not that courtly literature is just queer, which amounts to treating queerness like a sticker we can put in different places; or that it can be queered, which implies that queerness is a modern invention that is surprisingly pertinent, even when looking to the distant past. Rather, I see queerness as "the drive" that ironizes those narratives we have, such as that which holds that the most canonical medieval texts are largely complicit with patriarchy, with resistance only lurking at or beyond their margins. As we have seen, Edelman argues that "politics" always "works to *affirm* a structure, to *authenticate* social order, which it then intends to transmit to the future," whereas queerness and irony perform precisely the opposite work. Needless to say, I largely agree; yet I would stress how queerness and irony upset as profoundly our relationship to the past as they do that with the future. Could Edelman's, and/or normativity's, emphasis on futurism even be a tactic for not engaging with the (queer) disorder of the past? Dinshaw writes,

> It is important to assert medieval indeterminacy because such postmodern interventions [as Homi Bhabha's "postcolonial project"] are hampered by their binary blind spots; the point is not simply to claim that the medieval is postmodern *avant la lettre* but to argue that a more patient consideration of the Middle Ages would extend the range of their inventions and (I'll suggest) clarify their politics. (*Getting Medieval* 16)

Perhaps less generously, and certainly less constructively, I would suggest that the medieval may, in important ways, *ironize* postmodern politics, too.

CODA

~

Slashes

In the opening section of her brilliant *Queer/Early/Modern,* Carla Freccero reflects on the meaning of the slashes in the title. These slashes "interrupt" formulations like "early modern"; they "force a pause" on each term and on its relation to the others (3). "Inarticulable though they may be," they also allow for directional ambiguity, which is at the heart of her project, as it cannot be clear which terms are acting on each other—or how (3). "The slash between *early* and *modern,*" she thus writes, "allows me to admit considerable uncertainty about the question of whether what I do in queering 'back then' has anything to do with 'back then' or not" (4; original emphases).

Courtly and Queer is also, it seems to me, a book of slashes. There are those I have most advertised: courtly/queer, of course, and verse romance/*dits*. And there are others. As concerns the corpus: High/Late Middle Ages. As concerns the methodology: language and poetics/gender and sexual politics, even deconstruction/queer theory. Certain chapters are largely about slashes, too: the chapter on metalepsis, those that describe the knotty relations between narrative levels or segments; or the chapter on lyric insertion, those between the lyrics and the surrounding texts. No doubt the relationship between the chapters also takes a similar form. Indeed, studies of the interplay between narrative segments and levels, on the one hand, and lyric pieces and surrounding verse narratives, on the other, come together—in their methodology and ambitions—but are not the same thing. Likewise, the ambivalent reflexivity of the always-already reflexive subject intersects—in its emphasis on the illogical, the messy, the irresolvable, and the excessive—with the vicious irony of "the drive," without being identical to it. Arguably the most important slashes are, moreover, the countless fine ones within readings: not only those where I am considering different moments in texts alongside one another but also the slashes that position my reading of a given instance in relation to those of other critics.

Even if slashes are "inarticulable," it makes sense, then, to use this coda briefly to reflect on how I conceive of them: what can and cannot finally be known, and said, about the relations and juxtapositions at the core of this book. This despite a significant caveat: it would be inconsistent for all these relationships to be identical in form. If slashes stand for interactions that can be called queer insofar as they persistently embrace ambiguity, then of course one slash is not identical to the next. Rather, the relationship between them would seem necessarily to take the form of other slashes—meta-slashes—in all their resistance to determination.

It is nonetheless important to insist on how, on the whole, this book's engagement with what I am here calling slashes is in opposition to critical modes that privilege our distance from the past. As mentioned, this book resists the temptation of what Fradenburg has called "discontinuist historicism," "or the idea that different periods of time are simply and radically other to one another" (87). In the spirit of exciting work on "post-historicism" in medieval English studies, as well as Freccero's volume or Dinshaw's work, I am wary of approaches where the refrain can seem to be as follows: everything must be contextualized as carefully and locally as possible, and anachronism is the ultimate sin. As Maura Nolan warns, "It is possible to be influenced by a kind of 'pastism'—a refusal to see those moments at which the Middle Ages seem shockingly modern, out of step with the 'medieval' and surprisingly or painfully resonant with contemporary preoccupations" (68). Positing a fundamental difference between the medieval and the modern should, furthermore, give particular pause when it comes to sexuality studies; for heteronormativity's total fixation on difference when it comes to the gender of object-choice—and its tendency, as Edelman and others have shown (e.g., *No Future* 57–63), not to critically interrogate this notion of difference on which it claims to rely—has been so immensely problematic.

Yet, as I have insisted at various points, the juxtapositions of elements at the heart of this book do not reflect relations of identity either. There is an important difference between conceiving of the relation of courtliness and queerness, for instance, in terms of the slash (courtly/queer) rather than an equal sign (courtly=queer). (And the "and" in this book's title leaves crucial room, in my view, for the persistent ambiguity of the relations between courtliness and queerness). The slash and the equal sign even seem to me incompatible, since positing a relationship of identity between terms is in contrast to this book's understanding of queerness, according to which, to quote Edelman, "queerness can never define an identity; it can only ever disturb one" (*No Future* 17).

In part, then, my point is that "*both* sameness and difference are essential to grasping the past" (Nolan 67; original emphasis), or that the "choices" of "queer historians are not limited simply to mimetic identification with the past or blanket alterism" (Dinshaw, *Getting Medieval* 34). Yet, I would also go a step further, as many of the queer juxtapositions and relationships analyzed here take aim at this opposition of sameness and difference, scrambling and confusing it. Lyric insertion is a particularly clear example. I have argued that in Renart's *Rose, Le Roman du Châtelain de Coucy et de la Dame de Fayel*, and the *Dit de la Panthère*, the surrounding narratives are not identical to the inserted lyrics, but they extend their emphasis on the indeterminacy of language and desire. This sort of relational dynamic could perhaps be analyzed in psychoanalytic terms, which I have acknowledged but not particularly privileged in this book. For example, Edmondson (following others) draws on Lacan's concept of *extimité*, the paradox whereby "we experience the most intimate part of ourselves as something exterior, located in the neighbor" (148). The relationship (not) articulated by the slash can also be described in the deconstructive ways that I have emphasized. Indeed, I have been interested in the confusion, unraveling, jamming of notions of similarity and difference, inside and outside, self and other, whether in relation to elements within texts or among baggier concepts like courtliness and queerness. And in my view, queer theory does a particularly good job at, well, queering these oppositions. While I have principally engaged with Butler and Edelman, we also, of course, encounter elsewhere queer desire's radical potential to destabilize, which muddles the opposition between sameness and difference. Perhaps most famously, "shattering, with its connotation of shock and fragmentation—and the implication that that which is shattered can never be repaired—has been," as Adam Phillips writes, Leo "Bersani's word for the ego's darker design in which the satisfaction more truly sought" in sexual relations "is a fortifying dissolution not a monumental achievement" (Bersani and Phillips 93). Bersani also imagines relations "in which the very opposition between sameness and difference becomes irrelevant as a structuring category of being" (Bersani and Phillips 86). Similarly, I would argue that the relationship between, say, the courtly and the queer or between verse romances and *dits*—as well as other juxtapositions in this book—foments a "fortifying dissolution" in relation to each element, and the point is that this "shattering" is not amenable to any neat opposition between sameness and difference, self and other, inside and outside.

This book has, therefore, staged juxtapositions that (I hope) trouble, deconstruct, queer relations between elements in and among verse romances and *dits*—and between these courtly texts and today's queerness. It thus makes sense, in signing off, to consider the sort of relations I envision this book having with other work in the field. Perhaps not surprisingly, they take the form of what I am here calling slashes. This book has advanced the argument that a queerness, which is inextricable from poetic indeterminacy, lurks at the (perverse) heart of—or drives—the tradition of courtly verse narratives from the High and Late Middle Ages. Yet, in advancing this big thesis, I do not mean to denigrate work that operates differently: for example, studies focused on material culture or more local historical issues, or inspired by the work of Marx or Foucault. It seems to me that there can be a tendency, in some theoretical work, to argue that one's approach encompasses all others: think Fredric Jameson's assertion, in the *Political Unconscious*, that Marxism is "that 'untranscendable horizon' that subsumes . . . apparently antagonistic or incommensurable critical operations, assigning them an undoubted sectoral validity within itself" (10). No doubt one could similarly argue that the seductive horror of poetic indeterminacy underlies all critical endeavors, while always complexly engaging the critic's desires—even when s/he is not thematizing indeterminacy or desire. Yet, this sort of argument, which is perhaps unfairly associated with deconstruction, is not particularly productive in my view—and it is presumptuous. There can also be a tendency to view one's approach as haunting others, which won't dare look it in the eye. Scala, for example, argues that in medieval English studies, "psychoanalysis forms the unconscious desire of historicism—its language appears everywhere yet is never recognized as such by the critical subject that speaks it" ("Historicists" 122). Maybe the indeterminacy of language and of desire haunt (some or many) critical endeavors looking for something more determinate in medieval texts. And with Freccero (esp. 17–30), I do think there is a danger in overemphasizing the material to the detriment of the immaterial. But this is also not really the contribution I see this book as making. Rather, while this study embraces the unredeemable negativity of queerness, which puts it in a perverse relationship to various received narratives about medieval French literature—a sort of monumental literary history or critical meta-narrative of courtly literature that I have elaborately critiqued—my sincerest desire is that juxtapositions that I have (and have not) developed here will be useful in other work with different orientations. That aspects of my thesis and/or different readings will enter into indeterminate relations with other approaches: interactions that don't add up but are perversely engaging. Slashes I have not pursued or foreseen.

BIBLIOGRAPHY

PRIMARY SOURCES

Adam de la Halle. *Œuvres complètes*. Edited by Pierre-Yves Badel, Lettres gothiques, 1995.

Benoît de Sainte-Maure. *Le Roman de Troie*. Edited by Emmanuèle Baumgartner and Françoise Vielliard, Lettres gothiques, 1998.

Bernard de Ventadour. *Les Chansons d'amour*. Edited by Moshé Lazar, Klincksieck, 1966.

[Châtelain de Coucy]. *Chansons attribuées au Chastelain de Couci (fin du XIIe-début du XIIIe siècle)*. Edited by Alain Lerond, Presses universitaires de France, 1964.

Chrétien de Troyes. *Le Chevalier au lion ou le roman d'Yvain*. Edited by David Hult, Lettres gothiques, 1994.

———. *Le Chevalier de la charrette ou le roman de Lancelot*. Edited by Charles Méla, Lettres gothiques, 1992.

———. *Cligès*. Edited by Charles Méla and Olivier Collet, Lettres gothiques, 1994.

———. *Erec et Enide*. Edited by Jean-Marie Fritz, Lettres gothiques, 1992.

Christine de Pizan. *Le Livre de l'Advision Cristine*. Edited by Christine Reno and Liliane Dulac, Honoré Champion, 2001.

———. *Le Livre des Trois Vertus*. Edited by Charity Cannon Willard with Eric Hicks, Honoré Champion, 1989.

———. *Le Livre du Duc des vrais amants*. Edited by Dominique Demartini and Didier Lechat, Champion, 2013.

Copeland, Rita and Ineke Sluiter, editors. *Medieval Grammar & Rhetoric: Language Arts and Literary Theory, AD 300–1475*. Oxford UP, 2009.

[Gratian]. *Décret de Gratien: Causes 27 à 36. Le Mariage*. Edited by Jean Werckmeister, Cerf, 2011.

Guillaume de Machaut. *The Complete Poetry and Music, Volume 1: The Debate Poems. Le Jugement dou Roy de Behaingne, Le Jugement dou Roy de Navarre, Le Lay de Plour*. Edited by R. Barton Palmer et al., Medieval Institute, 2016.

———. *La Fontaine Amoureuse*. Edited by Jacqueline Cerquiglini-Toulet, Stock, 1993.

———. *Le Livre du Voir Dit*. Edited by Paul Imbs with Jacqueline Cerquiglini-Toulet, Lettres gothiques, 1999.

[Heldris de Cornuälle]. *Silence: A Thirteenth-Century Romance*. Edited by Sarah Roche-Mahdi, Michigan State UP, 1992.

Jakemés. *Le Roman du Châtelain de Coucy et de la Dame de Fayel*. Edited by Catherine Gaullier-Bougassas, Champions classiques, 2009.

[Jaufre Rudel]. *Les Chansons de Jaufré Rudel*. Edited by Alfred Jeanroy, 2nd ed., Honoré Champion, 1965.

Jean Froissart. *La Prison amoureuse*. Edited by Anthime Fourrier, Klincksieck, 1974.

Jean Renart. *Le Roman de la Rose ou de Guillaume de Dole*. Edited by Félix Lecoy; presentation by Jean Dufournet, Champion Classiques, 2008.

Isidore of Seville. *Etymologiae*. Edited by W. M. Lindsay, 2 vols., Clarendon, 1919.

[Marie de France]. *Lais de Marie de France*. Edited by Karl Warnke; presentation by Laurence Harf-Lancner, Lettres gothiques, 1990.

Nicole de Margival. *Le Dit de la panthère*. Edited by Bernard Ribémont, Honoré Champion, 2000.

———. *Le Dit de la panthère d'amours*. Edited by Henry Todd, Firmin Didot, 1883.

Partonopeu de Blois. Edited by Olivier Collet and Pierre-Marie Joris, Lettres gothiques, 2005.

Partonopeus de Blois: An Electronic Edition. Edited by Penny Eley et al., HriOnline, 2005, https://www.dhi.ac.uk/partonopeus/main.html

Peter Lombard. *The Sentences, Book 4: On the Doctrine of Signs*. Translated by Giulio Silano, Pontifical Institute of Mediaeval Studies, 2010.

Renaud de Beaujeu. *Le Bel Inconnu*. Edited by Michèle Perret, Champion Classiques, 2003.

[Saint Jerome]. *Adversus Jovinianum*. Partially translated in *Jankyn's Book of Wikked Wyves*, edited by Ralph Hanna and Traugott Lawler, U of Georgia P, 1997, vol. 1, pp. 157–93.

SECONDARY SOURCES

Adams, Tracy. "'Pour un petit de nice semblant': Desire and Distance in Christine de Pizan's *Le Livre du Duc des Vrais Amans*." *French Forum*, vol. 28, n. 3, 2003, pp. 1–24.

Akbari, Suzanne Conklin. "Nature's Forge Recast in the *Roman de Silence*." *Literary Aspects of Courtly Culture. Selected Papers from the Seventh Triennial Conference of the International Courtly Literature Society. U of Massachusetts, Amherst, 27 July-1 August 1992*, edited by Donald Maddox and Sara Sturm-Maddox, D. S. Brewer, 1994, pp. 39–46.

Allen, Anthony. "La Mélancolie du biographe: *Le Roman du Castelain de Couci* et le deuil de la voix." *Neophilologus*, vol. 85, n. 1, 2001, pp. 25–41.

Altmann, Barbara. "'Trop peu en sçay': The Reluctant Narrator in Christine de Pizan's Works on Love." *Chaucer's French Contemporaries: The Poetry/Poetics of Self and Tradition*, edited by R. Barton Palmer, AMS Press, 1999, pp. 217–49.

Armstrong, Adrian, and Sarah Kay. *Knowing Poetry: Verse in Medieval France from the Rose to the Rhétoriqueurs*, Cornell UP, 2011.

Armstrong, Grace. "Enide and Solomon's Wife: Figures of Romance *Sapientia*." *French Forum*, vol. 14, 1989, pp. 401–18.

———. "Women of Power: Chrétien de Troyes's Female Clerks." *Women in French Literature: A Collection of Essays*, edited by Michael Guggenheim, Stanford French and Italian Studies, ANMA Libri, 1988, pp. 29–46.

Attwood, Catherine. "The Image in the Fountain: Fortune, Fiction and Femininity in the *Livre du Voir Dit* of Guillaume de Machaut." *Nottingham French Studies*, vol. 38, n. 2, 1999, pp. 137–49.

———. "Temps et lieux du souvenir: le *Voir Dit* de Guillaume de Machaut." Reprinted in *Comme mon cœur désire*, edited by Denis Hüe, pp. 235–56.

Baldwin, John W. *The Language of Sex: Five Voices from Northern France around 1200*. U of Chicago P, 1994.

Bateman, J. Chimène. "Problems of Recognition: The Fallible Narrator and the Female Addressee in *Partonopeu de Blois*." *Partonopeus in Europe: An Old French Romance and Its Adaptations*, edited by Catherine Hanley et al., *Medievalia*, vol. 25, n. 2, 2004, pp. 163–79.

Baumgartner, Emmanuèle. *Le Récit médiéval*. Hachette, 1995.

———. "Trouvères et *losengiers*." *Cahiers de civilisation médiévale*, vol. 25, nn. 99–100, 1982, pp. 171–78.

Benvensite, Emile. *Problèmes de linguistique générale*. Vol. 1, Gallimard, 1966–74.

Bersani, Leo. *Is the Rectum a Grave?: And Other Essays*. U of Chicago P, 2010.

Bersani, Leo, and Adam Phillips. *Intimacies*. U of Chicago P, 2008.

Berthelot, Anne. "Nicole de Margival lecteur d'Adam de la Halle: 'tel qu'en lui-même.'" *Perspectives médiévales*, vol. 20, 1994, pp. 4–14.

Bloch, R. Howard. *The Anonymous Marie de France*. U of Chicago P, 2003.

———. *Etymologies and Genealogies: A Literary Anthropology of the French Middle Ages*. U of Chicago P, 1983.

———. *Medieval French Literature and Law*. U of California P, 1977.

Blumreich, Kathleen. "Lesbian Desire in the Old French *Roman de Silence*." *Arthuriana*, vol. 7, n. 2., 1997, pp. 47–62.

Bolduc, Michelle. "Images of Romance: The Miniatures of *le Roman de Silence*." *Arthuriana*, vol. 12, n. 1, 2002, pp. 101–12.

Boulton, Maureen. "L'Idéologie de la forme: le *Voir Dit* de Guillaume de Machaut." Reprinted in *Comme mon cœur désire*, edited by Denis Hüe, pp. 199–207.

———. *The Song in the Story: Lyric Insertion in French Narrative Fiction, 1200–1400*. U of Pennsylvania P, 1993.

Boutet, Dominique. "L'Éloge du prince et l'expérience de la mélancolie. Réflexions sur les facteurs de cohérence du *Jugement du roi de Navarre* de Guillaume de Machaut." *Penser le pouvoir au Moyen Âge (VIIIe-XVe siècle). Études d'histoire et de littérature offertes à Françoise Autrand*, edited by Dominique Boutet and Jacques Verger, ENS rue d'Ulm, 2000, pp. 33–46.

Brown, Catherine. *Contrary Things: Exegesis, Dialectic, and the Poetics of Didacticism*. Stanford UP, 1998.

Brown, Thomas. "The Relationship between *Partonopeus de Blois* and the Cupid and Psyche Tradition." *BYU Studies Quarterly*, vol. 5, n. 3, 1964, pp. 193–202.

Brownlee, Kevin. "Ovide et le moi poétique 'moderne' à la fin du Moyen Âge: Jean Froissart et Christine de Pizan." *Modernité au Moyen Âge. Le Défi du passé*, edited by Brigitte Cazelles and Charles Méla, Droz, 1990, pp. 153–73.

———. *Poetic Identity in Guillaume de Machaut*. U of Wisconsin P, 1984.

———. "Rewriting Romance: Courtly Discourse and Auto-Citation in Christine de Pizan." *Gender and Text in the Later Middle Ages*, edited by Jane Chance, U of Florida P, 1996, pp. 172–94.

———. "Transformations of the *Charrete*: Godefroi de Leigni Rewrites Chrétien de Troyes." *Stanford French Review*, vol. 14, nn. 1–2, 1990, pp. 161–78.

———. "Widowhood, Sexuality, and Gender in Christine de Pizan." *Romanic Review*, vol. 86, n. 2, 1995, pp. 339–54.

Bruckner, Matilda Tomaryn. "*Le Chevalier de la Charrette (Lancelot)*." *The Romances of Chrétien de Troyes: A Symposium*, edited by Douglas Kelly, UP of Kentucky, 1985, pp. 132–81.

———. "*Le Chevalier de la Charrette*: That Obscure Object of Desire, Lancelot." *A Companion to Chrétien de Troyes*, edited by Norris Lacy and Joan Tasker Grimbert, D. S. Brewer, 2005, pp. 137–55.

———. "An Interpreter's Dilemma: Why Are There So Many Interpretations of Chrétien's *Chevalier de la charrette?*" *Romance Philology*, vol. 40, n. 2, 1986, pp. 159–80.

———. "Of *Cligés* and Cannibalism." *Arthuriana*, vol. 18, n. 3, 2008, pp. 19–32.

———. *Shaping Romance: Interpretation, Truth, and Closure in Twelfth-Century French Fictions*. U of Pennsylvania P, 1993.

Brundage, James. *Law, Sex, and Christian Society in Medieval Europe*. U of Chicago P, 1987.

Buckbee, Edward. "*Erec et Enide*." *The Romances of Chrétien de Troyes: A Symposium*, edited by Douglas Kelly, UP of Kentucky, 1985, pp. 48–88.

Burch, Sally. "*Amadas et Ydoine*, *Cligès*, and the Impediment of Crime." *Forum for Modern Language Studies*, vol. 36, n. 2, 2000, pp. 185–95.

Burgwinkle, William. "État présent: Queer Theory and the Middle Ages." *French Studies*, vol. 60, n. 1, 2006, pp. 79–88.

———. *Sodomy, Masculinity, and Law in Medieval Literature: France and England, 1050–1230*. Cambridge UP, 2004.

Burns, E. Jane. *Bodytalk: When Women Speak in Old French Literature*. U of Pennsylvania P, 1993.

Busby, Keith. "Froissart's Poetic Prison: Enclosure as Image and Structure in the Narrative Poetry." *Froissart Across the Genres*, edited by Donald Maddox and Sara Sturm-Maddox, U of Florida P, 1998, pp. 81–100.

Butler, Judith. "Critically Queer." *GLQ*, vol. 1, n. 1, 1993, pp. 17–32.

———. *Gender Trouble: Feminism and the Subversion of Identity*. Routledge Classics, 2007.

———. *The Psychic Life of Power: Theories in Subjection*. Stanford UP, 1997.

Butterfield, Ardis. "Pastoral and the Politics of Plague in Machaut and Chaucer." *Studies in the Age of Chaucer*, vol. 16, 1994, pp. 3–27.

———. *Poetry and Music in Medieval France: From Jean Renart to Guillaume de Machaut*. Cambridge UP, 2002.

Callahan, Christopher. "Lyric Discourse and Female Vocality: On the Unsilencing of Silence." *Arthuriana*, vol. 12, n. 1, 2002, pp. 123–31.

Calin, William. *A Poet at the Fountain: Essays on the Narrative Verse of Guillaume de Machaut*. UP of Kentucky, 1974.

Cerquiglini-Toulet, Jacqueline. "Le Clerc et l'écriture: Le *Voir Dit* de Guillaume de Machaut et la définition du *dit*." Reprinted in *Comme mon cœur désire*, edited by Denis Hüe, pp. 133–56.

———. "*Un Engin si Soutil*": *Guillaume de Machaut et l'écriture au XIVe siècle*. Honoré Champion, 2001.

———. "Fullness and Emptiness: Shortages and Storehouses of Lyric Treasure in the Fourteenth and Fifteenth Centuries." *Yale French Studies*, 1991, pp. 224–35.

———. "Polyphème et l'antre de la voix." Reprinted in *Comme mon cœur désire*, edited by Denis Hüe, pp. 221–34.

———. "Pour une typologie de l'insertion lyrique." *Perspectives médiévales*, vol. 3, 1997, pp. 9–14.

Cheyette, Fredric and Howell Chickering. "Love, Anger, and Peace: Social Practice and Poetic Play in the Ending of *Yvain*." *Speculum*, vol. 80, n. 1, 2005, pp. 75–117.

Clark, Robert L. A. "Queering Gender and Naturalizing Class in the *Roman de Silence*." *Arthuriana*, vol. 12, n. 1, 2002, pp. 50–63.

Cohn, Dorrit. "Metalepsis and Mise en Abyme." Translated by Lewis Gleich, *Narrative*, vol. 20, n. 1, 2012, pp. 105–40.

Colby-Hall, Alice. "Frustration and Fulfillment: The Double Ending of the *Bel Inconnu*." *Yale French Studies*, vol. 67, 1984, pp. 120–34.

Dällenbach, Lucien. *Le Récit spéculaire: essai sur la mise en abyme*. Seuil, 1977.

De Looze, Laurence. "From Text to Text and from Tale to Tale: Jean Froissart's *Prison Amoureuse*." *The Centre and Its Compass: Studies in Medieval Literature in Honor of Professor John Leyerle*, edited by Robert Taylor, Medieval Institute, 1993, pp. 87–110.

———. "The Gender of Fiction: Womanly Poetics in Jean Renart's *Guillaume de Dole*." *French Review*, vol. 64, n. 4, 1991, pp. 596–606.

———. "Generic Clash, Reader Response, and the Poetics of Non-Ending in *le Bel Inconnu*." *Courtly Literature: Culture and Context. Selected Papers from the Fifth Triennial Congress of the International Courtly Literature Society, Dalfsen, the Netherlands, 9–16 August 1986*, edited by Keith Busby and Erik Kooper, Benjamins, 1990, pp. 113–23.

———. "Guillaume de Machaut and the Writerly Process." *French Forum*, vol. 9, n. 2, 1984, pp. 145–61.

———. "Masquage et démasquage de l'auteur dans *les Jugements* de Guillaume de Machaut." *Masques et déguisements dans la littérature médiévale*, edited by Marie-Louise Ollier, Presses de l'Université de Montréal, 1988, pp. 203–9.

———. *Pseudo-Autobiography in the Fourteenth Century: Juan Ruiz, Guillaume de Machaut, Jean Froissart, and Geoffrey Chaucer*. U of Florida P, 1997.

de Man, Paul. *Aesthetic Ideology*. U of Minnesota P, 1996.

———. *Allegories of Meaning: Figural Language in Rousseau, Nietzsche, Rilke, and Proust*. Yale UP, 1979.

———. *Blindness and Insight: Essays in the Rhetoric of Contemporary Criticism*. 2nd ed., U of Minnesota P, 1983.

Demartini, Dominique. "Figures du poète dans *le Livre du duc des vrais amants* de Christine de Pizan ou l'amour démasqué." *Bien dire et bien aprandre*, n. 25, 2007, pp. 87–104.

Derrida, Jacques. *De la Grammatologie*. Minuit, 1967.

———. *Psyché: Inventions de l'autre*. 2 vols. Galilée, 1987.

Dinshaw, Carolyn. *Chaucer's Sexual Poetics*. U of Wisconsin P, 1989.

———. *Getting Medieval: Sexualities and Communities, Pre- and Postmodern*. Duke UP, 1999.

———. *How Soon Is Now? Medieval Texts, Amateur Readers, and the Queerness of Time*. Duke UP, 2012.

Dragonetti, Roger. *Le Mirage des sources: l'art du faux dans le roman médiéval*. Seuil, 1987.

———. *La Technique poétique des trouvères dans la chanson courtoise: contribution à l'étude de la rhétorique médiévale*. Slatkine, 1979.

———. *La Vie de la lettre au moyen âge*, Le Conte du Graal. Seuil, 1980.

Dulac, Liliane. "Peut-on comprendre les relations entre Erec et Enide?" *Le Moyen Age*, vol. 100, 1994, pp. 37–50.

Edelman, Lee. *Homographesis: Essays in Gay Literary and Cultural Theory*. Routledge, 1994.

———. *No Future: Queer Theory and the Death Drive*. Duke UP, 2004.

Edmondson, George. "Naked Chaucer." *The Post-Historical Middle Ages*, edited by Elizabeth Scala and Sylvia Federico, Palgrave, 2009, pp. 139–60.

Ehrhart, Margaret. "Machaut's *Dit de la fonteinne amoureuse*, the Choice of Paris, and the Duties of Rulers." *Philological Quarterly*, vol. 59, n. 2, 1980, pp. 119–39.

———. "Only Connect: Machaut's *Book of Morpheus* and the Powers of the Weak." *Chaucer's French Contemporaries: The Poetry/Poetics of Self and Tradition*, edited by R. Barton Palmer, AMS Press, 1999, pp. 137–62.

Eley, Penny. Partonopeus de Blois: *Romance in the Making*. D. S. Brewer, 2011.

Fenster, Themla. "La *fama*, la femme, et la dame de la tour: Christine de Pizan et la médisance." *Au champ des escriptures*, edited by Eric Hicks et al., Honoré Champion, 2000, pp. 461–77.

Findley, Brooke Heidenreich. "Deadly Words, Captive Imaginations: Women and Poetic Creation in Jean Froissart's *Prison Amoureuse*." *French Forum*, vol. 32, n. 3, 2007, pp. 1–21.

Fischel, Joseph J. *Sex and Harm in the Age of Consent*. U of Minnesota P, 2016.

Foucault, Michel. "Qu'est-ce qu'un auteur?" *Bulletin de la société française de philosophie*, vol. 63, n. 3, 1969, pp. 73–104.

Fourrier, Anthime. *Le Courant réaliste dans le roman courtois en France au Moyen Âge*. Nizet, 1960.

Fradenburg, Aranye. "(Dis) Continuity: A History of Dreaming." *The Post-Historical Middle Ages*, edited by Elizabeth Scala and Sylvia Federico, Palgrave, 2009, pp. 87–115.

Frappier, Jean. "Le Prologue du *Chevalier de la Charrette* et son interprétation." *Romania*, vol. 93, n. 371, 1972, pp. 337–77.

Freccero, Carla. *Queer/Early/Modern*. Duke UP, 2006.

Freeman, Michelle A. "*Cligés*." *The Romances of Chrétien de Troyes: A Symposium*, edited by Douglas Kelly, UP of Kentucky, 1985, pp. 89–131.

Gaunt, Simon. *Gender and Genre in Medieval French Literature*. Cambridge UP, 1995.

———. *Love and Death in Medieval French and Occitan Courtly Literature: Martyrs to Love*. Oxford UP, 2006.

———. "The Significance of *Silence*." *Paragraph*, vol. 13, n. 2, 1990, pp. 202–16.

———. *Troubadours and Irony*. Cambridge UP, 1989.

Genette, Gérard. *Figures III*. Seuil, 1972.

Gide, André. *Journal 1889–1939*. Gallimard, 1948.

Gilbert, Jane. *Living Death in Medieval French and English Literature*. Cambridge UP, 2011.

Gilmore, Gloria. "*Le Roman de Silence*: Allegory in Ruin or Womb of Irony?" *Arthuriana*, vol. 7, n. 2, 1997, pp. 111–28.

Gingras, Francis. *Le Bâtard conquérant: essor et expansion du genre romanesque au Moyen Âge*. Honoré Champion, 2011.

Girard, René. *Le Bouc émissaire*. B. Grasset, 1982.

Gravdal, Kathryn. *Ravishing Maidens: Writing Rape in Medieval French Literature and Law*. U of Pennsylvania P, 1991.

Green, D. H. *Irony in the Medieval Romance*. Cambridge UP, 1979.

Greene, Virginie. *Logical Fictions in Medieval Literature and Philosophy*. Cambridge UP, 2014.

———. *Le Sujet et la mort dans la Mort Artu*. Librairie Nizet, 2002.

———. "What Happened to Medievalists After the Death of the Author?" *The Medieval Author in Medieval French Literature*, edited by Virginie Greene, Palgrave, 2006, pp. 205–27.

Grigsby, John. "The Narrator in *Partonopeu de Blois, le Bel Inconnu*, and *Joufroi de Poitiers*." *Romance Philology*, vol. 21, n. 4, 1968, pp. 536–43.

Grimbert, Joan Tasker. "*Cligés* and the *Chansons*: A Slave of Love." *A Companion to Chrétien de Troyes*, edited by Norris Lacy and Joan Tasker Grimbert, D. S. Brewer, 2005, pp. 120–36.

Grossweiner, Karen. "A Tripartite Model for Determining Narratorial Subjectivity in Medieval Romance: The Composite Subject in *Partonope of Blois*." *Studies in Philology*, vol. 109, n. 4, 2012, pp. 381–408.

Guynn, Noah. *Allegory and Sexual Ethics in the High Middle Ages*. Palgrave, 2007.

Haas, Kurtis. "Erec's Ascent: The Politics of Wisdom in Chrétien's *Erec et Enide*." *Romance Quarterly*, vol. 46, n. 3, 1999, pp. 131–40.

Haidu, Peter. *Aesthetic Distance in Chrétien de Troyes: Irony and Comedy in* Cligès *and* Perceval. Droz, 1968.

———. "The Episode as Semiotic Module in Twelfth-Century Romance." *Poetics Today*, vol. 4, n. 4, 1983, pp. 655–81.

———. "Realism, Convention, Fictionality, and the Theory of Genres in *Le Bel Inconnu*." *L'Esprit créateur*, vol. 12, n. 1, 1972, pp. 37–60.

———. *The Subject Medieval/Modern: Text and Governance in the Middle Ages*. Stanford UP, 2004.

———. *The Subject of Violence: The Song of Roland and the Birth of the State*. Indiana UP, 1993.

Hanf, Georg. "Sur le *Voir Dit* de Guillaume de Machaut." Translated and reprinted in *Comme mon coeur désire*, edited by Denis Hüe, pp. 7–61.

Hanning, Robert. *The Individual in Twelfth-Century Romance*. Yale UP, 1977.

Hoepffner, Ernest. "Crestien de Troyes und Guillaume de Machaut." *Zeitschrift für romanische Philologie*, vol. 39, 1919, pp. 627–29.

———. "Les poésies lyriques du *Dit de la Panthère* de Nicole de Margival." *Romania*, vol. 46, nn. 182/3, 1920, pp. 204–30.

Huchet, Jean-Charles. *L'Amour discourtois: la 'fin'amors' chez les premiers troubadours*. Privat, 1987.

Hüe, Denis, editor. *Comme mon cœur désire: le Livre du Voir Dit*. Paradigme, 2001.

Hughes, Laura. "Machaut's Virtual *Voir Dit* and the Moment of Heidegger's Poetry." *Exemplaria*, vol. 25, n. 3, 2013, pp. 192–210.

Hult, David. "Author/Narrator/Speaker: The Voice of Authority in Chrétien's *Charrete*." *Discourses of Authority in Medieval and Renaissance Literature*, edited by Kevin Brownlee and Walter Stephens, UP of New England, 1989, pp. 76–96.

Hunt, Tony. "Abelardian Ethics and Béroul's *Tristan*." *Romania*, vol. 98, n. 392, 1977, pp. 501–40.

———. "Chrétien's Prologues Reconsidered." *Conjunctures: Medieval Studies in Honor of Douglas Kelly*, edited by Keith Busby and Norris Lacy, Rodopi, 1994, pp. 153–68.

Huot, Sylvia. *From Song to Book: The Poetics of Writing in Old French Lyric and Lyrical Narrative Poetry*. Cornell UP, 1987.

———. "Guillaume de Machaut and the Consolation of Poetry." *Modern Philology*, vol. 100, n. 2, 2002, pp. 165–95.

———. "Reading the Lies of the Poets: The Literal and the Allegorical in Machaut's *Fonteinne amoureuse*." *Philological Quarterly*, vol. 85, 2006, pp. 25–48.

———. "Reliving the *Roman de la Rose*: Allegory and Irony in Machaut's *Voir Dit.*" *Chaucer's French Contemporaries: The Poetry/Poetics of Self and Tradition*, edited by R. Barton Palmer, AMS Press, 1999, pp. 47–69.

Jaeger, C. Stephen. *The Origins of Courtliness: Civilizing Trends and the Formation of Courtly Ideals, 939–1210*. U of Pennsylvania P, 1985.

Jameson, Fredric. *The Political Unconscious: Narrative as a Socially Symbolic Act*. Cornell UP, 1981.

Jewers, Caroline. "Fabric and Fabrication: Lyric and Narrative in Jean Renart's *Roman de la Rose*." *Speculum*, vol. 71, n. 4, 1996, pp. 907–24.

———. "The Non-Existent Knight: Adventure in *Le Roman de Silence*." *Arthuriana*, vol. 7, n. 2, 1997, pp. 87–110.

Karras, Ruth Mazo. *Sexuality in Medieval Europe: Doing unto Others*. Routledge, 2017.

Kay, Sarah. *The Chansons de Geste in the Age of Romance: Political Fictions*. Clarendon, 1995.

———. "The Contradictions of Courtly Love and the Origins of Courtly Poetry: The Evidence of the *lauzengiers*." *Journal of Medieval and Early Modern Studies*, vol. 26, n. 2, 1996, pp. 209–53.

———. *Courtly Contradictions: The Emergence of the Literary Object in the Twelfth Century*. Stanford UP, 2001.

———. *The Place of Thought: The Complexity of One in Late Medieval French Didactic Poetry*. U of Pennsylvania P, 2007.

———. *Subjectivity in Troubadour Poetry*. Cambridge UP, 1990.

———. "Who was Chrétien de Troyes?" *Arthurian Literature*, vol. 15, 1997, pp. 1–35.

Kelly, Douglas. *The Art of Medieval French Romance*. U of Wisconsin P, 1992.

———. *Christine de Pizan's Changing Opinion: A Quest for Certainty in the Midst of Chaos*. D. S. Brewer, 2007.

———. "The Genius of the Patron: The Prince, the Poet, and Fourteenth-Century Invention." *Studies in the Literary Imagination*, vol. 20, n. 1, 1987, pp. 77–97.

———. "Honor, Debate, and *Translatio Imperii* in *Cligés*." *Arthuriana*, vol. 18, n. 3, 2008, pp. 33–47.

———. *Machaut and the Medieval Apprenticeship Tradition: Truth, Fiction, and Poetic Craft*. D. S. Brewer, 2014.

———. *Sens and Conjointure in the* Chevalier de la charrette. Mouton, 1966.

———. "The Source and Meaning of 'Conjointure' in Chrétien's *Erec* 14." *Viator*, vol. 1, 1970, pp. 179–200.

Kinoshita, Sharon. "Heldris de Cornuälle's *Roman de Silence* and the Feudal Politics of Lineage." *PMLA*, vol. 110, n. 3, 1995, pp. 397–409.

———. "Male-Order Brides: Marriage, Patriarchy, and Monarchy in the *Roman de Silence*." *Arthuriana*, vol. 12, n. 1, 2002, pp. 64–75.

———. "The Poetics of *Translatio*: French-Byzantine Relations in Chrétien de Troyes's *Cligés*." *Exemplaria*, vol. 8, n. 2, 1996, pp. 315–54.

Klassen, Norman. "The Lover's *Largesce*: Agency and Selfhood in Chrétien's *Le Chevalier de la Charrette* (Lancelot)." *French Forum*, vol. 24, n. 1, 1999, pp. 5–20.

Koehler, Erich. "Observations historiques et sociologiques sur la poésie des troubadours." *Cahiers de civilisation médiévale*, vol. 7, n. 25, 1964, pp. 27–51.

Krueger, Roberta L. "The Author's Voice: Narrators, Audiences, and the Problem of Interpretation." *The Legacy of Chrétien de Troyes*, edited by Norris Lacy et al., Rodopi, 1987, vol. 1, pp. 115–40.

———. "Textuality and Performance in *Partonopeu de Blois*." *Assays*, vol. 3, 1985, 57–72.

———. *Women Readers and the Ideology of Gender in Old French Verse Romance*. Cambridge UP, 1993.

Kocher, Zan [Suzanne]. "Narrative Structure of the *Roman de Silence*: Lessons in Interpretation." *Romance Notes*, vol. 42, n. 3, 2002, pp. 349–58.

Lacy, Norris. "'Amer par oïr dire': *Guillaume de Dole* and the Drama of Language." *French Review*, vol. 54, n. 6, 1981, pp. 779–87.

———. *The Craft of Chrétien de Troyes: An Essay on Narrative Art*. Brill, 1980.

———. "Narrative, Point of View, and the Problem of Erec's Motivation." *Kentucky Romance Quarterly*, vol. 18, 1971, pp. 355–62.

———. "Thematic Structure in the *Charrette*." *L'Esprit créateur*, vol. 12, n. 1, 1972, pp. 13–18.

Laird, Judith, and Earl Jeffrey Richards. "'Tous parlent par une mesmes bouche': Lyrical Outbursts, Prosaic Remedies, and Voice in Christine de Pizan's *Livre du Duc des vrais amans*." *Christine de Pizan and Medieval French Lyric*, edited by Earl Jeffrey Richards, U of Florida P, 1998, pp. 103–31.

Lanoue, David. "History as Apocalypse: The 'Prologue' of Machaut's *Jugement dou Roy de Navarre*." *Philological Quarterly*, vol. 60, n. 1, 1981, pp. 1–12.

Laranjinha, Ana Sofia. "L'Ironie comme principe structurant chez Chrétien de Troyes." *Cahiers de civilisation médiévale*, vol. 41, n. 162, 1998, pp. 175–82.

Lazar, Moshé. "Lancelot et la *mulier mediatrix*: la Quête de soi à travers la femme." *L'Esprit créateur*, vol. 9, n. 4, 1969, pp. 243–56.

Leach, Elizabeth Eva. *Guillaume de Machaut: Secretary, Poet, Musician*. Cornell UP, 2014.

Lechat, Didier. *"Dire par fiction": métamorphoses du je chez Guillaume de Machaut, Jean Froissart, et Christine de Pizan*. Honoré Champion, 2005.

Léonard, Monique. *Le dit et sa technique littéraire, des origines à 1340*. Honoré Champion, 1996.

Leupin, Alexandre. *Fiction et incarnation: littérature et théologie au Moyen Age*. Flammarion, 1993.

Libera, Alain de. *La Naissance du sujet. L'Archéologie du sujet*, vol. 1, Vrin, 2007.

———. *La Quête de l'identité. L'Archéologie du sujet*, vol. 2, Vrin, 2008.

Lochrie, Karma. *Heterosyncrasies: Female Sexuality When Normal Wasn't*. U of Minnesota P, 2005.

Lottin, D. O. "Les Théories du péché originel au XIIe siècle." *Recherches de théologie ancienne et médiévale*, vol. 12, 1940, pp. 78–103.

Lucey, Michael. "Proust's Queer Metalepses." *MLN*, vol. 116, n. 4, 2001, pp. 795–815.

Lukács, György. *The Theory of the Novel: A Historico-Philosophical Essay on the Forms of Great Epic Literature*. Translated by Anna Bostock, MIT P, 1971.

Luttrell, Claude. *The Creation of the First Arthurian Romance: A Quest*. Edward Arnold, 1974.

Maddox, Donald. *Structure and Sacring: The Systematic Kingdom in Chrétien's Erec et Enide*, UP of Kentucky, 1978.

Maddox, Donald, and Sara Sturm-Maddox. "*Erec et Enide*: The First Arthurian Romance." *A Companion to Chrétien de Troyes*, edited by Norris Lacy and Joan Tasker Grimbert, D. S. Brewer, 2005, pp. 103–19.

Malina, Debra. *Breaking the Frame: Metalepsis and the Construction of the Subject*. The Ohio State UP, 2002.

Marcus, Sharon. "Queer Theory for Everyone: A Review Essay." *Signs*, vol. 31, n. 1, 2005, pp. 191–218.

Marnette, Sophie. *Narrateur et points de vue dans la littérature française médiévale: une approche linguistique*. Peter Lang, 1998.

McCracken, Peggy. "'The Boy Who Was a Girl': Reading Gender in the *Roman de Silence*." *Romanic Review*, vol. 85, n. 4, 1994, pp. 515–34.

———. "Love and War in *Cligés*." *Arthuriana*, vol. 18, n. 3, 2008, pp. 6–18.

———. *The Romance of Adultery: Queenship and Sexual Transgression in Old French Literature*. U of Pennsylvania P, 1998.

———. "Silence and the Courtly Wife: Chrétien de Troyes's *Erec et Enide*." *Arthurian Yearbook*, vol. 3, 1993, pp. 107–26.

McGrady, Deborah. *Controlling Readers: Guillaume de Machaut and His Late Medieval Audience*. U of Toronto P, 2006.

———. "Machaut and His Material Legacy." *A Companion to Guillaume de Machaut*, edited by Deborah McGrady and Jennifer Bain, Brill, 2012, pp. 361–85.

———. "Textual Bodies, the Digital Surrogate, and Desire: Guillaume de Machaut's Judgment Cycle and His Protean Corpus." *Digital Philology*, v. 5, n. 1, 2016, pp. 8–27.

———. "'Tout son païs m'abandonna': Reinventing Patronage in Machaut's *Fonteinne amoureuse*." *Yale French Studies*, n. 110, 2006, pp. 19–31.

———. "What Is a Patron? Benefactors and Authorship in Harley 4431, Christine de Pizan's Collected Works." *Christine de Pizan and the Categories of Difference*, edited by Marilynn Desmond, U of Minnesota P, 1998, pp. 195–214.

Medeiros, Marie-Thérèse de. "Du dit comme divertissement: le cas de *la Prison amoureuse* de Froissart." *L'Imaginaire courtois et son double*, edited by Giovanna Angeli and Luciano Formisano, Edizioni scientifiche italiane, 1992, pp. 165–72.

Miller, Anne-Hélène. "Guillaume de Machaut and the Forms of Pre-Humanism in Fourteenth-Century France." *A Companion to Guillaume de Machaut*, edited by Deborah McGrady and Jennifer Bain, Brill, 2012, pp. 33–48.

Mills, Robert. *Seeing Sodomy in the Middle Ages*. U of Chicago P, 2015.

Moreau, J. M. *Eschatological Subjects: Divine and Literary Judgment in Fourteenth-Century French Poetry*. The Ohio State UP, 2014.

Nichols, Stephen. "Amorous Imitations: Bakhtin, Augustine, and *Le Roman d'Enéas*." *Romance: Generic Transformations from Chrétien de Troyes to Cervantes*, edited by Kevin Brownlee and Marina Scordilis Brownlee, UP of New England, 1985, pp. 47–73.

Nightingale, Jeanne. "Erec in the Mirror: The Feminization of the Self and the Reinvention of the Chivalric Hero in Chrétien's First Romance." *Arthurian Romance and Gender. Selected Proceedings of the 17th International Arthurian Congress*, edited by Friedrich Wolfzettel, Rodopi, 1995, pp. 130–46.

Nolan, Maura. "Historicism after Historicism." *The Post-Historical Middle Ages*, edited by Elizabeth Scala and Sylvia Federico, Palgrave, 2009, pp. 63–85.

Nouvet, Claire. "Pour une économie de la dé-limitation: la *Prison amoureuse* de Jean Froissart." *Neophilologus*, vol. 70, n. 3, 1986, pp. 341–56.

———. "Writing (in) Fear." *Gender and Text in the Later Middle Ages*, edited by Jane Chance, U of Florida P, 1996, pp. 279–305.

Palmer, R. Barton. "Guillaume de Machaut and the Classical Tradition: Individual Talent and (Un)Communal Tradition." *A Companion to Guillaume de Machaut*, edited by Deborah McGrady and Jennifer Bain, Brill, 2012, pp. 239–60.

———. "The Metafictional Machaut: Self-Reflexivity and Self-Mediation in the Two Judgment Poems." *Studies in the Literary Imagination*, vol. 20, n. 1, 1987, pp. 23–39.

———. "Transtextuality and the Producing-I in Guillaume de Machaut's *Judgement* Series." *Exemplaria*, vol. 5, n. 2, 1993, pp. 283–304.

Paupert, Anne. "Le 'je' lyrique féminin dans l'œuvre poétique de Christine de Pizan." *Et c'est la fin pour quoy nous sommes ensemble: Hommage à Jean Dufournet,* edited by Jean-Claude Aubailly, vol. 3, Champion, 1993, pp. 1057-71.

Peraino, Judith. *Giving Voice to Love: Song and Self-Expression from the Troubadours to Guillaume de Machaut.* Oxford UP, 2011.

Perret, Michèle. "Atemporalités et effet de fiction dans *Le Bel Inconnu.*" *Le nombre du temps. En hommage à Paul Zumthor,* edited by Emmanuèle Baumgartner et al., Honoré Champion, 1988, pp. 225-35.

Picherit, Jean-Louis. "Les Exemples dans *le Jugement dou Roy de Navarre* de Guillaume de Machaut." *Lettres Romanes,* vol. 36, n. 2, 1982, pp. 103-16.

Poirion, Daniel. "Le Monde imaginaire de Guillaume de Machaut." Reprinted in *Comme mon cœur désire,* edited by Denis Hüe, pp. 173-86.

Polak, Lucie. *Chrétien de Troyes: Cligés.* Grant and Culter, 1982.

Pomel, Fabienne. "Les Sens enclos: potentialités allégoriques de la métaphore carcérale dans *la Prison amoureuse* de Jean Froissart." *Réalités, images, écritures de la prison au Moyen Âge,* edited by Jean-Marie Fritz and Silvère Menegaldo, Editions universitaires de Dijon, 2012, pp. 119-33.

Pratt, Karen. "Humour in the *Roman de Silence.*" *Arthurian Literature,* vol. 19, 2002, pp. 87-104.

Prince, Gerald. *Dictionary of Narratology.* U of Nebraska P, 2003.

Prior, Sandra Pierson. "The Love That Dares Not Speak Its Name: Displacing and Silencing the Shame of Adultery in *Le Chevalier de la Charrete.*" *Romanic Review,* vol. 97, n. 2, 2006, pp. 127-52.

Purcell, William. "*Transsumptio*: A Rhetorical Doctrine of the Thirteenth Century." *Rhetorica,* vol. 5, n. 4, 1987, pp. 369-410.

Psaki, F. Regina. "The Modern Editor and Medieval 'Misogyny': Text Editing and *Le Roman de Silence.*" *Arthuriana,* vol. 7, n. 2, 1997, pp. 78-86.

Ramey, Lynn Tarte. "Representations of Women in Chrétien's *Erec et Enide*: Courtly Literature or Misogyny?" *Romanic Review,* vol. 84, n. 4, 1993, pp. 377-86.

Ramm, Ben. "A Rose by Any Other Name?: Queering Desire in Jean Renart's *Le roman de la Rose, ou de Guillaume de Dole.*" *Exemplaria,* vol. 19, n. 3, 2007, pp. 402-19.

Reiss, Edmond. "Medieval Irony." *Journal of the History of Ideas,* vol. 42, n. 2, 1981, pp. 209-226.

Reydners, Anne. "Le Roman de *Partonopeu de Blois* est-il l'œuvre d'un précurseur de Chrétien de Troyes?" *Le Moyen Âge,* vol. 111, nn. 3-4, 2005, pp. 479-502.

Reynolds, Philip. *How Marriage Became One of the Sacraments: The Sacramental Theology of Marriage from Its Medieval Origins to the Council of Trent.* Cambridge UP, 2016.

Richards, J. Earl. "Rejecting Essentialism and Gendered Writing: The Case of Christine de Pizan." *Gender and Text in the Later Middle Ages,* edited by Jane Chance, U of Florida P, 1996, pp. 96-131.

Rosenfeld, Jessica. *Ethics and Enjoyment in Late Medieval Poetry: Love after Aristotle.* Cambridge UP, 2011.

Rychner, Jean. "Encore le prologue du *Chevalier de la charrette.*" *Vox Romanica,* vol. 31, 1972, pp. 263-71.

———. "Le prologue du *Chevalier de la charrette.*" *Vox Romanica,* vol. 26, 1967, pp. 1-23.

Salih, Sarah. "Unpleasures of the Flesh: Medieval Marriage, Masochism, and the History of Heterosexuality." *Studies in the Age of Chaucer,* vol. 33, 2011, pp. 125-47.

Samuelson, Charlie. "Affirming Absence and Embracing Nothing: on the Paradoxical Place of Heterosexual Sex in Medieval French Verse Romance." *Arthurian Literature*, vol. 36, 2021, pp. 79–104.

———. "De la filiation à la subversion: les modalités et enjeux des répétitions dans *Aucassin et Nicolette* et *le Roman de Silence*." *Florilegium*, vol. 30, 2015, pp. 1–25.

Scala, Elizabeth. "The Gender of Historicism." *The Post-Historical Middle Ages*, edited by Elizabeth Scala and Sylvia Federico, Palgrave, 2009, pp. 192–214.

———. "Historicists and Their Discontents: Reading Psychoanalytically in Medieval Studies." *Texas Studies in Literature and Language*, vol. 44, n. 1, 2002, pp. 108–31.

Scanlon, Larry. "Unspeakable Pleasures: Sexual Regulation and the Priesthood of Genius." *Romanic Review*, vol. 86, n. 2, 1995, pp. 213–42.

Schmolke-Hasselmann, Beate. *The Evolution of Arthurian Romance: The Verse Tradition from Chrétien to Froissart*. Translated by Margaret and Roger Middleton, Cambridge UP, 1998.

Schultz, James. *Courtly Love, the Love of Courtliness, and the History of Sexuality*. U of Chicago P, 2006.

Segre, Cesare. "What Bakhtin Left Unsaid: The Case of the Medieval Romance." *Romance: Generic Transformation from Chrétien de Troyes to Cervantes*, edited by Kevin Brownlee and Marina Scordilis Brownlee, UP of New England, 1985, pp. 23–46.

Shirt, David. "*Cligés*: A Twelfth-Century Matrimonial Case-book?" *Forum for Modern Language Studies*, vol. 18, n. 1, 1982, pp. 75–89.

Simons, Penny, and Penny Eley. "Male Beauty and Sexual Orientation in *Partonopeus de Blois*." *Romance Studies*, vol. 17, n. 1, 1999, pp. 41–56.

———. "*Partonopeus de Blois* and Chrétien de Troyes: A Re-Assessment." *Romania*, v. 117, nn. 467–78, 1999, pp. 316–41.

———. "The Prologue to *Partonopeus de Blois*: Text, Context, and Subtext." *French Studies*, vol. 49, n. 1, 1995, pp. 1–16.

———. "A Subtext and Its Subversion: The Variant Endings to *Partonopeu de Blois*." *Neophilologus*, vol. 82, n. 2, 1998, pp. 181–97.

Simpson, James. *Troubling Arthurian Histories: Court Culture, Performance and Scandal in Chrétien de Troyes's Erec et Enide*. Peter Lang, 2007.

Singer, Julie. *Blindness and Therapy in Late Medieval French and Italian Poetry*. D. S. Brewer, 2011.

Solterer, Helen. "At the Bottom of Mirage, a Woman's Body: *Le Roman de la Rose* of Jean Renart." *Feminist Approaches to the Body in Medieval Literature*, edited by Linda Lomperis and Sarah Stanbury, U of Pennsylvania P, 1993, pp. 213–33.

———. "Dismembering, Remembering the Châtelain de Couci." *Romance Philology*, vol. 46, n. 2, 1992, pp. 103–24.

———. *The Master and Minerva: Disputing Women in French Medieval Culture*. Berkeley: U of California P, 1995.

Spearing, A. C. *The Medieval Poet as Voyeur: Looking and Listening in Medieval Love-Narratives*. Cambridge UP, 1993.

———. *Textual Subjectivity: The Encoding of Subjectivity in Medieval Narratives and Lyrics*. Oxford UP, 2005.

Stahuljak, Zrinka. "Chrétien de Troyes: moralisateur impossible." *La Revue littéraire*, vol. 19, 2005, pp. 115–31.

Stahuljak, Zrinka, et al. *Thinking through Chrétien de Troyes*. D. S. Brewer, 2011.

Stock, Lorraine. "The Importance of Being Gender 'Stable': Masculinity and Feminine Empowerment in *le Roman de Silence*." *Arthuriana*, vol. 7, n. 2, 1997, pp. 7–34.

Sullivan, Nikki. *A Critical Introduction to Queer Theory*. UP of Edinburgh, 2003.

Sullivan, Penny. "The Education of the Heroine in Chrétien's *Erec et Enide*." *Neophilologus*, vol. 69, n. 3, 1985, pp. 321–31.

Swift, Helen. "Picturing Narrative Voice: Communication and Displacement." *Digital Philology*, v. 5, n. 1, 2016, 28–46.

———. "The Poetic 'I.'" *A Companion to Guillaume de Machaut*, edited by Deborah McGrady and Jennifer Bain, Brill, 2012, pp. 13–32.

Taylor, Jane H. M. "The Lyric Insertion: Towards a Functional Model." *Courtly Literature: Culture and Context, Selected Papers from the Fifth Triennial Congress of the International Courtly Literature Society, Dalfsen, the Netherlands, 9–16 August 1986*, edited by Keith Busby and Eric Kooper, John Benjamins, 1990, pp. 539–48.

Thiry, Claude. "Allégorie et histoire dans *la Prison amoureuse* de Froissart." *Studi francesi*, vv. 61–62, 1977, pp. 15–29.

Thomas, Antoine. "Guillaume de Machaut et *l'Ovide moralisé*." *Romania*, vol. 41, n. 163, 1912, pp. 382–400.

Uhlig, Marion. "Métalepse et flux narratif au Moyen Âge: le récit à tiroirs, un Éden d'avant la transgression." *Fabula-LhT*, n. 20, 2018. http://www.fabula.org/lht/20/uhlig.html.

Valls, Jose Luis. *Freudian Dictionary: A Comprehensive Guide to Freudian Concepts*, translated by Susan Rogers. Routledge, 2019.

Vance, Eugene. *From Topic to Tale: Logic and Narrativity in the Middle Ages*. U of Minnesota P, 1987.

———. *Mervelous Signals: Poetic and Sign Theory in the Middle Ages*. U of Nebraska P, 1986.

Vincensini, Jean-Jacques. "Figure de l'imaginaire et figure du discours: le motif du 'cœur mangé' dans la narration médiévale." *Le 'Cuer' au Moyen âge (Réalité et Senefiance)*. Senefiance, vol. 30, 1991, pp. 439–59.

Waters, Elizabeth. "The Third Path: Alternative Sex, Alternative Gender in *le Roman de Silence*." *Arthuriana*, vol. 7, n. 2, 1997, pp. 35–46.

Williams, Sarah Jane. "La dame, les chansons et les lettres." Translated and reprinted in *Comme mon cœur désire*, edited by Denis Hüe, pp. 83–92.

Wolfzettel, Friedrich. "La poésie lyrique en France comme mode d'appréhension de la réalité: Remarques sur l'invention du sens visuel chez Machaut, Froissart, Deschamps et Charles d'Orléans." Reprinted in *Comme mon coeur désire*, edited by Denis Hüe, pp. 157–72.

Zaddy, Z. P. "The Structure of Chrétien's *Erec*." *Modern Language Review*, vol. 62, n. 4, 1967, pp. 608–19.

Zingesser, Eliza. "The Vernacular Panther: Encyclopedism, Citation, and French Authority in Nicole de Margival's *Dit de la panthère*." *Modern Philology*, vol. 109, n. 3, 2012, pp. 301–11.

Zink, Michel. *Roman rose et roman rouge: le Roman de la Rose ou de Guillaume de Dole de Jean Renart*. Belles lettres, 2015.

———. *La Subjectivité littéraire: autour du siècle de Saint Louis*. PUF, 1985.

INDEX

Adversus Jovinianum (Jerome), 164
agency: discourse and, 55; in Edelman, 139; passive, 147, 150; patronage and, 45; reflexivity and, 38; sexuality and, 18
Alain de Lille, 7, 95
Allegories of Reading (de Man), 6
Aquinas, Thomas, 46
Aristotle, 28, 55–56
Augustine, 29–30
Averroes, 46

Baldwin, James, 116
Baldwin, John, 163
Bateman, Chimène, 78, 83
Battle of Baesweiler, 99, 101
Baudelaire, Charles, 16, 191
Baumgartner, Emmanuèle, 19
Bel Inconnu (Renard de Beaujeu), 70–73, 81, 84
Benveniste, Emile, 27–28
Bersani, Leo, 22, 209
Bloch, Howard, 11, 13

Boulton, Maureen, 113n2, 116
Bruckner, Matilda Tomaryn, 3–4, 8–10, 76, 87
Burgwinkle, William, 7–8, 18
Burke, Kenneth, 6
Burns, E. Jane, 17
Bush, Barbara, 139
Bush, George H. W., 139
Butler, Judith, 29–34, 37–38, 48, 50–52, 58–61, 65, 69, 73–74, 79–80, 88, 90, 93, 95, 97, 105–6, 209
Butterfield, Ardis, 117, 128, 149

Calin, William, 183, 202
Capellanus, Andreas, 154
Cerquiglini-Toulet, Jacqueline, 3–4, 14, 107, 141, 205
Chaucer, Geoffrey, 17
Chevalier de la Charrette, Le (Chrétien de Troyes), 9–12, 30, 54–68
Chrétien de Troyes, 1, 9, 11–12, 29, 54–68, 160–81
Christine de Pizan, 12, 16, 20, 24–25, 29–44
Clark, Robert, 88, 88n15

· 225 ·

Cligés (Chrétien de Troyes), 11, 172–81
Comte d'Anjou (Maillart), 5
congé, 133
conjointure, 3, 161
Copeland, Rita, 6
crossdressing, 88, 88n16, 92

Dällenbach, Lucien, 72, 109
de Libera, Alain, 28–29, 48
de Man, Paul, 6, 12–13, 16, 23, 26, 140, 159–60, 173, 181, 191, 205–6
Demartini, Dominique, 34
De planctu Naturae (Alain de Lille), 7
Derrida, Jacques, 7–8, 21, 113–14, 120, 155
De Trinitate (Augustine), 29
deviance: indeterminacy and, 138; of language, 7, 120; *losengiers* and, 20, 22; normativity and, 141; in rhetoric, 6; romance and, 9; sexual, 52, 99–100, 126, 137–38, 150–51, 153
Dinshaw, Carolyn, 16–17, 22, 110, 208
discontinuity, 3–4, 19, 208
discursive resignification, 105–6
displacement, 35, 64, 105, 115–16, 122–24, 131
dispossession, 57, 116, 133
Dit de la Panthère (Nicole de Margival), 14, 16, 141–54
dits, 1–6; first person in, 27; poetic indeterminacy in, 14–16; *romans* vs., 2
drag, 88, 88n16, 97
Dragonetti, Roger, 12–13, 126n6, 130
Duc de Vrais Amans (Christine de Pizan), 12, 23–24, 30–44

Edelman, Lee, 17–18, 21, 25, 114, 116, 120, 124, 126, 135–39, 150–53, 156–57, 160–61, 163, 169, 181, 187–88, 191, 198, 200, 202, 205–6, 208
Edmondson, George, 19, 209
Eley, Penny, 74, 78, 87
Epistre Othea (Christine de Pizan), 20
Erec et Enide (Chrétien de Troyes), 10–12, 161–72, 177
Escoufle (Renart), 5

Essay Concerning Human Understanding (Locke), 47

Fables (Ponge), 7
Fall of Man, 164
faux amants, 19–20
fear, 146, 176–77
feminist philosophy, 16, 19–21, 137–38, 168, 190
fils a vilain, 78–79, 81, 85
fin'amor, 73, 99, 109, 113–14, 128, 141, 152, 194–96
Findley, Brooke Heidenreich, 107
Fonteinne amoureuse, La (Machaut), 14, 25, 44–54
Foucault, Michel, 12, 30, 52, 159, 195, 210
Fourrier, Anthime, 74, 87, 99n17, 106
Fradenburg, Aranye, 19, 208
Freccero, Carla, 110, 207–8, 210
Froissart, Jean, 3, 14, 73–74, 98–109

Gaunt, Simon, 138, 158, 163, 174
gender identity, 52, 65–66, 74, 88n16, 97, 102
Genette, Gérard, 70
Gide, André, 72
Gilmore, Gloria, 95
Gingras, Francis, 2
grammar, 6–7, 27–30
Gratian, 164–65
Green, D. H., 158–59
Greene, Virginie, 12
Guillaume de Lorris, 128
Guynn, Noah, 7, 13, 15

Haidu, Peter, 61, 95, 158, 172–73, 176, 179
Hegel, Georg, 33–34, 37–38, 59, 61
heteronormativity, 18–19, 21
Homographesis (Edelman), 17, 25, 114, 151–52
homosexuality. *See also* queer theory; sexuality: *losengiers* and, 19–22; masculinity and, 153; in *La Prison Amoureuse*, 99–100; rhetoric and, 17–18; security and, 137; sodomy and, 18
Hughes, Laura, 15

Hugh of Saint Victor, 3–4
Hunbaut (anon.), 5
Hunt, Tony, 162, 171
Huon de Mery, 5
Huot, Sylvia, 53, 113n2, 183, 202

identity, gender, 52, 65–66, 74, 88n16, 97, 102
indeterminacy: of desire, 123; deviance and, 138; masculinity and, 153; medieval, 206; poetic, 6–16, 44, 108, 210; queer sexuality and, 114; reflexivity and, 25; sexual, 16–23, 108, 123; subjectivity and, 29
irony, 12, 16, 157; aesthetics and, 173–74; in Chrétien de Troyes, 161–81; in *Cligés*, 172–81; constructive, 169, 175–76, 196; deconstructive, 169, 172–74, 181; defined, 158–59; de Man, 159–60; in Isidore of Seville, 193; in *Jugements*, 181–92; lyric insertion and, 155; in Machaut, 181–205; in *Roman de Silence*, 97; in Schlegel, 159–60; sexuality and, 160; temporality and, 181; in *Voir Dit*, 192–205
Isidore of Seville, 193

Jaeger, Stephen, 8
Jakemés, 128–42
Jameson, Fredric, 210
Jean de Meun, 44, 128
Jerome, 164
Jugement dou roy de Behaingne (Machaut), 181–92
Jugement dou roy de Navarre (Machaut), 181–92
Just Above My Head (Baldwin), 116

Kay, Sarah, 9, 189
Kelly, Douglas, 2–4, 9
Kinoshita, Sharon, 174
Kocher, Zan, 89
Krueger, Roberta, 13, 34–35, 124, 135, 137–39

Lacan, Jacques, 139, 160, 163, 177, 188, 195–96, 201, 204, 209
Lacy, Norris, 8–9
Laura (film), 124, 126
Lechat, Didier, 27
Leigni, Godefroi de, 30

Léonard, Monique, 2n5
Lettenhove, Kervyn de, 99n17
Lochrie, Karma, 18–19
Locke, John, 47
logic, 6, 29–30, 68–69. See also metalepsis
Lombard, Peter, 164
losengiers, 19–22, 54–55, 120
love, 16, 77, 102–3, 114, 142, 147–48, 176–77, 179, 181, 192, 202
Lucey, Michael, 73
Lucinde (Schlegel), 159–60
Lukács, Georg, 4, 158
Luttrell, Claude, 3
lyric insertion: as deconstructive, 113, 120; dispossession and, 116; in *Dit de la Panthère*, 141–54; *fin'amor* and, 113–14; narrative and, 119–20; queerness of, 114; queer sexuality and, 114–15; in *Roman de la Rose ou de Guillaume de Dole* (Renart), 111–13, 115–28; in *Roman du Châtelain de Couci et de la Dame de Fayel*, 128–41

Machaut, Guillaume de, 1–2, 14–15, 29, 44–54, 155, 181–205
Maillart, Jean, 5
Malina, Debra, 25, 72
Marnette, Sophie, 27
marriage, 19, 164–65, 167–68, 177
Marxism, 210
masculinity, 114, 153, 191
McCracken, Peggy, 94–95, 174
McGrady, Deborah, 4, 15, 190
metalepsis: in *Bel Inconnu*, 70–72; as deconstructive, 72; defined, 70, 72–73; history of concept, 72–73; mise en abyme vs., 72–73; in *Partonopeu de Blois*, 74–87; in *La Prison Amoureuse*, 98–109; queer theory and, 73–74; rhetoric and, 73–74; in *Roman de Silence*, 87–98
meta-literariness, 4
Mills, Robert, 18
mise en abyme, 72–73
mixtions, 3, 99
Miyazawa, Kiichi, 139
mouvance, 74–75

narrator, 4, 16, 76–78, 84, 191
Nicole de Margival, 14, 141–54
Nietzsche, Friedrich, 52
No Future (Edelman), 26, 152, 160–61
normativity, 18–19
Nouvet, Claire, 20–21, 103

onanism, 113
Origins of Courtliness (Jaeger), 8
Ovid, 102

Palmer, R. Barton, 2–3, 45, 183
Partonopeu de Blois, 11–12, 74–87
passive agency, 147, 150
Peirce, Charles Sanders, 6
Peraino, Judith, 155–56
person: first, 27–28; third, 27–28
personhood, 46–47
Phillips, Adam, 209
Pizan, Christine de, 3, 5, 12, 23–24, 30–44
poetic indeterminacy, 6–16, 44, 108, 210
Ponge, Francis, 7
postmodernism, 14, 22, 25, 69, 110, 206
poststructuralism, 25, 69, 157, 194
Preminger, Otto, 124
Prison amoureuse, La (Froissart), 3, 14, 73–74, 98–109
Psychic Life of Power, The (Butler), 29–30, 33, 52
Purcell, William, 73
Pyramus, 102

queer subversion, 87, 104
queer theory, 16, 20–21, 68–69, 73–74, 79–80, 110, 156. *See also* homosexuality
Quintilian, 72–73
reflexivity: in Butler, 33–34, 52, 58–59; in *Le Chevalier de la Charrette*, 57–60, 63–64, 67; in *Duc des Vrais Amans*, 31–44; in *La Fonteinne Amoureuse*, 44–54; subjectivity and, 30

Renart, Jean, 5, 22, 111–13, 115–28, 202–3, 209
Renaud de Beaujeu, 70–73, 81, 84

repetition, 72, 91–93, 160, 201–2. *See also* metalepsis
Reynolds, Philip, 163
rhetoric: love and, 21–22; metalepsis and, 73–74; sexuality and, 17–18
Richards, J. Earl, 44
Roman de la Rose ou de Guillaume de Dole (Renart), 22, 111–13, 115–28, 132, 202–3, 209
Roman de Silence, 73–74, 87–98
Roman du Châtelain de Couci et de la Dame de Fayel, Le (Jakemés), 128–42
Rousseau, Jean-Jacques, 113

Salih, Sarah, 19
salut d'amour, 133
Scala, Elizabeth, 23
Scheler, Auguste, 99n17
Schlegel, Friedrich, 159–60
Schultz, James, 18
semiologics, 4–5
sex scenes, 83
sexual deviance, 52, 99–100, 126, 137–38, 150–51, 153
sexual indeterminacy, 16–23, 123
sexuality. *See also* homosexuality: discourse and, 195; irony and, 160; lyric insertion and, 114–15; marriage and, 19; poetry and, 195–96; rhetoric and, 17–18
Sluiter, Ineke, 6
sodomy, 18–19, 94, 114
Solterer, Helen, 125, 131–32, 138–39
Spearing, A. C., 12, 73, 82
Stahuljak, Zrinka, 9
subjectivity: in Butler, 29–30, 32, 37–38, 50; in *Le Chevalier de la Charrette*, 54–68; in de Libera, 28–29; in *Duc des Vrais Amans*, 31–44; in *La Fonteinne Amoureuse*, 44–54; grammar and, 29–30; reflexivity and, 30; third-person pronouns and, 27
Swift, Helen, 14–15

Thisbé, 102
Thomas of Chobham, 6
Tournoiement Antechrist (Mery), 5

Trinity, 29
troubador songs, 3
trouvère songs, 3

Ventadorn, Bernart de, 21
verse romance, 1–6; poetic indeterminacy in, 8–13; third person in, 27
virelai, 133–35, 133n8
Voir Dit, Le (Machaut), 3, 14, 192–205

Wencelas of Brabant, 99, 101
William VI of Jülich, 101
Wittig, Monique, 81

Yvain, the Knight of the Lion (Chrétien de Troyes), 11–12

Zingesser, Eliza, 153–54
Zink, Michael, 3–4, 115, 118n5, 122

INTERVENTIONS: NEW STUDIES IN MEDIEVAL CULTURE
Ethan Knapp, Series Editor

Interventions: New Studies in Medieval Culture publishes theoretically informed work in medieval literary and cultural studies. We are interested both in studies of medieval culture and in work on the continuing importance of medieval tropes and topics in contemporary intellectual life.

Courtly and Queer: Deconstruction, Desire, and Medieval French Literature
CHARLIE SAMUELSON

Continental England: Form, Translation, and Chaucer in the Hundred Years' War
ELIZAVETA STRAKHOV

Material Remains: Reading the Past in Medieval and Early Modern British Literature
EDITED BY JAN-PEER HARTMANN AND ANDREW JAMES JOHNSTON

Translation Effects: Language, Time, and Community in Medieval England
MARY KATE HURLEY

Talk and Textual Production in Medieval England
MARISA LIBBON

Scripting the Nation: Court Poetry and the Authority of History in Late Medieval Scotland
KATHERINE H. TERRELL

Medieval Things: Agency, Materiality, and Narratives of Objects in Medieval German Literature and Beyond
BETTINA BILDHAUER

Death and the Pearl Maiden: Plague, Poetry, England
DAVID K. COLEY

Political Appetites: Food in Medieval English Romance
AARON HOSTETTER

Invention and Authorship in Medieval England
ROBERT R. EDWARDS

Challenging Communion: The Eucharist and Middle English Literature
JENNIFER GARRISON

Chaucer on Screen: Absence, Presence, and Adapting the Canterbury Tales
EDITED BY KATHLEEN COYNE KELLY AND TISON PUGH

Chaucer, Gower, and the Affect of Invention
STEELE NOWLIN

Fragments for a History of a Vanishing Humanism
EDITED BY MYRA SEAMAN AND EILEEN A. JOY

The Medieval Risk-Reward Society: Courts, Adventure, and Love in the European Middle Ages
WILL HASTY

The Politics of Ecology: Land, Life, and Law in Medieval Britain
EDITED BY RANDY P. SCHIFF AND JOSEPH TAYLOR

The Art of Vision: Ekphrasis in Medieval Literature and Culture
EDITED BY ANDREW JAMES JOHNSTON, ETHAN KNAPP, AND MARGITTA ROUSE

Desire in the Canterbury Tales
ELIZABETH SCALA

Imagining the Parish in Late Medieval England
ELLEN K. RENTZ

Truth and Tales: Cultural Mobility and Medieval Media
EDITED BY FIONA SOMERSET AND NICHOLAS WATSON

Eschatological Subjects: Divine and Literary Judgment in Fourteenth-Century French Poetry
J. M. MOREAU

Chaucer's (Anti-)Eroticisms and the Queer Middle Ages
TISON PUGH

Trading Tongues: Merchants, Multilingualism, and Medieval Literature
JONATHAN HSY

Translating Troy: Provincial Politics in Alliterative Romance
ALEX MUELLER

Fictions of Evidence: Witnessing, Literature, and Community in the Late Middle Ages
JAMIE K. TAYLOR

Answerable Style: The Idea of the Literary in Medieval England
EDITED BY FRANK GRADY AND ANDREW GALLOWAY

Scribal Authorship and the Writing of History in Medieval England
MATTHEW FISHER

Fashioning Change: The Trope of Clothing in High- and Late-Medieval England
ANDREA DENNY-BROWN

Form and Reform: Reading across the Fifteenth Century
EDITED BY SHANNON GAYK AND KATHLEEN TONRY

How to Make a Human: Animals and Violence in the Middle Ages
KARL STEEL

Revivalist Fantasy: Alliterative Verse and Nationalist Literary History
RANDY P. SCHIFF

Inventing Womanhood: Gender and Language in Later Middle English Writing
TARA WILLIAMS

Body Against Soul: Gender and Sowlehele *in Middle English Allegory*
MASHA RASKOLNIKOV

www.ingramcontent.com/pod-product-compliance
Lightning Source LLC
Chambersburg PA
CBHW030110010526
44116CB00005B/185